OpenJDK Cookbook

Over 80 recipes to build and extend your very own version
of Java platform using OpenJDK project

Alex Kasko

Stanislav Kobylyanskiy

Alexey Mironchenko

BIRMINGHAM - MUMBAI

OpenJDK Cookbook

First published: January 2015

Production reference: 1240115

Published by Packt Publishing Ltd.
Livery Place
35 Livery Street
Birmingham B3 2PB, UK.

ISBN 978-1-84969-840-5

www.packtpub.com

Cover image by Benoit Benedetti (benoit.benedetti@gmail.com)

Credits

About the Authors

Alex Kasko is a participant in the OpenJDK project. He maintains unofficial OpenJDK builds on his GitHub account and has 8 years' experience in enterprise and high-performance programming. He works in an OpenJDK development team at Red Hat Inc.

Stanislav Kobylyanskiy is a software developer with years of Java experience. He started his career with C++ and system programming in the late 90s with the Aelita software (now DELL). After a few years, he switched to Java and then moved to telecom. At that time, he joined T-Mobile, UK, to rebuild their Customer Service Web Portal, which lasted for about 4 years. Currently, he is with an investment bank where he is working on a strategic algorithmic trading platform. He is continuously looking for new challenges and to extend his knowledge of core Java technologies.

> I want to say thank you to my family—my two lovely daughters, Alyssa and Alexandra, and to my beloved wife, Natalia—for all their help and support in everything I do.

Alexey Mironchenko is a software developer with experience in scalable enterprise projects, involving Java EE, NoSQL databases, and various other frameworks. He has a mathematical background with some COQ and Maxima experience, and his hobby is to test cutting-edge technologies that are open source or in early access.

About the Reviewers

Usman Saleem is a seasoned software developer with special focus on Java, JEE, PostgreSQL, and utilizing open source tools in software development in general. He has worked with EnterpriseDB, OpenSCG, Red Hat, and Ventyx, Australia. He has taught object-oriented programming and enterprise software development in several public and private sector universities to undergraduate students. When he is not (re)writing his blog software, he likes trying out various strength training workouts or playing Angry Birds with his son.

Usman has an MSc (CS) degree and holds RHCSA, SCWCD, SCBCD, SCJD, and SCJP certifications. He maintains his blog at `http://www.usmans.info`.

Otávio Santana (`@otaviojava`) is a developer and enthusiast of open source. He is an evangelist and practitioner of agile philosophy and polyglot development in Brazil. Otávio is a JUG leader of JavaBahia and SouJava and a strong supporter of Java communities in Brazil, where he also leads the BrasilJUGs initiative to incorporate Brazilian JUGs into joint activities. He is a cocreator and is also responsible for the Linguagil Group—a merge of Java, Ruby, Python, and Agile groups that promote agility across language-focused communities. In the open source world, Otávio is a developer in OpenJDK and a creator of Apache Easy-Cassandra. He has also helped in JBoss Weld, Hibernate, Apache Commons, and other open source projects. Otávio is a very active speaker in Brazil, where he has participated in the largest Java events in the country. As an international speaker, Otávio has presented in JavaOne and the Cassandra tour events. Otávio is also a writer and has many articles and even a book on JVM Internals. Otávio Santana actually means "make the future Java", working in several Java Specification Request (JSR), JAR, as part of the Java Expert team. Otávio was recently nominated and won JCP's Outstanding Adopt-a-JSR Participant of the Year award for his very active role in several JSRs and OpenJDK.

Martin Toshev is a software engineer by profession and hobby. He has been working on a number of large enterprise projects for different companies for the past 5 years using mostly the Java technology stack. He has experience in the areas of social networking and J2EE middleware and is a contributor to the OpenJDK platform.

www.PacktPub.com

Support files, eBooks, discount offers, and more

For support files and downloads related to your book, please visit www.PacktPub.com.

Did you know that Packt offers eBook versions of every book published, with PDF and ePub files available? You can upgrade to the eBook version at www.PacktPub.com and as a print book customer, you are entitled to a discount on the eBook copy. Get in touch with us at service@packtpub.com for more details.

At www.PacktPub.com, you can also read a collection of free technical articles, sign up for a range of free newsletters, and receive exclusive discounts and offers on Packt books and eBooks.

https://www2.packtpub.com/books/subscription/packtlib

Do you need instant solutions to your IT questions? PacktLib is Packt's online digital book library. Here, you can search, access, and read Packt's entire library of books.

Why subscribe?

- Fully searchable across every book published by Packt
- Copy and paste, print, and bookmark content
- On demand and accessible via a web browser

Free access for Packt account holders

If you have an account with Packt at www.PacktPub.com, you can use this to access PacktLib today and view 9 entirely free books. Simply use your login credentials for immediate access.

Table of Contents

Preface

OpenJDK is a unique project that opens numerous and exciting opportunities for people who want to dive into the huge and complicated infrastructure behind the JVM. There is an incredible amount of things to learn and to explore. Almost anyone can find something in it as per their interest, starting from HTTP, Web, software dependency problems, and ending with hardware-specific JIT optimization techniques, and concurrency challenges. Such variety is very unique and it would be true to say that there is no other open source project that can provide something similar. The other factor is that there are not so many other open source projects on that scale; possibly only the Linux core. Such scale requires a non-trivial organizational approach and, to be involved in that process, to see how it works, is a very interesting insight.

This cookbook will lead you through steps to take you into the world of OpenJDK as smoothly as possible. It starts by explaining how to download the source code and how to build the different versions of OpenJDK, how to set it up on a machine, and what different options are available. Then, you will learn how to set up the development environment (IDE) required for editing and debugging C++ and Java source code, and how to start making changes. It will go through some examples, which you may decide to change in various parts of OpenJDK. Further, it will cover the tools available for testing, benchmarking, and ensuring that the changes you have made are not breaking the existing functionality. As OpenJDK is a big project with its own rules and processes, there will be a part covering the procedures that are involved in making changes or fixing bugs, the lifecycle of projects, JSRs, JEPs, and so on. At the end, there will be a section about future work that is planned to be included in forthcoming releases; that part will be the most interesting section for anyone who is interested in the future direction of OpenJDK and wants to try something new, which is not yet available in the stable product.

In addition, this book contains many practical examples which should be useful to any developer who is working with OpenJDK or any other Java technology. They are available in simple form, which allows you to quickly copy and use them for your own project.

What this book covers

Chapter 1, Getting Started with OpenJDK, provides an overview of OpenJDK, explains what it is, and covers the basic steps required to have OpenJDK running and properly configured on the machine.

Chapter 2, Building OpenJDK 6, covers the steps required to build OpenJDK Version 6. This build is very different from OpenJDK 7 and OpenJDK 8 and requires more manual work to be done.

Chapter 3, Building OpenJDK 7, covers the steps required to build OpenJDK Version 7. Building OpenJDK 7 is an easier and more enjoyable process, compared to OpenJDK 6.

Chapter 4, Building OpenJDK 8, covers the steps required to build OpenJDK Version 8.

Chapter 5, Building IcedTea, teaches you how to build a set of tools that are developed apart from OpenJDK. These tools are replaced with some proprietary bits that are not available as open source, which include a browser plugin, Java WebStart, and so on.

Chapter 6, Building IcedTea with Other VM Implementations, covers some interesting VM projects, which also can benefit from the features provided by IcedTea, and how to build that product using these VMs and non-x86 CPUs.

Chapter 7, Working with WebStart and the Browser Plugin, will cover the configuration and installation of WebStart and browser plugin components, which are the biggest parts of the IcedTea project.

Chapter 8, Hacking OpenJDK, covers some bits which are required to start digging into the OpenJDK source code. Such things are the installation and setup of IDE, debugging, and updating HotSpot source code. There are also some useful examples of what the developer can do, for example, implementing your own intrinsic details.

Chapter 9, Testing OpenJDK, will go through an approach used in OpenJDK to test the source code and, since writing code is not enough, we need to write high quality product on which the code has to be tested. This chapter will also show you some examples to use the latest available tools.

Chapter 10, Contributing to OpenJDK, explains how OpenJDK is changing and evolving, how changes are executed, and what one needs to do to participate or to facilitate changes in OpenJDK. Some of these changes, if they are big enough, can take years to appear in the production version.

Chapter 11, Troubleshooting, teaches you about one of the most important parts of any project: bug fixing. It is important to understand which tools and processes are involved. In this chapter, we will cover some important steps, from submitting defects, to pushing the fix into the shared repository.

Chapter 12, Working with Future Technologies, covers some future developments in OpenJDK. As with any big project, OpenJDK has a roadmap with some exciting and promising projects for the next releases. That is exactly what this chapter is about. It lists all the steps required to download sources, build, and run some examples, where possible.

Chapter 13, Build Automation, provides some useful tips for automating the build process. It will be useful for those developers who make frequent changes in OpenJDK or always want to have the build with all the latest changes.

What you need for this book

Generally, you will need nothing except a machine connected to the Internet, preferably to run Linux. If you are going to use a Windows machine, then you will need to install Cygwin.

There may also be additional specific requirements which come with each recipe separately.

Who this book is for

This book is for developers who want a deeper understanding of OpenJDK and want to start making changes. This could be someone who has some cool ideas and wants to contribute or who has found a bug that is tempting to fix. Also it will provide a good starting point to people who want to make changes to the existing VM, for some reason. This could be for research or tailoring VM for specific needs, like special hardware or some very specific requirements.

Overall, it will be useful to anyone who wants to simply have look inside OpenJDK, see what it is, and how it works.

Sections

This book contains the following sections:

Getting ready

This section tells us what to expect in the recipe, and describes how to set up any software or any preliminary settings needed for the recipe.

How to do it...

This section characterizes the steps to be followed for "cooking" the recipe.

How it works...

This section usually consists of a brief and detailed explanation of what happened in the previous section.

There's more...

It consists of additional information about the recipe in order to make the reader more curious about the recipe.

See also

This section may contain references to the recipe.

Conventions

In this book, you will find a number of styles of text that distinguish between different kinds of information. Here are some examples of these styles, and an explanation of their meaning.

Code words in text, database table names, folder names, filenames, file extensions, pathnames, dummy URLs, user input, and Twitter handles are shown as follows: "We can include other contexts through the use of the include directive."

A block of code is set as follows:

```
private static int doUpdateBytes(int crc, byte[] b, int off, int len)
{
    return updateBytes(crc, b, off, len);
}
```

Any command-line input or output is written as follows:

```
update-java-alternatives --list
```

New terms and **important words** are shown in bold. Words that you see on the screen, in menus or dialog boxes for example, appear in the text like this: "Then click on **Done**."

 Warnings or important notes appear in a box like this.

Tips and tricks appear like this.

Reader feedback

Feedback from our readers is always welcome. Let us know what you think about this book—what you liked or disliked. Reader feedback is important for us as it helps us develop titles that you will really get the most out of.

To send us general feedback, simply e-mail feedback@packtpub.com, and mention the book's title in the subject of your message.

If there is a topic that you have expertise in and you are interested in either writing or contributing to a book, see our author guide at www.packtpub.com/authors.

Customer support

Now that you are the proud owner of a Packt book, we have a number of things to help you to get the most from your purchase.

Downloading the example code

You can download the example code files from your account at http://www.packtpub.com for all the Packt Publishing books you have purchased. If you purchased this book elsewhere, you can visit http://www.packtpub.com/support and register to have the files e-mailed directly to you.

Errata

Although we have taken every care to ensure the accuracy of our content, mistakes do happen. If you find a mistake in one of our books—maybe a mistake in the text or the code—we would be grateful if you could report this to us. By doing so, you can save other readers from frustration and help us improve subsequent versions of this book. If you find any errata, please report them by visiting `http://www.packtpub.com/submit-errata`, selecting your book, clicking on the **Errata Submission Form** link, and entering the details of your errata. Once your errata are verified, your submission will be accepted and the errata will be uploaded to our website or added to any list of existing errata under the **Errata** section of that title.

To view the previously submitted errata, go to `https://www.packtpub.com/books/content/support` and enter the name of the book in the search field. The required information will appear under the **Errata** section.

Piracy

Piracy of copyrighted material on the Internet is an ongoing problem across all media. At Packt, we take the protection of our copyright and licenses very seriously. If you come across any illegal copies of our works in any form on the Internet, please provide us with the location address or website name immediately so that we can pursue a remedy.

Please contact us at `copyright@packtpub.com` with a link to the suspected pirated material.

We appreciate your help in protecting our authors and our ability to bring you valuable content.

Questions

If you have a problem with any aspect of this book, you can contact us at `questions@packtpub.com`, and we will do our best to address the problem.

1

Getting Started with OpenJDK

In this chapter, we will cover the following topics:

- ▶ Distinguishing OpenJDK from Oracle JDK
- ▶ Installing OpenJDK on Windows
- ▶ Configuring OpenJDK on Windows
- ▶ Installing OpenJDK on Linux
- ▶ Configuring OpenJDK on Linux
- ▶ Navigating through OpenJDK groups and projects

Introduction

OpenJDK is now an official Java 7 reference implementation, and is now one for Java 8 as well. This means that the most essential projects of the Java ecosystem are now open source. This also means that OpenJDK can be installed in various ways—from building from source to installing the binary package from the package manager, if any.

Sun's effort to release an open source JDK was the beginning of the project publicly stated in 2006, during the JavaOne conference. HotSpot was released under the GPLv2 license. The complete source code of the **Java Class Library** (**JCL**) was released in May 2007 under the GPL, except for several proprietary parts with GPL-incompatible licenses.

However, some proprietary parts (from 4 to 1 percent of the total code lines, depending on the update number) were required in OpenJDK in a separate proprietary bundle in the OpenJDK 7 b53 update in April 2009.

One may think that the initial installation and configuration are quite simple and do not need some sort of detailed explanation. In many ways, that's true; but there are some difficulties along the way.

We will start by distinguishing OpenJDK from Oracle JDK. The latter is based on the former, but not entirely. Each one has its own advantages and drawbacks. The primary OpenJDK advantage is the fact that it's open source while Oracle JDK is always recommended and is ready-to-use. Besides, OpenJDK 6 is the only maintainable Java 6 realization left, after the Java 6 discontinuation.

Then we will cover the installation process for Windows and possible issues with some Windows versions. After that, we will describe some typical profiles to configure an installed instance of OpenJDK for various needs, such as a server instance and developer instance.

Then we will go in to more complicated matters, such as installing OpenJDK on various Linux systems. There are at least two common ways to do it: the distribution-recommended way that depends on the distribution itself, and another way, which is common for all Linux systems.

Linux configuration is more or less the same as that of Windows, but there are some differences that need to be covered. The differences are, mainly, related to system philosophy, namely the way it's done and then what exactly is done.

Then we will proceed to OpenJDK internal structures—in an introductory way. We will consider OpenJDK projects that are already in use, and will learn how to use instruments that we will need later. Also, we will briefly look at OpenJDK groups and find out what they are doing and how they may influence OpenJDK's further evolution.

Last but not least, you will learn how to benefit from the Adopt OpenJDK program, which is also a part of the OpenJDK community. Adopt OpenJDK is an effort to improve OpenJDK usability readiness, test new language releases, and do whatever it needs to make OpenJDK more useful and welcoming among users as well as developers.

This chapter is written with an introductory purpose, and does not cover some details that are common to Oracle Java. However, it provides a necessary basis to work with.

We will use Java 7, as it is stable and the latest Java version available. All screenshots and processes are assuming that we use Java 7, if another is not explicitly mentioned.

If you already have OpenJDK built and installed as default and you are aware of the differences between OpenJDK and Oracle JDK, as well as of the existence of Adopt OpenJDK, you may skip this chapter entirely.

Distinguishing OpenJDK from Oracle JDK

Though OpenJDK is an official reference implementation for the Java platform, certain Oracle-provided software are not open source. The most famous of them is the Java browser plugin, but there are a lot more differences than just that. This recipe will show you how to distinguish OpenJDK from Oracle JDK.

Getting ready

To follow this recipe, you will need an installed OpenJDK instance. It will be good if you have an Oracle JDK instance as well, to feel the difference. Also, we will assume that you have a Linux installation and an `update-java-alternatives` command installed and ready to use. To know how to install OpenJDK on various systems, see the later recipes in this chapter. To know how to switch the system Java version, if you do not have `update-alternatives` installed (for Fedora, Gentoo, and so on), visit the *Configuring OpenJDK on Linux* recipe or refer to your distribution documentation/forums.

How to do it...

Please take a look at the following procedures to know the difference between OpenJDK and Oracle JDK:

1. We will open a terminal and type the following command:

    ```
    update-java-alternatives  --list
    ```

2. We will see a full list of installed Java implementations:

    ```
    $ update-java-alternatives  --list
    java-1.6.0-openjdk-amd64 1061 /usr/lib/jvm/java-1.6.0-openjdk-
    amd64
    java-1.7.0-openjdk-amd64 1071 /usr/lib/jvm/java-1.7.0-openjdk-
    amd64
    java-6-oracle 1073 /usr/lib/jvm/java-6-oracle
    java-7-oracle 1081 /usr/lib/jvm/java-7-oracle
    java-8-oracle 1082 /usr/lib/jvm/java-8-oracle
    ```

3. Let's set Oracle Java as default. We will run the following command with `root` access:

    ```
    update-java-alternatives  --set java-7-oracle
    ```

[🔆 This command may produce errors such as "no alternatives for apt". It's OK, just ignore them.]

4. Then we will go to `https://www.java.com/en/download/installed.jsp?detect=jre` and check our browser plugin version. We will see the activate link (following the name of the activating entity).

    We can see from the result of our actions that the Java browser plugin has been installed.

5. Let's try to set OpenJDK as the default Java environment (the actual instance name may differ in your case):

    ```
    update-java-alternatives  --set java-1.7.0-openjdk-amd64
    ```

6. Then we will go to our browser page and refresh it. It may be necessary to restart the browser so that the changes can take effect, as shown in the following screenshot:

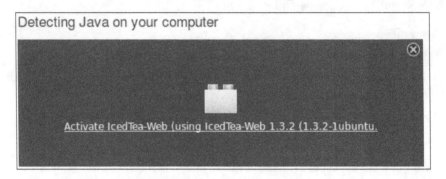

We can see that the plugin is not from the JDK itself but from a project named IcedTea.

IcedTea is an open source project, whose goal is to replace proprietary parts of the Java ecosystem as much as possible. The plugin itself is from IcedTea-Web, an open source implementation of the Java Web Start and Java browser plugins.

In most distributions, the `IcedTea` plugin is installed by default. But it is necessary to keep in mind that it's an open source plugin, and definitely not a referenced one. This means that its functionality might be slightly different from the Oracle plugin. It is also possible that some features may not work.

How it works...

Oracle JDK still has some proprietary components, and the browser plugin is one example. All we need in this chapter is to see the difference between the work of OpenJDK and Oracle JDK components that are different.

Also, the huge difference between OpenJDK and Oracle JDK lies in the license. OpenJDK is open source, while Oracle JDK contains proprietary pieces, and thus it is licensed under the Oracle binary license. The fact that OpenJDK is open source provides a whole new range of benefits (and exciting discoveries) through the ability to study and modify its source code. It is also worth mentioning that more than 90 percent of Oracle JDK is based on OpenJDK source code. This means the OpenJDK quality is not compromised in any way. The browser plugin is not the only thing that is missed in OpenJDK compared to Oracle JDK.

See also

▶ In *Chapter 5, Building IcedTea*, there is a detailed explanation of how to build IcedTea from source.

Installing OpenJDK on Windows

Windows is the most commonly used OS in the world, and many developers are using it as their primary system. Despite its popularity, Windows doesn't have such strong support by the OpenJDK development community, and installation of the product is not as easy as in Linux. This recipe will cover the steps required to install OpenJDK on Windows.

This recipe provides an easy but decentralized way to install programs, although the most recent versions provide package repositories of their own. However, on Windows, the only official way to install an up-to-date OpenJDK is to build it from source.

Getting ready

To follow this recipe, we will need an installed Windows system. Windows 7 or Windows 8 will be best, because Windows XP is already officially discontinued by Microsoft.

How to do it...

There is an official build of OpenJDK on Windows, but it exists for referential purposes only. It is official and easy to install, but it doesn't have any security updates or improvements. However, there are unofficial builds, maintained by Alex Casco. We will try to install OpenJDK in both ways:

1. We will start with an official reference build. To get it, we need to go to `https://jdk7.java.net/java-se-7-ri/` and accept the license terms. Then, download and run the installer.

Though the OpenJDK source code is licensed by an open license, this official build is licensed by the Oracle Binary Code license and by GPLv2. If you want to keep your OpenJDK open source, please use one licensed by GPLv2.

2. Unpack the downloaded file in a location you prefer. Let's name it `C:/OpenJDK`.

3. Open the Windows command line by navigating to **Start | Run**, type `cmd`, and click on the **Run** button.

4. Run the following command:

    `C:\OpenJDK\bin\java.exe -version`

    It will output the Java version information. The output should look like this:

    ```
    openjdk version 1.7.0
    OpenJDK Runtime Environment <build 1.7.0-b146>
    OpenJDK Client VM <build 21.0-b16, mixed mode>
    ```

Congratulations! We've just installed the OpenJDK official binary.

How it works...

The reference implementation is the only available official binary build of OpenJDK. But it lacks security and is used only for reference purposes. It is a simple archive that needs to be unpacked to use it.

To bypass this unpleasantness and give Windows users an opportunity to install OpenJDK as a binary without building it from source, one of the OpenJDK contributors established a completely unofficial but very useful OpenJDK build set for various platforms.

Moreover, this binary build, unlike the official one, is open source and licensed over GPL. So we can use it even in a completely open source environment without adding any proprietary pieces that will possibly get us in trouble.

 You will find an installer for Mac in those unofficial builds as well.

There's more...

Though an official reference binary is outdated, there is an unofficial project that provides OpenJDK builds from sources that are up to date.

Now we will install OpenJDK 7 from unofficial builds:

1. Go to `https://github.com/alexkasko/openjdk-unofficial-builds`.

2. Select an appropriate build for Windows and download it.

3. Unpack it and run `install.exe`.

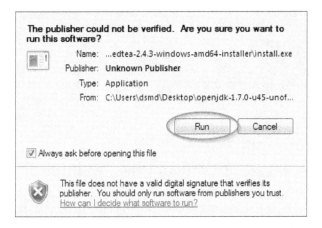

4. Click on the **Run** button when the preceding message appears.

5. Carefully read and accept the license and then click on **Next**.

6. Select the installation path in the next window. It will point to your home directory by default, so be careful—such an installation may be available to no one but yourself.

7. If the target directory does not exist, let the installer create it.

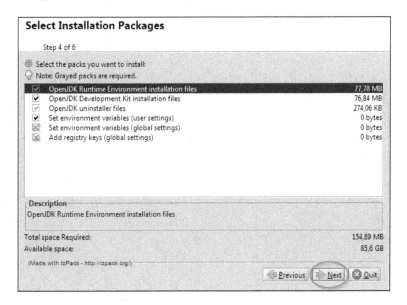

8. Check the red highlighted checkboxes in the preceding screenshot only if you want to set this JDK as default for all users in the system, not just for you. You may uncheck the fourth box if you don't need this JDK to be default at all.

9. Then click on the **Next** button and wait until the installation is finished.

10. Then click on the **Next** button for the last time.

11. Then click on **Done**.

See also

Although the simplest way to install OpenJDK is to unpack binaries, manually or in an automatic fashion, there is no doubt that working with the source code will give us more flexibility at all possible levels.

To know more, read the following chapters:

> ▸ *Chapter 2, Building OpenJDK 6* up to *Chapter 4, Building OpenJDK 8* to learn about building OpenJDK from source

> ▸ *Chapter 6, Building IcedTea with Other VM Implementations* to build OpenJDK using other VMs

> ▸ *Chapter 13, Build Automation* to work with future technologies, which will be unavailable in binary form for quite some time

Configuring OpenJDK on Windows

Although the initial configuration is sufficient for most tasks, it may still be required to do some configuration. In the case of OpenJDK, this is performed by setting system variables. Here we will touch only on the case that often occurs when JDK is unpacked manually—how to set it as default.

Getting ready

To follow this recipe, we will need an OpenJDK instance installed on our Windows system. Windows 7 or Windows 8 will be best, because Windows XP is already officially discontinued by Microsoft.

How to do it...

At first, we need to install our OpenJDK implementation as the default Java instance. This is often necessary for development:

1. In order to do so, we will go to **Start** | **Control Panel** | **System** | **Advanced** | **Environment Variables** | **User Variables** (or **System Variables** for system-wide configuration) and add the path to the Java executable to the PATH system variable, as shown:

 If there are other paths to other Java executables, we may need to delete them as well, but it will be better to remember them, since we may need to restore our old default Java settings.

2. If we were installing OpenJDK from unofficial builds, there may be no need to change the PATH variable at all.

3. To validate our newly configured variable, we will go to the Command Prompt and type the following:

```
java -version
```

4. The expected output is the version of our newly installed build.

How it works...

In order to set a newly installed OpenJDK instance as the default JDK, we need to change the system variable. After that change, our Java executables will be visible to the system.

There's more...

The same procedure is followed to set the CLASSPATH variable. It is not very necessary, and if you are using other libraries such as GNU classpath, you probably know about it.

Installing OpenJDK on Linux

The Linux operating system allows for many internal tweaks, as well as for changes to the system's source code. It is also known as a complicated OS, and not all distributions are user-friendly. There are many people using it, and it's open source, such as OpenJDK itself. The installation process varies between chosen distributions, and we will go through the process for the three most-used package managers, as well as through the process that will work for virtually all x86 Linux distributions.

Getting ready

To follow this recipe, you will need an installed Linux system. It will be better if it has the kernel version 2.6 or higher, though OpenJDK is reported workable on 2.4 kernels as well. Also, if you have the .deb, .rpm, or .ebuild package manager, the recommended way to install any package is to install it using those.

How to do it...

When the installation of various packages is concerned, the process is dependent on our Linux distribution.

For a Debian-based distribution:

1. Open a terminal and type:

```
apt-get install openjdk-7-jdk
```

We should have root permissions or use `sudo` to gain access to system files.

2. This will trigger the installation automatically. If we get an error message, indicating that the package is not found, we should Google an appropriate name for an OpenJDK package for our distribution.

For an RPM-based distribution, we'll need to first search for the package names, because package names are varied between different distributions, as shown here:

```
yum search openjdk
```

You will see an output like this:

```
java-1.6.0-openjdk.x86_64 : OpenJDK Runtime Environment
java-1.6.0-openjdk-demo.x86_64 : OpenJDK Demos
java-1.6.0-openjdk-devel.x86_64 : OpenJDK Development Environment
java-1.6.0-openjdk-javadoc.x86_64 : OpenJDK API Documentation
java-1.6.0-openjdk-src.x86_64 : OpenJDK Source Bundle
java-1.7.0-openjdk.x86_64 : OpenJDK Runtime Environment
java-1.7.0-openjdk-demo.x86_64 : OpenJDK Demos
java-1.7.0-openjdk-devel.x86_64 : OpenJDK Development Environment
java-1.7.0-openjdk-javadoc.noarch : OpenJDK API Documentation
java-1.7.0-openjdk-src.x86_64 : OpenJDK Source Bundle
```

You may install all of the packages that have the desired version. Then, we will run another command, using the package name we've just found:

```
yum install <a found package name>
```

This will also trigger an automatic download and installation.

If we have a Gentoo-based distribution, just type the following:

```
emerge openjdk-1.7
```

This will, depending on your distribution, unpack and install a binary package or, more probably, automatically build this package from source.

There's more...

Aside from the recommended ways, there is a generic installation procedure. It is quite simple, though it may do some damage to your operating system, so don't use it unless you really know what you're doing:

1. This is the way to unpack the OpenJDK system and then install it yourself. To get the builds, we will refer again to the unofficial build page, `https://github.com/alexkasko/openjdk-unofficial-builds`.

2. Then unpack the downloaded package into a folder and run the following command from it:

```
java -jar ./install.jar
```

3. A GUI installer window will appear. Read and accept the license, choose the directory, and allow OpenJDK to be created, if it does not exist, as shown:

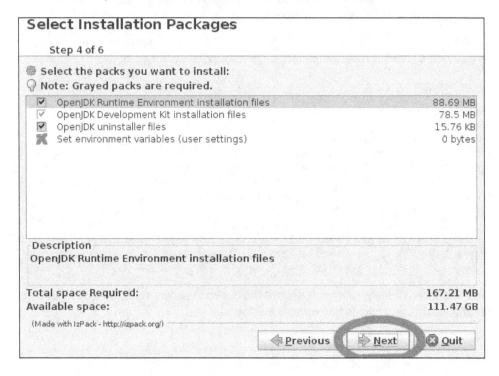

4. Check the preceding checkbox if you want to make this installation the default one. Then click on the **Next** button.

5. Wait for the installation to complete, and click on **Next** for the last time.

6. Then click on **Done**.

Configuring OpenJDK on Linux

Linux configuration profiles differ from the Windows ones, because those systems are working with resources as well as with hardware in a slightly different fashion. Here, we will briefly explain those differences and a way to overcome them. Moreover, different Linux distributions, as always, have different ways to deal with the configuration. We will try to pass through the most noticeable ones.

Getting ready

To follow this recipe, you will need an OpenJDK instance installed on a Linux system. The deb, rpm, or ebuild distributions will suite us really well, although we will see a method for generic Linux configuration also.

Also, we will need the bash startup files to be installed properly.

> In most Linux distributions, the generic way to configure anything that needs root access is not recommended, and the results of such an approach tend to vanish with each update. Usually, there are distribution-recommended how-to's where the problem solution is described.

How to do it...

First let's check whether your bash startup files are installed. The simplest possible way is to configure your OpenJDK using them. They are system-wide and easy to use, though there are drawbacks in their usage, such as update conflicts:

1. Type the following line in your terminal:

   ```
   cat /etc/profile
   ```

   If the file exists and contains some kind of shell script, then your bash startup file's setup is probably correct. If not, please set it up by following your distribution instructions.

2. Then add the /etc/profile.d/openjdk.sh file.

3. In order to configure different things, write the following:

   ```
   To set JAVA_HOME
   JAVA_HOME=<youJDK installation directory>
   export JAVA_HOME

   To append JAVA_HOME to PATH
   pathappend $JAVA_HOME/bin PATH

   To adjust CLASSPATH directory
   AUTO_CLASSPATH_DIR=<classpath dir>
   pathprepend . CLASSPATH

   for dir in `find ${AUTO_CLASSPATH_DIR} -type d 2>/dev/null`; do
       pathappend $dir CLASSPATH
   ```

```
    done

    for jar in `find ${AUTO_CLASSPATH_DIR} -name "*.jar" 2>/dev/null`;
    do
        pathappend $jar CLASSPATH
    done

    export CLASSPATH
```

> The CLASSPATH env variable should be avoided as much as
> possible. It is generally used by legacy Java applications mostly
> configured for JDK 1.2 and below. Use -classpath with java
> and javac commands instead.

The preceding code is quite simple—it just appends all JAR files to the classpath.

How it works...

This script is called during shell initialization, so whenever you perform shell initialization, these variables will be exported. The variables are thus system-wide, so be careful while playing with them, as they can cause your Java to fail permanently if you make some errors in this file.

There's more...

On Linux, you can see the directory structure of the installed OpenJDK using the tree command.

To do so, install the tree package (use your distribution's documentation if possible) and type:

```
    tree -L 1 <path-to-openjdk> -lah
```

You will see something like the following:

```
/usr/lib/jvm/java-7-openjdk-amd64
├── [  22]  ASSEMBLY_EXCEPTION -> jre/ASSEMBLY_EXCEPTION
├── [4.0K]  bin
├── [  41]  docs -> ../../../share/doc/openjdk-7-jre-headless
├── [4.0K]  include
├── [4.0K]  jre
```

```
├─── [4.0K]   lib
├─── [4.0K]   man
├─── [  20]   src.zip -> ../openjdk-7/src.zip
└─── [  22]   THIRD_PARTY_README -> jre/THIRD_PARTY_README
```

This is the first-level directory structure in which:

- ▸ ASSEMBLY_EXCEPTION is about licensing, and so is THIRD_PARTY_README.
- ▸ The docs folder is for various OpenJDK documentation (changelog, copyrights, authors, and so on).
- ▸ The include directory is to include paths (for JNI, for example).
- ▸ The jre directory is where the Java Runtime is placed.
- ▸ The lib directory is where various OpenJDK libraries are placed (such as Jigsaw or CORBA support; mainly, it consists of all OpenJDK code).
- ▸ The man command is a manual pages entry for OpenJDK. It contains OpenJDK classes, javadocs, and other manual entries. It may be extremely useful in the highly improbable event of Internet connection loss.

Navigating through OpenJDK groups and projects

OpenJDK is not one huge project. It consists of a large number of subprojects, and is developed by relatively small groups of developers. We will look at them and realize what is going on under the hood of OpenJDK.

Getting ready

To follow this recipe, you will need an OpenJDK instance installed and an established Internet connection. The recipe is more for the initial understanding of the process rather than for practical use, so if you are familiar with these matters, don't hesitate to skip this recipe entirely.

How to do it...

We will see what OpenJDK consists of:

1. Go to http://openjdk.java.net/.
2. In the right column, there are overviews of groups as well as projects.

3. We will select one of them to get through the process.

 The process will be described in detail in *Chapter 8, Hacking OpenJDK*.

4. Let the selected project be JDK9.

5. Go to the JDK9 project page at http://openjdk.java.net/projects/jdk9/.

There's not very much to see, because there is only the basic on-boarding information. Most of the project business is in the bug tracker.

After we read the information about the project on an official site, we will go to JDK JIRA to see what's happening here. We will go to the JDK9 part of JIRA at https://bugs.openjdk. java.net/browse/JDK/fixforversion/14949.

Here we can see various issues related directly to JDK9 and see how the process is going.

How it works...

Groups are sets of developers who may work on different projects but in one large scope. Developers participate in chosen projects, and projects are sponsored by groups.

 To participate in a group and become a contributor, follow the instructions at http://openjdk.java.net/contribute/.

There are four major types of projects:

- ▶ Feature
- ▶ Improvement
- ▶ Replacement
- ▶ Portability

For example, the JDK9 project is a featured one. The graphics rasterizer project is a replacement one, while the Swing group is a whole group that is focused on the improvement of Swing.

Various ports' projects are obviously the portability ones.

See also

- ▶ See *Chapter 8, Hacking OpenJDK*, *Chapter 11, Troubleshooting*, and *Chapter 13, Build Automation*—they will suit you just well
- ▶ Tails in *Chapter 4, Building OpenJDK 8*

2
Building OpenJDK 6

In this chapter, we will cover:

- ▸ Preparing CA certificates
- ▸ Building OpenJDK 6 on Ubuntu Linux 12.04 LTS
- ▸ Setting up the minimum build environment for the most compatible Linux builds
- ▸ Installing Cygwin for Windows builds
- ▸ Building 32-bit FreeType libraries for OpenJDK 6 on Windows
- ▸ Building 64-bit FreeType libraries for OpenJDK 6 on Windows
- ▸ Building 32-bit OpenJDK 6 on Windows 7 SP1
- ▸ Building 64-bit OpenJDK 6 on Windows 7 x64 SP1

Introduction

OpenJDK 6 is a free and open source implementation of the Java Platform, Standard Edition Version 6. Currently, this project is actively maintained by the community with the leading role held by Red Hat, Inc.

Among all Java Platform versions, Java 6 had the longest lifetime. Its Reference Implementation Sun Java 6 was released in December 2006, and OpenJDK 7, the Reference Implementation of the next version of the Java Platform, wasn't out until July 2011. During these 5 years, a lot of applications were built on this platform version.

Also, during these years the authors of Reference Implementation, Sun Microsystems, were acquired by the Oracle Corporation, and so the product was renamed Oracle Java. In February 2013, Oracle ended public support for Oracle Java 6, but it didn't mean the end of Java 6: Red Hat, Inc. took the leading role in OpenJDK 6 and now it continues to release new versions on a regular basis.

The OpenJDK 6 codebase differs greatly from both Oracle and Sun Java 6 and OpenJDK 7 codebases. It started as a fork of OpenJDK 7 build 20, and the first version that passed the Java Compatibility Kit test suite was released before the general availability of OpenJDK 7. The versioning scheme differs from the versioning of Oracle Java 6. Each release doesn't have an update number and only has a build number, such as b01 and b02. At the time of writing this book, the release from January 2014 is Version b30.

You can see the family tree of OpenJDK 6 in the following diagram:

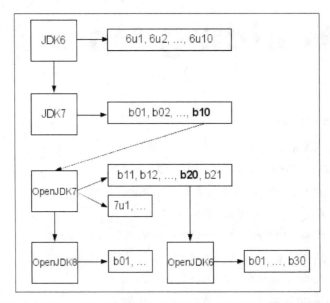

Diagram reference: https://blogs.oracle.com/darcy/entry/openjdk_6_genealogy

OpenJDK 6 is supported on Linux, Windows, and Solaris operating systems. Only Windows and Linux versions will be discussed further. For both Linux and Windows operating systems, x86 and x86_64 architectures are supported. To conform with the OpenJDK terminology, the **i586** term will be used for x86 architecture and **amd64** will be used for the x86_64 one. OpenJDK 6 does not support cross compilation, so the i586 operating system must be used to build the i586 version, and the same is true for amd64. The build process for both architectures is almost the same for the Linux version, but differs a lot for the Windows one.

Preparing CA certificates

Public-key cryptography is used widely on the Internet. When the web browser opens a secured website, it checks the server-side certificate against the website domain name. To perform such checks, all web browsers have a list of **Certificate Authority** (**CA**) certificates that may be used to sign server-side certificates of websites. Such checks may be disabled but they are a necessary part of secure web browsing, client banking, and so on.

When website access is used by a Java program (for example, to download a file from a secure site), programs such as the browser in the preceding example should check the site certificate. Such a check is usually performed by the underlying SSL API implementation, and with the browser, the list of CA certificates must be available to the OpenJDK runtime.

Such a list is stored in the `openjdk_directory/jre/security/cacerts` file in the **Java KeyStore** (**JKS**) format. In official OpenJDK 6 tarballs, the `cacerts` file contains no certificates. If runtime with such empty file is used to access a secured website, an obscure exception will be thrown.

The following code snippet will cause the exception with the root cause:

```
new URL("https://github.com/").openStream().close();
Caused by: java.security.InvalidAlgorithmParameterException:
    the trustAnchors parameter must be non-empty
      at java.security.cert.PKIXParameters.setTrustAnchors
        (PKIXParameters.java:...
          at java.security.cert.PKIXParameters.<init>
            (PKIXParameters.java:120)
          at java.security.cert.PKIXBuilderParameters.<init>
            (PKIXBuilderParameters....
          at sun.security.validator.PKIXValidator.<init>
            (PKIXValidator.java:73)
          ... 47 more
```

Getting ready

To prevent such an exception, a proper `cacerts` file should be prepared. It may be used during the OpenJDK build or added to the `jre/security` directory later. The list of CA certificates should be obtained and converted to the JKS format. To download and convert the CA list, we will need a recent version of the Ubuntu (or similar Linux-based) operating system with cURL and `keytool` utilities installed. You will also need `cat`, `awk`, and `csplit` standard utilities; these should be already installed as part of the `coreutils` package.

How to do it...

The following steps will help us to prepare CA certificates:

1. Install the cURL utility:

   ```
   sudo apt-get install curl
   ```

2. Install the `keytool` utility as part of the prebuilt OpenJDK package:

   ```
   sudo apt-get install openjdk-7-jdk
   ```

3. Download the CA list used by the Firefox web browser, preconverted in the PEM format from the cURL library website into the `cacert.pem` file:

```
curl -L http://curl.haxx.se/ca/cacert.pem -o cacert.pem
```

4. Split the `cacert.pem` file into multiple files with the `cert_` prefix. Each file will contain a single CA certificate:

```
cat cacert.pem | awk '/-----BEGIN CERTIFICATE-----/,
   /-----END CERTIFICATE-----/{ print $0; }'
     > cacert-clean.pem

csplit -k -f cert_ cacert-clean.pem "
   /-----BEGIN CERTIFICATE-----/" {*}
```

5. Create a JKS keystore and load all CA certificates there using `keytool`:

```
for CERT_FILE in cert_*; do
     ALIAS=$(basename ${CERT_FILE})
     echo yes | keytool -import -alias ${ALIAS}
        -keystore cacerts -storepass 'changeit'
        -file ${CERT_FILE} || :
done
```

6. Check the `cacerts` file's contents:

```
keytool -list -keystore cacerts -storepass 'changeit'
```

Now the `cacerts` file is ready to use.

How it works...

A list of CA certificates used by the Firefox web browser is freely available as part of the open source security library from Mozilla called NSS. This list is available in text format at `http://mxr.mozilla.org/mozilla/source/security/nss/lib/ckfw/builtins/certdata.txt`. We have used the same file but preconverted it in to PEM format, which is available at the cURL website.

The `keytool` utility understands certificates in the PEM format, but it can only load certificates one-by-one, so the big PEM file is split beforehand. Also, the `keytool` utility has strict requirements from the PEM files: no text content is allowed before /-----BEGIN CERTIFICATE-----/ and after /-----END CERTIFICATE-----/ strings. The `awk` utility is used to strip unneeded prefixes and postfixes.

Then the `csplit` utility is used to split the file using /-----BEGIN CERTIFICATE-----/ separators.

Next, the split files are loaded into the keystore one by one. The keystore is created on the first certificate load.

The `changeit` password is used for this keystore, which may be quite an unsecure choice for the password. However, this does not matter for the `cacerts` file because the CA certificates contain only public keys and need not be hidden behind the password.

There's more...

Most of this recipe is not specific to the Ubuntu operating system; any Unix-like environment (for example, Cygwin on Windows) would suffice.

Bash scripts in this recipe can be replaced by any other scripting language such as Python or PowerShell.

Instead of the CA list from Firefox, any other set of CA certificates may be used. Some CA certificates may be removed, for example a particular CA certificate not trusted by the user, or some additional CA certificates may be added, for example inner corporate CA certificates to access a company's intranet resources.

See also

- ► The source of the script used in this recipe is the `obuildfactory` project on GitHub at `https://github.com/hgomez/obuildfactory/blob/2075649116e32a5f 0bbf8fc7b2791769387eda92/openjdk7/macosx/build.sh#L54`
- ► The cURL utility manual at `http://curl.haxx.se/docs/manpage.html`
- ► The keytool utility manual at `http://docs.oracle.com/javase/6/docs/ technotes/tools/windows/keytool.html`

Building OpenJDK 6 on Ubuntu Linux 12.04 LTS

The build process of OpenJDK relies heavily on Unix-like development tools. Linux-based operating systems usually have top notch support for such tools, so building OpenJDK on Linux can be simpler than on Windows. For major distributions such as Fedora or Ubuntu, build toolchain and all dependencies are already included in distributions as packages and can be installed easily.

Ubuntu 12.04 LTS was chosen for this book because it is one of the most popular Linux distributions. For readers running other operating Ubuntu 12.04, virtual images may be found online for the most popular virtualization tools, such as Oracle VirtualBox or VMware.

To build binaries for i586 and amd64 architectures, corresponding versions of Ubuntu should be used. Build instructions are exactly the same for both architectures, so they won't be mentioned further in this recipe.

Getting ready

For this recipe, we will need a clean Ubuntu 12.04 (server or desktop version) running.

How to do it...

The following steps will help us to build OpenJDK:

1. Install prepackaged binaries of OpenJDK 6:

   ```
   sudo apt-get install openjdk-6-jdk
   ```

2. Install GCC toolchain and build dependencies:

   ```
   sudo apt-get build-dep openjdk-6
   sudo apt-get install libmotif-dev
   ```

3. Download and decompress official OpenJDK 6 build 30 tarball:

   ```
   mkdir openjdk-6-src-b30-21_jan_2014
   cd openjdk-6-src-b30-21_jan_2014
   wget https://java.net/projects/openjdk6/downloads/download/
   openjdk-6-src-b30-21_jan_2014.tar.xz
   tar xJf openjdk-6-src-b30-21_jan_2014.tar.xz
   rm openjdk-6-src-b30-21_jan_2014.tar.xz
   ```

4. Open the `jdk/make/javax/sound/jsoundalsa/Makefile` file with your favorite
   text editor and change line 68 from `LDFLAGS += -lasound` to:

   ```
   OTHER_LDLIBS += -lasound
   ```

5. Create a new text file `buildenv.sh` with the following environment settings:

   ```
   export LD_LIBRARY_PATH=
   export CLASSPATH=
   export JAVA_HOME=
   export LANG=C
   export ALT_BOOTDIR=/usr/lib/jvm/java-6-openjdk
   ```

6. Import the environment into the current shell session (note a dot and a space
   before it):

   ```
   . buildenv.sh
   ```

7. Start the build process from the `openjdk-6-src-b30-21_jan_2014` directory:

   ```
   make 2>&1 | tee make.log
   ```

8. Wait for the build to finish, and try to run the newly built binaries:

```
cd build/linux-amd64/j2sdk-image/
./bin/java -version
openjdk version "1.6.0-internal"
OpenJDK Runtime Environment (build 1.6.0-internal-ubuntu_22_
jan_2014_13_12-b00)
OpenJDK 64-Bit Server VM (build 23.25-b01, mixed mode)
```

How it works...

Prepackaged binaries of OpenJDK 6 are required because some of the build steps are run using the external Java runtime.

The `build-dep` command is used to install all the dependencies that are required to build the specified package. As Ubuntu packaged OpenJDK 6 is quite close to the official OpenJDK 6, this command will install almost all of the required dependencies.

The `libmotif-dev` package is the only additional package required. It contains the Motif GUI toolkit header files.

The `jdk/make/javax/sound/jsoundalsa/Makefile` file adjustment is required to conform with the Ubuntu 12.04 GCC 4.6 toolchain. It is not required for the original GCC 4.2 toolchain and may not be required for more recent OpenJDK 6 official sources, because this change is going to be included in OpenJDK 6 upstream.

The `tee` command is used to write output to the logfile and the screen simultaneously.

After a successful build on the amd64 platform, JDK files will be placed in `build/linux-amd64/j2sdk-image` and JRE files will be placed in `build/linux-amd64/j2re-image`. On the i586 platform, the `build/linux-i586` path will be used instead.

There's more...

Javadoc generation takes a lot of time and is the most memory consuming step of the build. It may be skipped with an additional environment variable:

```
export NO_DOCS=true
```

This build has generated a milestone tag and a build number `b00`. The predefined build number and milestone may be set using additional environment variables:

```
export MILESTONE=ubuntu-build
export BUILD_NUMBER=b30
```

The `cacerts` file may be provided during the build using an additional environment variable:

```
export ALT_CACERTS_FILE=path/to/cacerts
```

For amd64 builds, preinstalled Java provided by the `ALT_BOOTDIR` variable may be either the amd64 or i586 build. The i586 binaries consume less memory and may be used for amd64 builds on limited hardware.

The build process for OpenJDK 6 is effectively single-threaded; parallel builds (using `make -j N`) are not supported for this version.

See also

- ▸ The previous recipe *Preparing CA certificates*
- ▸ The official build instructions for OpenJDK 6 at `http://hg.openjdk.java.net/jdk6/jdk6/raw-file/tip/README-builds.html`
- ▸ The source bundles of the current OpenJDK 6 version from Red Hat, Inc. at `https://java.net/projects/openjdk6/downloads`
- ▸ The source bundles of older versions of OpenJDK 6 from Oracle at `http://download.java.net/openjdk/jdk6/promoted/`
- ▸ The mailing list thread about problems with `jsoundalsa` on Ubuntu 12.04 noted previously at `http://mail.openjdk.java.net/pipermail/jdk6-dev/2014-January/003222.html`

Setting up the minimum build environment for the most compatible Linux builds

OpenJDK 6 on Linux was developed for and most excessively tested with those GCC toolchains available at that time. Modern Linux distributions have newer toolchains, for example, Ubuntu 12.04 has GCC 4.6. Newer toolchains may have more advanced optimizations and provide slightly faster code, but older ones should be more stable for OpenJDK.

Oracle published the minimum build environment description for OpenJDK 6. It says:

> *"Building with the MBE will generate the most compatible bits that install on, and run correctly on, the most variations of the same base OS and hardware architecture."*

We are going to build OpenJDK 6 on one of the minimum build environment platforms—Debian Linux 5.0 Lenny. The build instructions are exactly the same for i586 and amd64 architectures, so they won't be mentioned further in this recipe.

The build steps are similar to the previous recipe so we'll concentrate on different steps.

Getting ready

In this recipe, we will need Debian Lenny running. Installation images may be downloaded from the Debian CDImage archive. Lenny may not be compatible with some of the hardware on newer laptops, but should run fine with virtualization tools such as Oracle VirtualBox or VMware.

How to do it...

The following steps will help us to set up the minimum build environment:

1. Add archive repositories to the `/etc/apt/sources.list` file:

   ```
   deb http://archive.kernel.org/debian-archive/debian
     lenny main contrib non-free

   deb-src http://archive.kernel.org/debian-archive/debian
     lenny main contrib non-free
   ```

2. Install OpenJDK 6 binaries and build dependencies:

   ```
   sudo apt-get install openjdk-6-jdk

   sudo apt-get build-dep openjdk-6

   sudo apt-get install libmotif-dev
   ```

3. Download and decompress Apache Ant:

   ```
   wget http://archive.apache.org/dist/ant/binaries/apache-ant-1.8.4-
   bin.tar.gz

   tar xzf apache-ant-1.8.4-bin.tar.gz
   ```

4. Create a new text file `buildenv.sh` with environment settings, and import its content into the current bash shell:

   ```
   export LD_LIBRARY_PATH=

   export CLASSPATH=

   export JAVA_HOME=

   export LANG=C

   export ALT_BOOTDIR=/usr/lib/jvm/java-6-openjdk

   export ANT_HOME=path/to/apache-ant-1.8.4/

   export PATH=$ANT_HOME/bin:$PATH

   . buildenv.sh
   ```

5. Download and decompress the official OpenJDK 6 build 30 tarball:

   ```
   mkdir openjdk-6-src-b30-21_jan_2014

   cd openjdk-6-src-b30-21_jan_2014
   ```

```
wget https://java.net/projects/openjdk6/downloads/download/
openjdk-6-src-b30-21_jan_2014.tar.gz

tar xzf openjdk-6-src-b30-21_jan_2014.tar.gz

rm openjdk-6-src-b30-21_jan_2014.tar.gz
```

6. Start the build process from the `openjdk-6-src-b30-21_jan_2014` directory:

   ```
   make 2>&1 | tee make.log
   ```

7. Wait for the build to finish.

How it works...

Archive repository setup is required because the official Lenny repositories are no longer available.

A newer version of Apache Ant is required because the bundled Version 1.7.0 in Lenny is too old and OpenJDK 6 requires Ant 1.7.1 or higher.

There's more...

Other older Linux distributions such as Ubuntu 8.04 or Fedora 9 also may be used as the minimum build environment.

See also

▸ The *Building OpenJDK 6 on Ubuntu Linux 12.04 LTS* recipe

▸ The official build instructions for OpenJDK, 6 with the description of minimum build platforms, at `http://hg.openjdk.java.net/jdk6/jdk6/raw-file/tip/README-builds.html#MBE`

▸ The Debian CDImages archive at `http://cdimage.debian.org/cdimage/archive/`

Installing Cygwin for Windows builds

Like most of the other cross-platform open source projects, OpenJDK uses Unix-like tools for the build process. Tools such as `gmake`, `awk`, and `cpio` are ubiquitous for the Unix and Linux world and may be found on almost any Unix-like platform. However, these tools are based on Unix process behavior, and that becomes a problem when we want to run them on Windows.

Cygwin is a set of free and open source tools being developed by Red Had, Inc. and provides limited support for the Unix-like environment in Windows. It is required to build OpenJDK on Windows.

OpenJDK requires Cygwin i586 for both i586 and amd64 builds. The installation procedure is the same for both Windows 7 SP1 i586 and Windows 7 SP1 amd64 so we won't mention architecture further in this recipe.

Getting ready

To install and successfully use Cygwin, we'll need a clean installation of Windows 7 SP1 without antivirus software running.

How to do it...

The following steps will help us to install Cygwin:

1. Download `setup-x86.exe` from the `http://cygwin.com/` website.
2. Run the installer and choose `http://mirrors.kernel.org` as a packages' mirror.
3. Choose the additional packages:

    ```
    Devel/binutils
    Interpreters/m4
    Utils/cpio
    Archive/zip
    Archive/unzip
    System/procps
    ```

4. Perform the installation into the directory with the path in ASCII letters or numbers without spaces.

How it works...

Any antivirus software (or similar software that may scan the memory of other applications) is prohibited because it may interfere with Cygwin. Cygwin uses complex techniques to simulate the fork functionality of Unix on Windows. These techniques may not work with antivirus scanners running.

Only the i586 version on Cygwin is supported to build OpenJDK. The amd64 Cygwin may or may not work.

The Cygwin community hosts a lot of packages' mirrors worldwide. We use the `https://www.kernel.org/` mirror as one that should have the most complete set of prebuilt packages:

*   The `binutils` package is required for the `ar` utility. This is a special kind of archiver that may be used to create and update static libraries
*   The `m4` package is required to work with classic Unix macro processor scripts

- ▶ The `cpio` utility is used as an archiver because it may be much faster than the more popular tar utility in some environments

- ▶ The `procps` package is required for the free utility, which is used to get information about free and used memory

There's more...

OpenJDK 6 can also be built using commercial MKS toolkit. This method provides shorter build times, but is not supported for OpenJDK 8 and above.

A Cygwin installation may be copied from one Windows box to another without installation. This may be useful for builds on clean Windows boxes. Besides the usual windows binaries, Cygwin uses special kinds of symlink files, for example, `bin/awk` actually points to `bin/gawk.exe`. These symlinks may be crippled if loaded into or from version control systems such as Git. This problem may be circumvented by replacing symlinks with copies of actual binaries with symlink names: `gawk.exe` to `awk.exe` and so on.

See also

- ▶ The official build instructions for OpenJDK 6 with the list of required Cygwin packages at `http://hg.openjdk.java.net/jdk6/jdk6/raw-file/tip/README-builds.html#cygwin`

- ▶ The list of applications that may interfere with Cygwin at `https://cygwin.com/faq/faq.html#faq.using.bloda`

- ▶ The Cygwin user's guide at `https://www.cygwin.com/cygwin-ug-net/cygwin-ug-net.html`

Building 32-bit FreeType libraries for OpenJDK 6 on Windows

The majority of fonts used in modern software are encoded in vector format for proper scaling support. There are multiple standards for vector fonts, for example, Metafont from Professor Donald E. Knuth, Type1 from Adobe, TrueType from Apple and Microsoft, and OpenType from Adobe and Microsoft.

Rasterization of vector fonts is a remarkably complex task and most desktop software (such as web browsers or text processors) use third-party libraries to work with fonts.

Sun Microsystems licensed a third-party closed-source font library for use in Sun Java implementations. Sources of this library could not be released to public along with the initial release of OpenJDK. The Font Scaler Replacement Project was launched in the early days of OpenJDK to adopt an open source font library instead.

FreeType is a free and open source (under permissive license) font rasterization library. It is used widely in open source desktop software. FreeType was chosen by the OpenJDK team as a replacement for the closed-source font library and is now used by OpenJDK on all supported platforms. Prebuilt static and dynamic FreeType libraries are required for OpenJDK builds on Windows.

Getting ready

For this recipe we should have Windows 7 SP1 i586 running.

How to do it...

The following steps will help us in building FreeType:

1. Install Visual Studio.NET 2003 to the default installation path. Only Prerequisites and Visual C++ components are required.

2. Download the FreeType 2.5.2 source tarball from `http://freetype.org/` and decompress it.

3. Open the file `include\config\ftoption.h` and uncomment:

   ```
   #define FT_CONFIG_OPTION_SUBPIXEL_RENDERING
   ```

4. Change lines `/* #define FT_EXPORT(x) extern x */` and `/* #define FT_EXPORT_DEF(x)   x */` to:

   ```
   #define FT_EXPORT(x) __declspec(dllexport) x
   #define FT_EXPORT_DEF(x) __declspec(dllexport) x
   ```

5. Open the project file `builds\windows\visualc\freetype.dsw` in Visual Studio.NET 2003.

6. Change `Solution Configuration` to `Release Multithreaded` and build the solution. The `freetype252MT.lib` file will be placed into the `objs` directory.

7. Rename the file `freetype.lib` and save it for OpenJDK builds.

8. In **Project Properties** change **Configuration Type** to **Dynamic Library (.dll)** and build the solution. The `freetype.dll` and `freetype.exp` files will be placed into the `objs\release_mt` directory.

The directory with three result files will be denoted by the `ALT_FREETYPE_LIB_PATH` environment variable during OpenJDK builds.

How it works...

The `FT_CONFIG_OPTION_SUBPIXEL_RENDERING` macro enables subpixel rendering functionality in FreeType implementation.

The `FT_EXPORT` and `FT_EXPORT_DEF` macros should be adjusted with the calling conventions for the current platform. We changed them to use Windows-specific calling conventions.

FreeType has no predefined project file for Visual Studio.NET 2003. Instead, we are using the project file created for Visual Studio 6.

See also

- ▶ The *Building 64-bit FreeType libraries for OpenJDK 6 on Windows* recipe
- ▶ The FreeType official website `http://freetype.org/`
- ▶ Professor Donald E. Knuth's interview covering Metafont and TrueType at `http://www.advogato.org/article/28.html`
- ▶ The *OpenJDK: Font Scaler Replacement Project* page at `http://openjdk.java.net/projects/font-scaler/`

Building 64-bit FreeType libraries for OpenJDK 6 on Windows

The FreeType build for Windows amd64 is similar to the i586 build but has a much more complex configuration. Contrary to the i586 version, the amd64 library can be built with freely available tools using Microsoft Visual Studio 2005 Express Edition with the Windows Server 2003 SP1 Platform SDK.

Getting ready

For this recipe, we need to have Windows 7 SP1 amd64 running.

How to do it...

The following steps will help us in building FreeType:

1. Download the Visual Studio 2005 Express Edition from `http://www.microsoft.com/en-in/default.aspx` and install it to the default location. The messages about Windows 7 compatibility problems may be ignored.
2. Install `VS80sp1-KB926748-X86-INTL` and `VS80sp1-KB932232-X86-ENU` Visual Studio updates.

3. Download Windows Server 2003 SP1 Platform SDK from `http://www.microsoft.com/en-in/default.aspx` and install it using the default installation path. AMD-64 components are required for the build.

4. Perform steps 2, 3, and 4 from the previous recipe to download and adjust FreeType sources.

5. From the **Start** menu go to **Microsoft Platform SDK for Windows Server 2003 SP1 | Open Build Environment Window | Windows Server 2003 64-bit Build Environment | Set Win Svr 2003 x64 Build Env (Retail)**.

6. From the `cmd.exe` window that appears, run (the administrator permissions warning may be ignored):

```
>"C:\Program Files (x86)\Microsoft Visual Studio 8\Common7\IDE\VCExpress.exe"
```

7. In the main menu navigate to **Tools | Options | Projects and Solutions | VC++ Directories** and adjust the following directories:

Executable files:

```
C:\Program Files\Microsoft Platform SDK\Bin\win64\x86\AMD64
C:\Program Files\Microsoft Platform SDK\Bin
C:\Windows\System32
```

Include files:

```
C:\Program Files\Microsoft Platform SDK\Include
C:\Program Files\Microsoft Platform SDK\Include\crt
```

Library files:

```
C:\Program Files\Microsoft Platform SDK\Lib\AMD64
```

8. Open the FreeType solution at this path `freetype-2.5.2\builds\windows\vc2005\freetype.sln`.

9. In the menu, navigate to **Project | Properties | Configuration Properties | Configuration Manager** and choose **<New ...>** under **Active solution platform**.

10. Type `new platform x64` and choose **Win32** from **Copy settings from**.

11. On the **Configuration Manager** form, navigate to **Active solution configuration | LIB Release Multithreaded** and then go to **Active solution platform | x64**.

12. On the same form, in the grid for the FreeType project, navigate to **Configuration | Release multithreaded** and leave the **Win32** value under the **Platform** menu.

13. In the **Configuration Properties** menu, check whether **Configuration Type** is set to **Static Library (.lib)**.

14. Navigate to **Configuration Properties | C/C++ | Preprocessor** and change the **WIN32** value in the **Processor Definitions** string to **WIN64**.

15. Run **Build Solution** under **Build**, the `freetype252MT.lib` library will be placed into the `freetype-2.5.2\objs\win32\vc2005` directory. Rename it to `freetype.lib`, and save it for later.

16. In the **Configuration Properties** menu, change **Configuration Type** to **Dynamic Library (.dll)** and choose **Apply**.

17. Navigate to **Configuration Properties | Linker | Input** and put `bufferoverflowU.lib` into the **Additional Dependencies** field.

18. Navigate to **Configuration Properties | Linker | Command Line** and put `/MACHINE:AMD64` into the **Additional options** field.

19. Clean and build the solution. Target libraries `freetype.dll` and `freetype.exp` will be placed into the `freetype-2.5.2\objs\release_mt` directory.

The directory with three result files will be denoted by the `ALT_FREETYPE_LIB_PATH` environment variable during OpenJDK builds.

How it works...

Visual Studio 2005 Express does not support amd64 architecture, so the setup to use amd64 compilers from Windows SDK takes most of this recipe.

See also

▶ The *Building 32-bit FreeType libraries for OpenJDK 6 on Windows* recipe

▶ The FreeType official website `http://freetype.org/`

Building 32-bit OpenJDK 6 on Windows 7 SP1

Windows builds are much more cumbersome than Linux ones. Despite that, GCC toolchain is available on Windows. Through the MinGW project, OpenJDK uses official Microsoft compilers from Visual Studio and Windows SDK. This brings a lot of complications because the Microsoft toolchain doesn't work well with the Unix-like environment provided by Cygwin.

Visual Studio.NET 2003 is required to build i586 binaries. OpenJDK 6 on Windows i586 is the only version in this book that cannot be built using freely available tools. VS 2003 was chosen for OpenJDK 6 because it supports Windows 2000, which was critical at the time of Sun Java 6's development.

Getting ready

For this recipe, we should have Windows 7 SP1 i586 running with no antivirus software installed. Antivirus software is not allowed because it may interfere with the Cygwin runtime.

How to do it...

The following steps will help us to build OpenJDK 6:

1. Install Visual Studio.NET 2003 to the default installation path. Only the prerequisites and the Visual C++.NET component are required.

2. Install or copy the preinstalled version of Cygwin to `c:\cygwin`.

3. Download and install Microsoft DirectX 9.0 SDK (Summer 2004) to the default installation path. Note that this distribution is not available anymore from the `http://www.microsoft.com/en-in/default.aspx` website. We can download it from some other places online and check the file details:

   ```
   name: dxsdk_sum2004.exe
   size: 239008008 bytes
   sha1sum: 73d875b97591f48707c38ec0dbc63982ff45c661
   ```

4. Download Platform Software Development Kit Redistributable: Microsoft Layer for Unicode on Windows 95, 98, and Me Systems, 1.1.3790.0 from `http://www.microsoft.com/en-in/default.aspx` and install it into the `c:\unicows` directory.

5. Download `unicows.lib` from the `openjdk-unofficial-builds` GitHub project and put this into the `c:\unicows` directory too.

6. Download the Apache Ant version 1.8.4 ZIP distribution from the `http://apache.org/` website and decompress it into the `c:\ant` directory.

7. Download GNU make utility binary from the `http://www.cmake.org/` website using `http://www.cmake.org/files/cygwin/make.exe-cygwin1.7`, rename it to `make.exe`, and put it into the `c:\make` directory.

8. Create the `c:\path_prepend` directory and copy the `find.exe` and `sort.exe` files from the Cygwin installation.

9. Download the prebuilt FreeType libraries from the `openjdk-unofficial-builds` GitHub project (directory `6_32`) and put the binaries into the `c:\freetype` directory and header files into the `c:\freetype\include` directory.

10. Install OpenJDK 6 binaries or Oracle Java 6 into `c:\jdk6`.

11. Download the official OpenJDK 6 build 30 sources tarball from the `https://java.net/projects/openjdk6/downloads` web page and decompress it into the `c:\sources` directory (warning: the tarball does not include the `root` directory)

12. In the `sa.make` file at `hotspot\make\windows\makefiles`, change line 100 from `SA_CFLAGS = $(SA_CFLAGS) /ZI` to:

```
SA_CFLAGS = $(SA_CFLAGS) /Zi
```

13. Create a `build.bat` batch file and write the following environment variables settings there:

```
@echo off
set LD_LIBRARY_PATH=
set CLASSPATH=
set JAVA_HOME=
set PATH=c:/path_prepend;C:/WINDOWS/system32;C:/WINDOWS;C:/
WINDOWS/System32/Wbem;c:/make;c:/cygwin/bin;c:/jdk6/bin;c:/ant/bin
set ALT_BOOTDIR=c:/jdk6
set ALT_FREETYPE_LIB_PATH=c:/freetype
set ALT_FREETYPE_HEADERS_PATH=c:/freetype/include
set ALT_UNICOWS_LIB_PATH=c:/unicows
set ALT_UNICOWS_DLL_PATH=c:/unicows
call "C:/Program Files/Microsoft Visual Studio .NET 2003/Common7/
Tools/vsvars32.bat"
bash
echo Press any key to close window ...
pause > nul
```

14. Run `build.bat` from Windows Explorer. The `cmd.exe` window should appear with bash launched.

15. From the bash Command Prompt run the following commands:

```
cd /cygdrive/c/sources
chmod -R 777
make > make.log 2>&1
```

16. Launch another Cygwin console and run the following commands:

```
cd /cygdrive/c/sources
tail -f make.log
```

17. Wait for the build to finish.

How it works...

Cygwin installation is covered in the *Installing Cygwin for Windows builds* recipe of this chapter.

Directories in the root of disk C are used here for brevity. Generally, arbitrary paths consisting of ASCII letters or numbers and without spaces can be used.

Visual Studio 2003 is not officially supported on Windows 7. It warns about possible compatibility problems and may have glitches in the GUI interface, but its command-line tools work fine and the GUI interface is not needed for the OpenJDK build.

The newer version of DirectX SDK may also be used.

Different GNU make versions may have different problems on Windows. This particular version from the `cmake` project was tested on different Windows versions and works fine.

This recipe uses prebuilt FreeType 2.4.10 libraries from the `openjdk-unofficial-builds` GitHub project. FreeType may be built from sources using Visual Studio 2003. Please see the *Building 32-bit FreeType libraries for OpenJDK 6 on Windows* recipe in this chapter.

A patch for HotSpot serviceability `Makefile` file is required to circumvent the VS2003 bug discovered after one of the recent security updates. This change is going to be upstreamed into official OpenJDK 6 sources and may not be required for more recent source tarballs.

In environment settings, additional attention should be paid to the order of the contents of the `PATH` variable order. The `sort` and `find` Cygwin utilities go at the start of the `PATH` variable so they are not overshadowed by Windows utilities with the same name but a different functionality. The `make` utility is going goes before Cygwin to not be so they are not overshadowed by another version of make that may be included in the Cygwin installation.

The `chmod 777` command is required to fix Cygwin file permissions that may cause errors in later stages of the build.

The `make` output will be redirected to the `make.log` file. The `2>&1` statement ensures that both `stdout` and `stderr` will be redirected.

The `tail -f` command allows us to watch the contents of the `make.log` file as they are written during the build process.

The `pause > nul` command is added at the end of the batch file to prevent the `cmd.exe` window from disappearing in the case of runtime errors.

There's more...

To build the most compatible binaries, the same recipe should be used, but the Windows 2000 operating system should be used instead of Windows 7.

In Windows 2000, the `chmod 777` command is not required.

See also

- The *Installing Cygwin for Windows builds* recipe
- The *Building OpenJDK 6 on Ubuntu Linux 12.04 LTS* recipe, for information about build tuning
- The *Building 32-bit FreeType libraries for OpenJDK 6 on Windows* recipe
- The *Preparing CA certificates* recipe

- ▸ The official build instructions for OpenJDK 6 at `http://hg.openjdk.java.net/jdk6/jdk6/raw-file/tip/README-builds.html`
- ▸ The mailing list thread about the Serviceability HotSpot patch at `http://mail.openjdk.java.net/pipermail/jdk6-dev/2013-December/003163.html`

Building 64-bit OpenJDK 6 on Windows 7 x64 SP1

The amd64 build on Windows 7 is similar to the i586 build, but has additional complications.

Cygwin (at least the more common i586 version) works much worse on amd64 Windows. Due to a much bigger address space size, Cygwin fork techniques work much slower and are less reliable.

Visual Studio.NET 2003 does not support the amd64 architecture so the Windows Server 2003 SP1 Platform SDK is used instead.

Getting ready

For this recipe, we should have Windows 7 SP1 i586 running with no antivirus software installed. Antivirus software is not allowed because it may interfere with the Cygwin runtime.

How to do it...

The following steps will help us to build OpenJDK:

1. Download the Windows Server 2003 SP1 Platform SDK from the Microsoft website and install it using the default installation path. AMD-64 and MDAC (Microsoft Data Access Services) components are required for the build.

2. Perform steps 2 to 11 from the *Building 32-bit OpenJDK 6 on Windows 7 SP1* recipe (for FreeType libraries use `6_64` directory).

3. Step 12 from the previous recipe is not required for the amd64 build and may be skipped.

4. Create a `build.bat` batch file and write the following environment variables settings:

```
@echo off
set LD_LIBRARY_PATH=
set CLASSPATH=
set JAVA_HOME=
set PATH=C:/path_prepend;C:/WINDOWS/system32;C:/WINDOWS;C:/
WINDOWS/System32/Wbem;C:/make;C:/cygwin/bin;C:/jdk6/bin;C:/ant/bin
set ALT_BOOTDIR=c:/jdk6
set ALT_FREETYPE_LIB_PATH=c:/freetype
```

```
set ALT_FREETYPE_HEADERS_PATH=c:/freetype/include
set ALT_UNICOWS_LIB_PATH=c:/unicows
set ALT_UNICOWS_DLL_PATH=c:/unicows
call "C:/Program Files/Microsoft Platform SDK"/SetEnv.cmd /X64 /
RETAIL
bash
echo Press any key to close window ...
pause > nul
```

5. Follow steps 14 to 17 from the previous recipe.

How it works...

Most of the notes from the i586 build are also valid for the amd64 build except those specific to VS2003.

Patch to serviceability `Makefile` is not required because that part of `Makefile` is specific to i586 builds.

There's more...

To build the most compatible binaries, the same recipe should be used, but the Windows 2003 Server amd64 operating system should be used instead of Windows 7.

In Windows 2003, the `chmod 777` command is not required.

See also

▸ The *Installing Cygwin for Windows builds* recipe

▸ The *Building OpenJDK 6 on Ubuntu Linux 12.04 LTS* recipe, for information about build tuning

▸ The *Building 64-bit FreeType libraries for OpenJDK 6 on Windows* recipe

▸ The *Preparing CA certificates* recipe

▸ The official build instructions for OpenJDK 6 at `http://hg.openjdk.java.net/jdk6/jdk6/raw-file/tip/README-builds.html`

3
Building OpenJDK 7

In this chapter, we will cover:

- ► Building OpenJDK 7 on Ubuntu Linux 12.04 LTS
- ► Building OpenJDK 7 on Mac OS X
- ► Building 32-bit FreeType libraries for OpenJDK 7 on Windows
- ► Building 64-bit FreeType libraries for OpenJDK 7 on Windows
- ► Building 32-bit OpenJDK 7 on Windows 7 SP1
- ► Building 64-bit OpenJDK 7 on Windows 7 x64 SP1
- ► Preparing a standalone toolchain for 32- and 64-bit Windows builds

Introduction

OpenJDK 7 is a free and open source implementation of Java Platform, Standard Edition Version 7. At the time of writing this book, it is the latest version of OpenJDK that was ready for the production usage.

Initially, a lot of advanced changes were planned for OpenJDK 7, such as the modular VM and lambda expression support, but due to various technical and organizational reasons, after Sun Microsystems' acquisition by Oracle, most of the new features were postponed for the next versions of OpenJDK. This expedited the release. It reached **General Availability** status on 28 July 2011 and was the first OpenJDK version released as a Reference Implementation for the Java platform.

The major updates to OpenJDK 7 numbered update 2, update 4, and update 6 were released during the next year. After that, version numbering was changed and the next update 40, which is the latest version at the time of writing, was released in September 2013. The following update 60 was planned for May 2014 and the lifetime of OpenJDK 7 will end with update 80 in early 2015.

OpenJDK 7 release cycle differ from Oracle Java release cycles. Oracle Java updates are released for regular security-related changes and for OpenJDK updates. Oracle security changes are propagated to OpenJDK 7 (and to OpenJDK 6 where applicable) but OpenJDK is not released immediately after that. Instead, releases are done on major changes and cumulative security changes usually contain updated versions of HotSpot VM.

OpenJDK 7 is supported on Linux, Windows, Mac OS X, and Solaris operating systems. Only Windows, Linux, and Mac OS X versions will be discussed further. For both Linux and Windows operating systems, x86 and x86_64 architectures are supported. For Mac OS X only x86_64 is supported. To conform with OpenJDK terminology, the **i586** term will be used for x86 architecture and **amd64** will be used for the x86_64 one. OpenJDK 7 does not support cross-compilation, so the i586 operating system must be used to build the i586 version and the same is true for amd64. The build process for both architectures is almost the same for Linux version, but differs greatly for the Windows one.

In this chapter, we will use sources from the official OpenJDK 7 update 40 tarball.

Building OpenJDK 7 on Ubuntu Linux 12.04 LTS

This recipe is similar to recipe *Building OpenJDK 6 on Ubuntu Linux 12.04 LTS* from *Chapter 2, Building OpenJDK 6*.

The build process of OpenJDK relies heavily on Unix-like development tools. Linux-based operating systems usually have top notch support for such tools, so building OpenJDK on Linux (and on Mac OS X) can be simpler than on Windows. For major distributions such as Fedora or Ubuntu, the build toolchain and all the dependencies are already included in distributions as packages and can be installed easily.

Ubuntu 12.04 LTS was chosen for this book because it is one of the most popular Linux distributions. For readers running other operating systems, Ubuntu 12.04 virtual images may be found online for the most popular virtualization tools, such as Oracle VirtualBox or VMware.

To build binaries for i586 and amd64 architectures, corresponding versions of Ubuntu should be used. The build instructions are exactly the same for both architectures so they won't be mentioned further in this recipe.

Getting ready

For this recipe, we will need clean Ubuntu 12.04 (server or desktop version) running.

How to do it...

The following instructions will help us to build OpenJDK 7:

1. Install the prepackaged binaries of OpenJDK 6:

   ```
   sudo apt-get install openjdk-6-jdk
   ```

2. Install the GCC `toolchain` and build dependencies:

   ```
   sudo apt-get build-dep openjdk-6
   ```

3. Download and decompress the official OpenJDK 7 update 40 archive (results will be placed into the `openjdk` directory):

   ```
   wget http://download.java.net/openjdk/jdk7u40/
     promoted/b43/openjdk-7u40-fcs-src-b43-26_aug_2013.zip

   unzip -q openjdk-7u40-fcs-src-b43-26_aug_2013.zip
   ```

4. Create a new text file `buildenv.sh` with the following environment settings:

   ```
   export LD_LIBRARY_PATH=
   export CLASSPATH=
   export JAVA_HOME=
   export LANG=C
   export ALT_BOOTDIR=/usr/lib/jvm/java-6-openjdk
   ```

5. Import the environment into the current shell session (note a dot and a space before it):

   ```
   . buildenv.sh
   ```

6. Start the build process from the `openjdk` directory:

   ```
   make 2>&1 | tee make.log
   ```

7. Wait for the build to finish, and try to run the newly built binaries:

   ```
   cd build/linux-amd64/j2sdk-image/

   ./bin/java -version

   openjdk version "1.7.0-internal"

   OpenJDK Runtime Environment (build 1.7.0-internal-
     ubuntu_2014_02_08_08_56-b00)

   OpenJDK 64-Bit Server VM (build 24.0-b56, mixed mode)
   ```

How it works...

The prepackaged binaries of OpenJDK 6 are required because some of the build steps are run using the external Java runtime.

The `build-dep` command is used to install all the dependencies that are required to build the specified package. As Ubuntu packaged OpenJDK 6 is quite close to the official OpenJDK 6, this command will install almost all the required dependencies.

After a successful build on the amd64 platform, JDK files will be placed into `build/linux-amd64/j2sdk-image` and JRE files will be placed into `build/linux-amd64/j2re-image`. On the i586 platform, the `build/linux-i586` path will be used instead. An additional package of Server JRE that contains JDK without demos and samples will be placed into the `j2sdk-server-image` directory.

There's more...

The Javadoc generation takes a lot of time and is the most memory consuming step of the build. It may be skipped with an additional environment variable:

```
export NO_DOCS=true
```

Contrary to previous version, OpenJDK 7 supports parallel (multicore) native library compilation. The following environment variables may be used for the `jdk` and `hotspot` modules respectively:

```
PARALLEL_COMPILE_JOBS=N
HOTSPOT_BUILD_JOBS=N
```

This build has generated a milestone tag and build number `b00`. Predefined build numbers and milestones may be set using additional environment variables:

```
export MILESTONE=ubuntu-build
export BUILD_NUMBER=b30
```

The `cacerts` file may be provided during the build, using additional environment variable:

```
export ALT_CACERTS_FILE=path/to/cacerts
```

For amd64 builds preinstalled Java provided by variable `ALT_BOOTDIR` may be either the amd64 or i586 build. The i586 binaries consume less memory and may be used for amd64 builds on limited hardware.

OpenJDK 7 has the same minimum build requirements on Linux as the previous version, so Debian 5.0 Lenny may be used to build the most compatible version.

See also

▶ The *Preparing CA certificates* recipe from *Chapter 2, Building OpenJDK 6*

▶ The *Building OpenJDK 6 on Ubuntu Linux 12.04 LTS* recipe from *Chapter 2, Building OpenJDK 6*

▶ The *Setting up the minimum build environment for the most compatible Linux builds* recipe from *Chapter 2, Building OpenJDK 6*

▶ The official build instructions for OpenJDK 7 at `http://hg.openjdk.java.net/jdk7u/jdk7u/raw-file/tip/README-builds.html`

Building OpenJDK 7 on Mac OS X

OpenJDK 7 supports the Mac OS X platform as a *first class citizen* and building it using the proper version of `toolchain` is almost as easy as on Linux.

Historically, Java had first class support on Mac OS X. JDK was based on Sun codebase but built by Apple and integrated fully into their operating system environment. Up to Mac OS X 10.4 Tiger, graphical user interface applications written using the standard Swing toolkit had access to most of the Cocoa native interface features. Applications written in Java were very close to native ones, while still being cross-platform.

But with the next releases, the level of Java support went down. Starting from Mac OS X 10.5 Leopard, newer Cocoa features became unsupported for Java. Release of Apple Java 6 was postponed (comparing to Sun releases for other platforms) for more than a year. Java 6 was released in December 2006 but was not available for Mac OS X users until April 2008. Finally in October 2010, Apple officially announced discontinuation of Java support. Apple Java 6 is still being updated with security updates and may be installed on Mac OS X 10.9 Mavericks (the latest version at the time of writing) but no future Java versions will be released by Apple.

Third-party open source Java distributions existed for Mac OS X. The most notable is the SoyLatte—X11-based port of the FreeBSD Java 1.6 patchset to Mac OS X Intel machines. SoyLatte predated OpenJDK, was licensed under Java Research License, and supported Java 6 builds. Now it is part of the OpenJDK BSD-Port project.

Currently the official latest stable Java version for Mac OS X is Oracle Java 7 which matches closely with OpenJDK. In this recipe, we will build an OpenJDK 7 update 40 on Mac OS X 10.7.5 Lion. This operating system version was chosen because 10.7.3 is the official minimum build requirement platform that should provide the most compatible binaries for Mac OS X, and 10.7.5 matches it quite closely, but may run on newer Intel Ivy Bridge processors and may also be virtualized relatively easily using popular virtualization tools such as Oracle VirtualBox or VMware.

Getting ready

For this recipe, we will need clean Mac OS X 10.7.5 Lion running.

How to do it...

The following procedures will help us to build OpenJDK 7:

1. Download Xcode 3.4.2 for Lion (March 22, 2012) from `https://developer.apple.com/xcode/` (an Apple developer's account is required, registration is free) and install it.

2. Download the Command Line Tools for Xcode—late March 2012 (March 21, 2012) using the same download link mentioned previously and install it.

3. Run this command from the terminal to set up the command line tools:

   ```
   sudo xcode-select -switch /Applications/Xcode.app/Contents/
   Developer/
   ```

4. Navigate to **Applications | Utilities** and run **X11.app** to install it as an additional download.

5. Install the JDK 7—Oracle distribution, or prebuilt OpenJDK binaries may be used.

6. Download Apache Ant 1.8.4 from `http://archive.apache.org/dist/ant/binaries/` and decompress it.

7. Download the source archive `openjdk-7u40-fcs-src-b43-26_aug_2013.zip` from `http://download.java.net/openjdk/jdk7u40/promoted/b43/` and decompress it.

8. Create a new text file `buildenv.sh` with the following environment settings:

   ```
   export LD_LIBRARY_PATH=
   export CLASSPATH=
   export JAVA_HOME=
   export LANG=C
   export ANT_HOME=path/to/ant
   export PATH=path/to/ant/bin:$PATH
   export ALT_BOOTDIR=path/to/jdk7
   ```

9. Import the environment into the current terminal session (note a dot and a space before it):

   ```
   . buildenv.sh
   ```

10. Start the build process from the `openjdk` directory:

    ```
    make 2>&1 | tee make.log
    ```

11. Wait for the build to finish, and try to run the newly built binaries:

```
cd build/macosx-x86_64/j2sdk-image/
./bin/java -version
openjdk version "1.7.0-internal"
OpenJDK Runtime Environment (build 1.7.0-internal-
obf_2014_02_07_21_32-b00)
OpenJDK 64-Bit Server VM (build 24.0-b56, mixed mode)
```

How it works...

As well as the Xcode Command Line Tools that are used for the main part of the native source, Xcode itself is also required to build platform specific code.

OpenJDK on Mac OS X is moving away from using the X11 server, but it is still required for Version 7 builds. Mac OS X 10.7 Lion has X11 preinstalled, it just needs to be run once to be configured for the build.

Apple JDK6 may be used instead of OpenJDK7, but it requires additional configuration.

The Apache Ant build tool is required for some modules of the build.

There's more...

This recipe uses the official Apple builds of GCC (and G++) Version 4.2 as compilers. After that version, official Apple support for GCC was discontinued for licensing reasons. Clang—the open source compiler initially developed by Apple—is the default and preferred compiler in newer versions of Mac OS X. While newer versions of OpenJDK support Clang on Mac OS X, Version 7 still requires GCC.

OpenJDK 7 could be built on Mac OS X 10.8 Mountain Lion using the same steps. The only addition is that the X11 server should be installed separately using the XQuartz project.

Newer versions of Xcode and recent updates of Mac OS X 10.9 Mavericks may break the OpenJDK builds. If builds using newer OS / `toolchain` are desired, it is better to check the current situation with the build and proposed solutions on OpenJDK mailing lists.

See also

▶ The *Preparing CA certificates* recipe from *Chapter 2, Building OpenJDK 6*

▶ The *Building OpenJDK 6 on Ubuntu Linux 12.04 LTS* recipe from *Chapter 2, Building OpenJDK 6* for information about build tuning

▶ The official build instructions for Mac OS X on OpenJDK Wikipedia at `https://wikis.oracle.com/display/OpenJDK/Mac+OS+X+Port`

Building 32-bit FreeType libraries for OpenJDK 7 on Windows

The majority of fonts used in modern software are encoded in vector format for proper scaling support. There are multiple standards for vector fonts, for example Metafont from Professor Donald E. Knuth, Type1 from Adobe, TrueType from Apple and Microsoft, and OpenType from Adobe and Microsoft.

Rasterization of vector fonts is a remarkably complex task and most desktop software (such as web browsers or text processors) use third-party libraries to work with fonts.

Sun Microsystems licensed a third-party closed source font library for use in Sun Java implementation. The sources for this library could not be released to the public along with the initial release of OpenJDK. The Font Scaler Replacement Project was launched in the early days of OpenJDK to adopt the open source font library instead.

FreeType is a free and open source (under permissive license) font rasterization library. It is widely used in open source desktop software. FreeType was chosen by the OpenJDK team as a replacement for the closed source font library and is now used by OpenJDK on all supported platforms. Prebuilt static and dynamic FreeType libraries are required for OpenJDK builds on Windows.

FreeType may be built for OpenJDK 7 using the same Microsoft Windows SDK for Windows 7 and .NET Framework 4 (Version 7.1) that we will use for both i586 and amd64 OpenJDK builds. We will use the freely available Visual Studio 2010 Express Edition to configure the build settings for the FreeType project.

Getting ready

For this recipe, we should have Windows 7 SP1 i586 running.

How to do it...

The following procedure will help us to build FreeType:

1. Download Microsoft .NET Framework 4 from the Microsoft website and install it.

2. Download Microsoft Windows SDK for Windows 7 and .NET Framework 4 (Version 7.1) from the Microsoft website and install it to the default location with image filename `GRMSDK_EN_DVD.iso`.

3. Download Visual Studio 2010 Express Edition from the Microsoft website and install it to the default location. Only the Visual C++ component is required.

4. Download the FreeType 2.5.2 sources tarball from `http://freetype.org/` and decompress it.

5. Open the file `include\config\ftoption.h` and uncomment line 95:

    `#define FT_CONFIG_OPTION_SUBPIXEL_RENDERING`

6. Change lines 269 and 271 from `/* #define FT_EXPORT(x)        extern x */` and `/* #define FT_EXPORT_DEF(x)  x */` to `#define FT_EXPORT(x) __declspec(dllexport) x` and `#define FT_EXPORT_DEF(x) __declspec(dllexport) x.`

7. Open the solution `builds\windows\vc2010\freetype.sln` in Visual Studio.

8. In the main menu, go to **Project | Properties | Configuration Properties** and choose Windows7.1 SDK in the **Platform Toolset** field.

9. On the main screen choose **Release Multithreaded** as the **Solution Configuration**.

10. Run build, and the `freetype252MT.lib` library will be placed into the `freetype\objs\win32\vc2010` directory; rename it to `freetype.lib`, and save it for later use.

11. In the main menu, go to **Project | Properties | Configuration Properties**, change **Configuration Type** to **Dynamic Library (.dll)**, and build the solution. The `freetype252MT.dll` and `freetype252MT.exp` files will be placed into the `objs\release_mt` directory. Rename these files `freetype.dll` and `freetype.exp` and use them with the previously generated `freetype.lib` during the OpenJDK build.

How it works...

FreeType for i586 may be built using Visual Studio's own toolset, but we used the Windows SDK7.1 toolset to ensure compatibility with the OpenJDK build that uses the same toolset.

The `FT_CONFIG_OPTION_SUBPIXEL_RENDERING` macro enables subpixel rendering functionality in FreeType implementation.

The `FT_EXPORT` and `FT_EXPORT_DEF` macros should be adjusted with the calling conventions for the current platform. We changed them to use Windows-specific calling conventions.

See also

▶   The *Building 64-bit FreeType libraries for OpenJDK 7 on Windows* recipe

▶   The FreeType official website at `http://freetype.org/`

▶   Professor Donald E. Knuth's interview covering Metafont and TrueType at `http://www.advogato.org/article/28.html`

▶   The *OpenJDK: Font Scaler Replacement Project* page at `http://openjdk.java.net/projects/font-scaler/`

Building 64-bit FreeType libraries for OpenJDK 7 on Windows

The FreeType build for Windows amd64 is similar to the i586 build from the previous recipe. Only different steps will be written in this recipe. Please refer to the previous recipe, *Building 32-bit FreeType libraries for OpenJDK 7 on Windows* for more detailed instructions.

Getting ready

For this recipe, we should have Windows 7 SP1 amd64 running.

How to do it...

The following procedures will help us in building FreeType:

1. Download Microsoft .NET Framework 4 (Version 7.1), Microsoft Windows SDK for Windows 7 and Visual Studio 2010 Express Edition from the Microsoft website, and install them to default locations. The amd64 version of the SDK from the `GRMSDKX_EN_DVD.iso` file should be used.

2. Follow steps 4 to 9 from the previous recipe to download and adjust the FreeType sources and configure the project in Visual Studio.

3. On the main screen choose **x64** as the **Solution Platform**.

4. Follow steps 10 and 11 from the previous recipe. Libraries will be placed into the `freetype\builds\windows\vc2010\x64\Release Multithreaded` directory.

How it works...

FreeType amd64 cannot be built using the Express Edition of Visual Studio 2010. The Professional Edition or the Windows SDK toolset should be used. As we will use Windows SDK 7.1 for OpenJDK builds, we are also using it for appropriate FreeType builds.

See also

▶ The *Building 32-bit FreeType libraries for OpenJDK 7 on Windows* recipe

Building 32-bit OpenJDK 7 on Windows 7 SP1

The OpenJDK 7 build process on the Windows platform has undertaken major improvements in comparison to Version 6. Despite that, the build environment setup is still much more complex than on Linux and Mac OS X. Much of the complexity of the build comes from its usage of a Unix-like build environment through Cygwin tools.

The official compiler requirement for i586 builds is Microsoft Visual Studio C++ 2010 Professional Edition. The Express Edition of Visual Studio 2010 also may be used for the i586 build. While this edition is free (as in "free beer") it has an evaluation period of 30 days and requires registration after that. While registration is also free, this requirement may be problematic for some usage scenarios (for example, automated build services).

Instead of Visual Studio 2010, we will use Microsoft Windows SDK Version 7.1 for Windows 7. This SDK is also available for free from the Microsoft website and may be used without registration. It uses the same compiler as Visual Studio 2010 Express. It contains only Command Line Tools (no GUI) but may be used as an external toolset from Visual Studio 2010 if GUI is desired.

Getting ready

For this recipe, we should have Windows 7 SP1 i586 running with no antivirus software installed. Antivirus software is not allowed because it may interfere with Cygwin runtime.

How to do it...

The following procedure will help us to build OpenJDK:

1. Download Microsoft .NET Framework 4 from the Microsoft website and install it.
2. Download the Microsoft Windows SDK for Windows 7 from the Microsoft website and install it to the default location. The .NET Development and Common Utilities components are not required.
3. Download and install the Microsoft DirectX 9.0 SDK (Summer 2004) to the default installation path. Note that this distribution is not available any more on the Microsoft website. It may however be downloaded from other places. The file details are as follows:

   ```
   name: dxsdk_sum2004.exe
   size: 239008008 bytes
   sha1sum: 73d875b97591f48707c38ec0dbc63982ff45c661
   ```

4. Install or copy a preinstalled version of Cygwin to `c:\cygwin`.

5. Create the `c:\path_prepend` directory and copy into it `find.exe` and `sort.exe` files from the Cygwin installation.

6. Download GNU make utility binary from `http://www.cmake.org/` using `http://www.cmake.org/files/cygwin/make.exe-cygwin1.7`, rename it to `make.exe`, and put it in the `c:\make` directory.

7. Download the Apache Ant Version 1.8.4 zip distribution from `http://apache.org/` and decompress it to the `c:\ant` directory.

8. Download the prebuilt FreeType libraries from the `openjdk-unofficial-builds` GitHub project (directory `7_32`) and put the binaries into the `c:\freetype\lib` directory and the header files into the `c:\freetype\include` directory.

9. Install the OpenJDK 6 binaries or Oracle Java 6 into `c:\jdk6`.

10. Download the official OpenJDK 7 update 40 source archive from the `http://download.java.net/openjdk/jdk7u40/promoted/b43/` web page and decompress it to the `c:\sources` directory.

11. Create the `build.bat` batch file and write the following environment variables settings:

```
@echo off
rem clear variables
set LD_LIBRARY_PATH=
set CLASSPATH=
set JAVA_HOME=
rem ALT_* variables
set ALT_BOOTDIR=C:/jdk7
set ALT_FREETYPE_LIB_PATH=C:/freetype/lib
set ALT_FREETYPE_HEADERS_PATH=C:/freetype/include
set NO_DOCS=true
rem set compiler environment manually
set WINDOWSSDKDIR=C:/Program Files/Microsoft SDKs/Windows/v7.1/
set VSDIR=C:/Program Files/Microsoft Visual Studio 10.0/
set VS100COMNTOOLS=%VSDIR%/Common7/Tools
set Configuration=Release
set WindowsSDKVersionOverride=v7.1
set ToolsVersion=4.0
set TARGET_CPU=x86
set CURRENT_CPU=x86
set PlatformToolset=Windows7.1SDK
set TARGET_PLATFORM=WIN7
set LIB=%VSDIR%/VC/Lib;%WINDOWSSDKDIR%/Lib
set LIBPATH=%VSDIR%/VC/Lib
rem set path
```

```
set PATH=C:/path_prepend;%VSDIR%/Common7/
IDE;%VS100COMNTOOLS%;%VSDIR%/VC/Bin;%VSDIR%/VC/Bin/
VCPackages;%WINDOWSSDKDIR%/Bin;C:/WINDOWS/system32;C:/WINDOWS;C:/
WINDOWS/System32/Wbem;C:/make;C:/cygwin/bin;C:/jdk7/bin;C:/ant/bin
set INCLUDE=%VSDIR%/VC/INCLUDE;%WINDOWSSDKDIR%/
INCLUDE;%WINDOWSSDKDIR%/INCLUDE/gl;
bash
echo Press any key to close window ...
pause > nul
```

12. Run `build.bat` from Windows Explorer. The `cmd.exe` window should appear with bash launched.

13. From the bash Command Prompt run the following commands:

```
cd /cygdrive/c/sources
chmod -R 777 .
make > make.log 2>&1
```

14. Launch another Cygwin console and run the following commands:

```
cd /cygdrive/c/sources
tail -f make.log
```

15. Wait for the build to finish.

How it works...

Cygwin installation is covered in the *Installing Cygwin for Windows builds* recipe in *Chapter 2, Building OpenJDK 6*.

Directories in the root of disk C are used here for brevity. Generally, arbitrary paths consist of ASCII letters or numbers and no spaces may be used.

A newer version of the DirectX SDK also may be used.

Different GNU make versions might have different problems on Windows. This particular version from the cmake project was tested on different Windows versions and works fine.

This recipe uses prebuilt FreeType 2.4.10 libraries from the `openjdk-unofficial-builds` `GitHub` project. FreeType may be built from sources using the same Windows SDK 7.1 toolchain. Please see the *Building 32-bit FreeType libraries for OpenJDK 7 on Windows* recipe in this chapter.

In the environment settings, additional attention should be paid to the order of the PATH variable content. Sort and find Cygwin utilities should go at start of the PATH variable to avoid being overshadowed by the Windows' utilities with the same name but different functionality. Make goes before Cygwin to avoid being overshadowed by another version of make that may be included in the Cygwin installation.

The `chmod 777` command is required to fix Cygwin file permissions that may cause errors later stages of the build.

The make output will be redirected to the `make.log` file. The `2>&1` statement ensures that both `stdout` and `stderr` will be redirected.

The `tail -f` command allows us to watch the contents of the `make.log` file as they are written during the build process.

The `pause > nul` command is added at the end of the batch file to prevent the `cmd.exe` window disappearing in the case of runtime errors.

There's more...

To build the most compatible binaries, the same recipe should be used, but the Windows XP operating system should be used instead of Windows 7.

In Windows XP, the `chmod 777` command is not required.

The `tee` command may be used instead of `>` and `tail` to write the build log to file and console simultaneously.

The `SetEnv.Cmd` script from Windows SDK may be used (with proper flags) to set the compiler environment instead of setting variables manually.

Visual Studio 2010 Express or Professional edition may be used instead of Windows SDK 7.1.

Prebuilt OpenJDK 7 or Oracle Java 7 may be used as the boot JDK instead of 6.

See also

- The *Building 32-bit OpenJDK 6 on Windows 7 SP1* recipe from *Chapter 2, Building OpenJDK 6*
- The *Installing Cygwin for Windows builds* recipe from *Chapter 2, Building OpenJDK 6*
- The *Building OpenJDK 6 on Ubuntu Linux 12.04 LTS* recipe from *Chapter 2, Building OpenJDK 6* for information about build tuning
- The *Building 32-bit FreeType libraries for OpenJDK 7 on Windows* recipe from this chapter
- The *Preparing CA certificates* recipe from this chapter
- The official build instructions for OpenJDK 7 at `http://hg.openjdk.java.net/jdk7u/jdk7u/raw-file/tip/README-builds.html`

Building 64-bit OpenJDK 7 on Windows 7 x64 SP1

The amd64 build in Windows 7 is similar to the i586 build, but has additional complications.

Cygwin (at least the more common i586 version) works much worse on amd64 Windows. Due to the much bigger address space size, Cygwin fork techniques work much slower and are less reliable.

Visual Studio 2010 Express Edition does not support amd64 architecture, so Microsoft Windows SDK version 7.1 for Windows 7 or the Professional Edition of Visual Studio should be used.

Getting ready

For this recipe, we should have Windows 7 SP1 amd64 running with no antivirus software installed. Antivirus software is not allowed because it may interfere with Cygwin runtime.

How to do it...

The following procedures will help us to build OpenJDK:

1. Follow steps 1 to 10 from the previous recipe, *Building 32-bit OpenJDK 7 on Windows 7 SP1*, using the amd64 version of the Windows SDK and the FreeType libraries from the 7_64 directory.

2. Create a build.bat batch file and write the following environment variables settings there:

```
@echo off
rem clear variables
set LD_LIBRARY_PATH=
set CLASSPATH=
set JAVA_HOME=
rem ALT_* variables
set ALT_BOOTDIR=C:/jdk7
set ALT_FREETYPE_LIB_PATH=C:/freetype/lib
set ALT_FREETYPE_HEADERS_PATH=C:/freetype/include
set NO_DOCS=true
rem set compiler environment manually
set WINDOWSSDKDIR=C:/Program Files/Microsoft SDKs/Windows/v7.1/
set VSDIR=C:/Program Files (x86)/Microsoft Visual Studio 10.0/
set VS100COMNTOOLS=%VSDIR%/Common7/Tools
set Configuration=Release
set WindowsSDKVersionOverride=v7.1
set ToolsVersion=4.0
```

```
set TARGET_CPU=x64
set CURRENT_CPU=x64
set PlatformToolset=Windows7.1SDK
set TARGET_PLATFORM=WIN7
set LIB=%VSDIR%/VC/Lib/amd64;%WINDOWSSDKDIR%/Lib/x64
set LIBPATH=%VSDIR%/VC/Lib/amd64
rem set path
set PATH=C:/path_prepend;%VSDIR%/Common7/
IDE;%VS100COMNTOOLS%;%VSDIR%/VC/Bin/x86_amd64;%VSDIR%/VC/
Bin;%VSDIR%/VC/Bin/VCPackages;%WINDOWSSDKDIR%/Bin;C:/WINDOWS/
system32;C:/WINDOWS;C:/WINDOWS/System32/Wbem;C:/make;C:/cygwin/
bin;C:/jdk7/bin;C:/ant/bin
set INCLUDE=%VSDIR%/VC/INCLUDE;%WINDOWSSDKDIR%/
INCLUDE;%WINDOWSSDKDIR%/INCLUDE/gl;
bash
echo Press any key to close window ...
pause > nul
```

3. Follow steps 12 to 15 from the previous recipe.

How it works...

The amd64 build is similar to the i586 build, but can be much slower because Cygwin works slower on a 64-bit OS.

The build can be done using either the i586 or amd64 boot JDK, the only difference is amd64 requires more memory (not less than 1024MB).

For additional details, please see the *How it works...* section of the previous recipe *Building 32-bit OpenJDK 7 on Windows 7 SP1*.

There's more...

To build the most compatible binaries, the same recipe should be used, but the Windows 2003 Server amd64 operating system should be used instead of Windows 7.

In Windows 2003, the `chmod 777` command is not required.

A prebuilt OpenJDK 7 or Oracle Java 7 may be used as the boot JDK instead of 6.

See also

▶ The *Building 32-bit OpenJDK 7 on Windows 7 SP1* recipe from this chapter

▶ The *Building 64-bit OpenJDK 6 on Windows 7 x64 SP1* recipe from *Chapter 2, Building OpenJDK 6*

- ▶ The *Installing Cygwin for Windows builds* recipe from *Chapter 2, Building OpenJDK 6*

- ▶ The *Building OpenJDK 6 on Ubuntu Linux 12.04 LTS* recipe from *Chapter 2, Building OpenJDK 6*, for information about build tuning

- ▶ The *Building 64-bit FreeType libraries for OpenJDK 7 on Windows* recipe from this chapter

- ▶ The *Preparing CA certificates* recipe from *Chapter 2, Building OpenJDK 6*

- ▶ The official build instructions for OpenJDK 7 at `http://hg.openjdk.java.net/jdk7u/jdk7u/raw-file/tip/README-builds.html`

Preparing a standalone toolchain for 32- and 64-bit Windows' builds

In the previous recipes in this chapter, we built OpenJDK 7 for Windows using Windows SDK Version 7.1. This SDK requires installation prior to using it. The installation process requires .NET Framework 2 (to run the installer, included in Windows 7) and .NET Framework 4. Installation of these components may be very time consuming in some usage scenarios. For example, to automated builds it may be desirable to use completely clean Windows images for the builds. Besides being slow, the .NET Framework and SDK installers are graphical tools and may be hard to script for automatic installation.

In this recipe, we will create a set of files and an environment script that can be used to build OpenJDK 7 i586 and amd64 on completely clean Windows installations (with corresponding architecture) without installing any tools through GUI installers. Such a set of files may be put under the version control system to be checked out prior to the build.

Getting ready

For this recipe, we should have two clean images of Windows 7 SP1. One of them should have the i586 architecture and other should have the amd64 architecture.

How to do it...

The following procedure will help us to prepare a standalone toolchain:

1. Download the Microsoft Windows SDK for Windows 7 i586 (`GRMSDK_EN_DVD.iso`) from the Microsoft website and install it on the i586 Windows instance in the default location. The `.NET Development` and `Common Utilities` components are not required.

2. Create a `toolchain` directory. We will put various tools and libraries there and will refer to this directory as `<toolchain>`.

3. Copy the SDK files from the `C:\Program Files\Microsoft SDKs\Windows\v7.1` to `<toolchain>\winsdk71\sdk` directory.

4. Copy the Visual Studio files shipped with the SDK from the `C:\Program Files\Microsoft Visual Studio 10.0` to `<toolchain>\winsdk71\vs2010e` directory.

5. Download the Microsoft Windows SDK for Windows 7 amd64 (`GRMSDKX_EN_DVD.iso`) from the Microsoft website and install it on the amd64 Windows instance in the default location. The `.NET Development` and `Common Utilities` components are not required.

6. Copy the `C:\Program Files\Microsoft SDKs\Windows\v7.1\Bin\x64` directory from the SDK amd64 installation to the `<toolchain>\winsdk71\sdk/Bin/x64` directory.

7. Download and install the Microsoft DirectX 9.0 SDK (Summer 2004) to the default installation path on the i586 Windows instance. Note that this distribution is not available anymore on the Microsoft website. It may be downloaded from another place online, and the file details are as follows:

   ```
   name: dxsdk_sum2004.exe
   size: 239008008 bytes
   sha1sum: 73d875b97591f48707c38ec0dbc63982ff45c661
   ```

8. Copy files from the `C:\Program Files\Microsoft DirectX 9.0 SDK (Summer 2004)` directory to the `<toolchain>\directx` directory.

9. On the Windows i586 instance copy the files from the `C:\Windows\System32` directory to the `<toolchain>\msvcr/7_32` directory:

   ```
   msvcp100.dll
   msvcr100.dll
   msvcr100_clr0400.dll
   ```

10. On the Windows amd64 instance copy the same files as on the previous step (they should have the amd64 architecture) to the `<toolchain>\msvcr\7_64` directory.

11. Create an `env_32.bat` file with the following environment configuration that may be used for i586 builds:

    ```
    set TOOLCHAIN=<toolchain>
    set VS=%TOOLCHAIN%/winsdk71/vs2010e
    set WINSDK=%TOOLCHAIN%/winsdk71/sdk
    set ALT_COMPILER_PATH=%VS%/VC/Bin
    set ALT_WINDOWSSDKDIR=%WINSDK%
    set ALT_MSVCRNN_DLL_PATH=%TOOLCHAIN%/msvcr/7_32
    set ALT_DXSDK_PATH=%TOOLCHAIN%/directx
    set WINDOWSSDKDIR=%WINSDK%
    set VS100COMNTOOLS=%VS%/Common7/Tools
    set Configuration=Release
    ```

```
set WindowsSDKVersionOverride=v7.1
set ToolsVersion=4.0
set TARGET_CPU=x86
set CURRENT_CPU=x86
set PlatformToolset=Windows7.1SDK
set TARGET_PLATFORM=XP
set LIB=%VS%/VC/Lib;%WINSDK%/Lib
set LIBPATH=%VS%/VC/Lib
set PATH=%VS%/Common7/IDE;%VS%/Common7/Tools;%VS%/VC/Bin;%VS%/VC/
Bin/VCPackages;%WINSDK%/Bin;C:/WINDOWS/system32;C:/WINDOWS;C:/
WINDOWS/System32/Wbem;%TOOLCHAIN%/msvcr/7_32
set INCLUDE=%VS%/VC/INCLUDE;%WINSDK%/INCLUDE;%WINSDK%/INCLUDE/gl;
```

12. Create an `env_64.bat` file with the following environment configuration that may be used for amd**64** builds:

```
set TOOLCHAIN=...
set VS=%TOOLCHAIN%/winsdk71/vs2010e
set WINSDK=%TOOLCHAIN%/winsdk71/sdk
set ALT_COMPILER_PATH=%VS%/VC/Bin/x86_amd64
set ALT_WINDOWSSDKDIR=%WINSDK%
set ALT_MSVCRNN_DLL_PATH=%TOOLCHAIN%/msvcr/7_64
set ALT_DXSDK_PATH=%TOOLCHAIN%/directx
set WINDOWSSDKDIR=%WINSDK%
set VS100COMNTOOLS=%VS%/Common7/Tools
set Configuration=Release
set WindowsSDKVersionOverride=v7.1
set ToolsVersion=4.0
set TARGET_CPU=x64
set CURRENT_CPU=x64
set PlatformToolset=Windows7.1SDK
set TARGET_PLATFORM=XP
set LIB=%VS%/VC/Lib/amd64;%WINSDK%/Lib/x64
set LIBPATH=%VS%/VC/Lib/amd64
set PATH=%VS%/Common7/IDE;%VS%/Common7/Tools;%VS%/VC/Bin/
x86_amd64;%VS%/VC/Bin;%VS%/VC/Bin/VCPackages;%WINSDK%/Bin;C:/
WINDOWS/System32;C:/WINDOWS;C:/WINDOWS/System32/wbem;%LIBS_DIR%/
msvcr/7_64;%TOOLCHAIN%/msvcr/7_32;%VS%/Common7/IDE
set INCLUDE=%VS%/VC/INCLUDE;%WINSDK%/INCLUDE;%WINSDK%/INCLUDE/gl;
```

13. Add the `toolchain` directory to the source control repository. This file set is a standalone toolchain and may be used to build both the i**586** and amd**64** versions of OpenJDK 7 (and OpenJDK 8) on clean Windows images with corresponding architectures.

How it works...

The process in this recipe is quite straightforward: collect the installed files that are to be copied later on clean Windows images and prepare the environment for them.

One possible problem is that, while the Microsoft linker tool `link.exe` from the Windows SDK 7.1 does not require .NET 4 runtime to link native binaries, it requires the .NET shared library, `msvcr100_clr0400.dll` (see step 7 of this recipe). This library must be found in `PATH`, otherwise the build will fail at the HotSpot VM link stage with an unclear error.

There's more...

The OpenJDK configuration not specific to the Microsoft toolchain (Cygwin, FreeType, and so on) was removed from the environment files in this recipe for brevity. It should be added back to the environment files to perform the OpenJDK builds.

The result standalone toolchain is not specific to OpenJDK and may be used to build other software on Windows.

See also

▶ The *Building 32-bit OpenJDK 7 on Windows 7 SP1* recipe and the *Building 64-bit FreeType libraries for OpenJDK 7 on Windows* recipe from this chapter. They can be adjusted to use the standalone toolchain from this recipe

▶ A question from `http://stackoverflow.com/` about the linker dependencies on .NET4 runtime at `http://stackoverflow.com/questions/13571628/compiling-c-code-using-windows-sdk-7-1-without-net-framework-4-0`

4
Building OpenJDK 8

In this chapter, we will cover:

- ▶ Working with GNU Autoconf
- ▶ Building OpenJDK 8 on Ubuntu Linux 12.04 LTS
- ▶ Using ccache to speed up the OpenJDK 8 build process
- ▶ Building OpenJDK 8 on Mac OS X
- ▶ Building OpenJDK 8 on Windows 7 SP1

Introduction

The Java 8 specification brings a lot of innovations to the Java platform. Besides new language features such as functional interfaces and Lamda expression support, and library features such as streams and a new date/time API, OpenJDK 8 has a new build system. As this chapter is about building OpenJDK, we will explore the last innovation in depth.

For a long time, the Sun Java and OpenJDK build system grew around the release process. Requirements from the release engineers always came before the developers' requirements, and developers' requirements for the build process differ greatly from release ones. For the release preparation, the build process must be stable. Release builds are usually built from scratch, they always include the whole project and speed, and environment configuration complexities are not issues for them. On the contrary, partial, incremental, and fast as possible builds are required as air for the development. Also, build scripts must be as clean and manageable as possible to allow easy changes and fine tuning.

Up to the time when OpenJDK 7 was released, the build process had all the following *misfeatures* of the huge cross-platform project, listed as follows:

- ▶ Complex environment setup
- ▶ No reliable incremental builds
- ▶ Broken support for parallel builds
- ▶ No support for compilation cache
- ▶ Unreasonably slow builds in some parts
- ▶ Different types of build scripts (some for GNU, some for Apache Ant)
- ▶ Implicit compilation of Java sources with limited source list selection abilities
- ▶ Too-strict checks for the environment (required for release, but encumbering in the non-standard environment)
- ▶ *Drops* of additional binary components
- ▶ Dependency on specific versions of build tools
- ▶ No support for cross-compilation

Public access to the build caused by the appearance of the OpenJDK project triggered the evolution of the build system to become more developer and "casual builder" friendly. In the timeline of OpenJDK 7, the build process has undergone some cleanup, the builds became easier but fundamental issues stayed the same.

At last, a huge effort was made during the OpenJDK 8 development. The build system was completely rewritten, with major parts of it rewritten from scratch. Besides the cleanup and restructuring of the Makefiles and the removal of Apache Ant, the main problems were addressed: speed, multicore support, partial and incremental builds, cross–compilation, and a much easier environment setup.

The latter improvement was largely caused by the introduction of the prebuild step that prepares the project for the current environment. This build configuration step is performed using the GNU Autoconf build system. We will explore it more closely in the following recipe.

OpenJDK 8 is supported on Linux, Windows, Mac OS X, and Solaris operating systems. Only Windows, Linux, and Mac OS X versions will be discussed further. On both Linux and Windows operating systems, x86 and x86_64 architectures are supported. On Mac OS X, only x86_64 is supported.

Processor architecture configuration is changed in OpenJDK 8. Previously the x86 architecture was named i586 and x86_64 was named amd64. But now the x86 and x86_64 names are used as is. Also, due to the cross-compilation support, x86 versions can be built on x86_64 operating systems with minor configuration changes. So in this chapter, we will focus on x86_64 and will mention x86 builds where required.

Working with GNU Autoconf

GNU Autoconf, or simply the GNU build system, is a suite of build tools designed to assist in making source code packages portable across multiple Unix-like systems.

Autoconf contains multiple build-related tools and generally acts as a Makefile generator. Makefile templates are processed in the configure build step using environment information and configuration options specified by the user.

The Autoconf system is quite complex and there exists some controversy about its usage in modern projects. For some projects it may be too old, too complex, and too directed towards Unix-like systems compared to the cost of other platforms. But for OpenJDK, the highly cross-platform project that already heavily relies on Unix-like tools, autotool adoption for the configure build step is well justified.

The Autoconf system uses GNU make for the actual build step, but in contrast to the make tool, the whole Autoconf package is less portable, and a particular build setup may have restrictions on required versions of the Autoconf packages. Fortunately, this burden can be moved from developers to build system engineers. For the build configuration step, Autoconf generates a standalone shell script. Such a script, usually named configure, can not only be used without other build system tools, but also run in limited Unix-like environments such as Cygwin on the Windows platform.

In OpenJDK, the configure script is prepared beforehand and added to the source code tarball, so the build process does not require any of the autotools' build tools besides GNU make.

In this recipe, we will explore the OpenJDK 8 build configuration with different options.

Getting ready

For this recipe, you will need an operating system with a Unix-like environment: Linux, Mac OS X, or Windows with Cygwin installed. Please see the *Installing Cygwin for Windows builds* recipe from *Chapter 2, Building OpenJDK 6* about installing Cygwin.

How to do it...

The following procedures will help us to configure the OpenJDK 8 build environment:

1. Install the JDK 7 from Oracle or the prebuilt OpenJDK binaries.
2. Download and decompress the official OpenJDK 8 source code archive (this archive was not available at the time of writing this book).

3. Run the build configuration script with the `--help` option:

   ```
   bash ./configure --help
   ```

   You can now see the list of available configuration options. Let's try some of them.

4. Run the following command to directly specify the JDK to use as the boot JDK during the build:

   ```
   bash ./configure --with-boot-jdk=path/to/jdk
   ```

5. Run the following command to take the default restrictions off the included cryptographic algorithm implementation:

   ```
   bash ./configure --enable-unlimited-crypto
   ```

6. Run the following command to not generate debug symbols during the build and not include them in target distribution:

   ```
   bash ./configure --disable-debug-symbols --disable-zip-debug-info
   ```

7. Run the following command to force bundle the FreeType libraries with OpenJDK on all platforms:

   ```
   bash ./configure --enable-freetype-bundling
   ```

8. Run the following command to specify CA certificates to the `keystore` file. Please see the *Preparing CA certificates* recipe about preparing such a file in *Chapter 2, Building OpenJDK 6*:

   ```
   bash ./configure --with-cacerts-file=path/to/cacerts
   ```

9. Run the following command to specify the milestone and build number for the build instead of the generated ones:

   ```
   bash ./configure -with-milestone=my-milestone --with-build-number=b42
   ```

How it works...

In OpenJDK, the configure script is not marked as executable by default due to the OpenJDK source repository policy. So `bash` is used explicitly to run the script in this recipe.

The `configure` script prepares the build configuration in the `build` directory. It performs a lot of checks and writes the environment-specific details, and the user provides options in the form of environment variables. These variables will be read automatically during the actual build.

There's more...

OpenJDK supports a lot of options; most of the options may be specified to configure the script simultaneously.

- ▸ The following recipes in this chapter for actually building of OpenJDK 8
- ▸ The official website of GNU Autoconf project at `http://www.gnu.org/software/autoconf/`
- ▸ The mailing list thread with a discussion about adopting Autoconf at `http://mail.openjdk.java.net/pipermail/build-infra-dev/2011-August/000030.html`

Building OpenJDK 8 Ubuntu Linux 12.04 LTS

This recipe is similar to the recipe *Building OpenJDK 7 on Ubuntu Linux 12.04 LTS* from *Chapter 3, Building OpenJDK 7*.

The build process of OpenJDK relies heavily on Unix-like development tools. Linux-based operating systems usually have top notch support for such tools, so building OpenJDK on Linux (and on Mac OS X) can be simpler than on Windows. For major distributions such as Fedora or Ubuntu, the build toolchain and all the dependencies are already included in distributions as packages and can be installed easily.

Ubuntu 12.04 LTS was chosen for this book because it is one of the most popular Linux distributions. For readers running other operating systems, Ubuntu 12.04 virtual images may be found online for the most popular virtualization tools like Oracle VirtualBox or VMware.

To build binaries for x86 and x86_64 architectures, corresponding versions of Ubuntu should be used. The build instructions are exactly the same for both architectures so they won't be mentioned further in this recipe. OpenJDK 8 supports cross-compilation, so the x86 version may be built on the x86_64 operating system. But such cross-compilation requires non-trivial library configurations and we will not use it in this recipe.

The minimum build environment that should produce the most compatible OpenJDK 8 binaries on Linux is Oracle Linux 6.4 amd64 with GCC Version 4.7. We will configure Ubuntu 12.04 to use GCC 4.7 to be close to the minimum build environment.

Getting ready

For this recipe, we will need clean Ubuntu 12.04 (server or desktop version) running.

How to do it...

The following procedures will help us to build OpenJDK 8:

1. Install the prepackaged binaries of OpenJDK 7:

   ```
   sudo apt-get install openjdk-7-jdk
   ```

2. Install the GCC toolchain and build dependencies:

   ```
   sudo apt-get build-dep openjdk-7
   ```

3. Add an additional packages repository:

   ```
   sudo add-apt-repository ppa:ubuntu-toolchain-r/test
   sudo apt-get update
   ```

4. Install the C and C++ compilers, Version 4.7:

   ```
   sudo apt-get install gcc-4.7
   sudo apt-get install g++-4.7
   ```

5. Go to the /usr/bin directory and set up default compiler-symbolic links:

   ```
   sudo rm gcc
   sudo ln -s gcc-4.7 gcc
   sudo rm g++
   sudo ln -s g++-4.7 g++
   ```

6. Download and decompress the official OpenJDK 8 source code archive (this archive was not available at the time of writing this book)

7. Run the autotools configuration script:

   ```
   bash ./configure
   ```

8. Start the build:

   ```
   make all 2>&1 | tee make_all.log
   ```

9. Run the build binaries:

   ```
   cd build/linux-x86_64-normal-server-release/images/
   ./bin/java -version
   openjdk version "1.8.0-internal"
   OpenJDK Runtime Environment (build 1.8.0-internal-
   ubuntu_2014_02_22_08_51-b00)
   OpenJDK 64-Bit Server VM (build 25.0-b69, mixed mode)
   ```

10. Go back to the source's root and build the compact profile's images:

    ```
    make profiles 2>&1 | tee make_profiles.log
    ```

11. Check the profiles images in the `build/linux-x86_64-normal-server-release/images` directory:

```
j2re-compact1-image
j2re-compact2-image
j2re-compact3-image
```

How it works...

The prepackaged binaries of OpenJDK 7 are required because some of the build steps are run using the external Java runtime.

The `build-dep` command is used to install all the dependencies that are required to build the specified package. As Ubuntu packaged OpenJDK 6 is quite close to the official OpenJDK 6, this command will install almost all the required dependencies.

Ubuntu 12.04 does not have the GCC 4.7 compilers in a default packages repository, so additional repository configuration is required.

There's more...

Default GCC 4.6 compilers also may be used to build OpenJDK 8.

OpenJDK 8 supports cross-compiling x86 binaries on a x86_64 host platform. But the `build-dep -a i386 openjdk-7` command to install all the required x86 dependencies won't work (some of the x86 dependencies are not installable on x86_64 OS) and manual dependencies installation may be non-trivial. It may be easier to build x86 binaries on a separate instance of x86 Ubuntu 12.04 using exactly the same steps from this recipe.

See also

- ▶ The *Working with GNU Autoconf* recipe from this chapter
- ▶ The *Preparing CA certificates* recipe from *Chapter 2, Building OpenJDK 6*
- ▶ The official instructions about building OpenJDK 8 at `http://hg.openjdk.java.net/jdk8u/jdk8u/raw-file/2f40422f564b/README-builds.html`
- ▶ Unofficial instructions about building OpenJDK 8 packages for Linux distributions at `https://github.com/hgomez/obuildfactory/wiki/How-to-build-and-package-OpenJDK-8-on-Linux`

Using ccache to speed up the OpenJDK 8 build process

Besides the Java source code, the OpenJDK source repository contains a lot of native C and C++ source code. Native code compilation is much longer than Java and may take a lot of time. During development, the same code may be compiled multiple times with minor changes. Intermediate binary results for parts of the code may be completely equal between the compilations, but usually parts of the code are recompiled even if no changes are added in those parts. It is natural to expect a more clever approach to code recompiling from modern advanced compilation/linking toolchains.

The **ccache** tool provides such cleverness for native compilation. This tool caches the output of C/C++ compilation so that the next time, the same compilation can be avoided and the results can be taken from the cache. This can greatly speed up recompiling time. The detection is done by hashing different kinds of information that should be unique for the compilation, and then using the hash sum to identify the cached output.

OpenJDK 8 supported ccache on Linux and Mac OS X but did not support Windows at the time of writing this book.

In this recipe, we will set up ccache for the OpenJDK 8 build on Ubuntu 12.04.

Getting ready

For this recipe, we will need Ubuntu 12.04 (server or desktop version) set up to build OpenJDK 8 (please see the previous recipe).

How to do it...

The following procedure will help us in enabling ccache:

1. Install the `ccache` package:

   ```
   sudo apt-get install ccache
   ```

2. Reconfigure the project, running the following command from the OpenJDK 8 source directory:

   ```
   bash ./configure
   ```

3. Check this line in the `configure` script output:

   ```
   ccache status:  installed and in use
   ```

How it works...

In OpenJDK 8, the `configure` script checks the cache availability and automatically enables its use during further builds.

There's more...

For product-like builds when result binaries are going to be used in production, it may be safer to reconfigure the project disabling `ccache` with the `--disable-ccache` option.

See also

- ▶ The previous recipe *Building OpenJDK 8 on Ubuntu Linux 12.04 LTS* from this chapter
- ▶ The official website of ccache at `http://ccache.samba.org/`

Building OpenJDK 8 on Mac OS X

OpenJDK 8 supports Mac OS X platform as a first class citizen and building it (using a proper version of toolchain) is almost as easy as on Linux.

Historically, Java had first class support on Mac OS X. JDK was based on the Sun code base but built by Apple and integrated finely into operating system environment. Up to Mac OS X 10.4 Tiger, graphical user interface applications written using the standard Swing toolkit had access to most of the Cocoa native interface features. Applications written in Java were felt to be very close to native ones, while still being cross-platform.

However, for the next releases, the level of Java support went down. Starting from Mac OS X 10.5 Leopard, newer Cocoa features became unsupported for Java. The release of Apple Java 6 was postponed (comparing to Sun releases for other platforms) for more than a year. Java 6 was released in December 2006 but was not available for Mac OS X users until April 2008. Finally, in October 2010, Apple officially announced its decision to discontinue Java support. Apple Java 6 is still being updated with security updates and may be installed on Mac OS X 10.9 Mavericks (the latest version at the time of writing this book) but no following Java versions will be released by Apple.

Third-party open source Java distributions do exist for Mac OS X. The most notable one is the SoyLatte X11-based port of the FreeBSD Java 1.6 patch set to Mac OS X Intel machines. SoyLatte predated OpenJDK, was licensed under the Java Research license and supported Java 6 builds. Now it is part of the OpenJDK BSD Port project.

Full support for Mac OS X on a par with other platforms was added in OpenJDK 7 and was continued in OpenJDK 8.

Getting ready

For this recipe, we will need clean Mac OS X 10.7.5 Lion (or any later version that supports Xcode 4) running.

How to do it...

The following procedures will help us to build OpenJDK 8:

1. Download Xcode 4.6.2 for Lion (April 15, 2013) from `https://developer.apple.com/xcode/` (an Apple developer's account is required, registration is free) and install it.

2. Download the Command Line Tools for Xcode, April 2013 (April 15, 2013) using the same download link as mentioned in the previous point, and install it.

3. Run this command from the terminal to set up the Command Line Tools:

    ```
    sudo xcode-select -switch /Applications/Xcode.app/Contents/
    Developer/
    ```

4. Navigate to **Applications | Utilities** and run **X11.app** to set up the X-server.

5. Install the JDK 7 Oracle distribution, or prebuilt OpenJDK binaries can be used.

6. Download and decompress the official OpenJDK 8 source code archive (this archive is not available at the time of writing this book).

7. Run the autotools configuration script:

    ```
    bash ./configure --with-boot-jdk=path/to/jdk7
    ```

8. Start the build:

    ```
    make all 2>&1 | tee make_all.log
    ```

9. Run the built binaries:

    ```
    cd build/macosx-x86_64-normal-server-release/images/j2sdk-image

    ./bin/java -version

    openjdk version "1.8.0-internal"

    OpenJDK Runtime Environment (build 1.8.0-internal-
    obf_2014_02_20_19_08-b00)

    OpenJDK 64-Bit Server VM (build 25.0-b69, mixed mode)
    ```

How it works...

Despite the Xcode Command Line Tools that are used for the main part of the native source, Xcode itself is also required to build the platform specific code.

OpenJDK on Mac OS X is moving from using the X11 server, but it is still required for Version 8 builds. Mac OS X 10.7 Lion has X11 preinstalled, it just needs to be run once to be configured for the build.

There's more...

This recipe uses the official Apple builds of GCC (and G++) Version 4.2 as compilers. After that version official Apple support for GCC was discontinued for licensing reasons. Clang—the open source compiler initially developed by Apple—is the default and preferred compiler in newer versions of Mac OS X.

Despite the initial developers' plans, OpenJDK 8 still requires GCC and cannot be built using Clang. This is the reason for using Version 4 of Xcode and not Version 5, which does not ship GCC at all. At the time of writing this book, Xcode 5 and Clang support was being added to the OpenJDK 9 project. Such support may be backported to OpenJDK 8 later; if you want to build Version 8 with Clang, it is best to check the OpenJDK mailing lists for up-to-date information.

On Mac OS X 10.8 Mountain Lion, a 10.9 Mavericks X11 server should be installed separately using the XQuartz project.

See also

- The *Working with GNU Autoconf* recipe from this chapter
- The *Preparing CA certificates* recipe from *Chapter 2, Building OpenJDK 6*
- Official instructions about building OpenJDK 8 at `http://hg.openjdk.java.net/jdk8u/jdk8u/raw-file/2f40422f564b/README-builds.html`
- Unofficial instructions about building OpenJDK 8 packages for Mac OS X at `https://github.com/hgomez/obuildfactory/wiki/Building-and-Packaging-OpenJDK8-for-OSX`

Building OpenJDK 8 on Windows 7 SP1

The OpenJDK 8 build process on Windows platform included major improvements compared to Version 7. Despite that, the build environment setup is still much more complex than on Linux and Mac OS X. Much of the complexity of the build comes from its usage of a Unix-like build environment through Cygwin tools.

The official compiler requirement for i586 builds is Microsoft Visual Studio C++ 2010 Professional Edition. The Express Edition of Visual Studio 2010 may also be used for the x86 build. For x86_64 builds, instead of Visual Studio 2010 Professional Edition, we will use the Microsoft Windows SDK Version 7.1 for Windows 7. This SDK is available for free from the Microsoft website. It uses the same compiler as Visual Studio 2010 Express. It contains only the Command Line Tools (no GUI) but may be used as an external toolset from Visual Studio 2010 if GUI is desired.

Getting ready

For this recipe, we should have Windows 7 SP1 amd64 running with no antivirus software installed. Antivirus software is not allowed because it may interfere with Cygwin runtime.

How to do it...

The following procedure will help us to build OpenJDK 8:

1. Download Microsoft .NET Framework 4 from the Microsoft website and install it.

2. Download the amd64 version of the Microsoft Windows SDK for Windows 7 (the `GRMSDKX_EN_DVD.iso` file) from the Microsoft website and install it to the default location. The `.NET Development` and `Common Utilities` components are not required.

3. Download Visual Studio 2010 Express Edition from the Microsoft website and install it to the default location. Only the Visual C++ component is required.

4. Download and install the Microsoft DirectX 9.0 SDK (summer 2004) to the default installation path. Note that this distribution is not available any more on the Microsoft website. It may be downloaded from another place online, and the file details are as follows:

   ```
   name: dxsdk_sum2004.exe
   size: 239008008 bytes
   sha1sum: 73d875b97591f48707c38ec0dbc63982ff45c661
   ```

5. Install or copy the preinstalled version of Cygwin to `c:\cygwin`.

6. Create a `c:\path_prepend` directory and copy to it the `find.exe` and `sort.exe` files from the Cygwin installation.

7. Download the GNU make utility binary from the `http://www.cmake.org/` website using `http://www.cmake.org/files/cygwin/make.exe-cygwin1.7`, rename it to `make.exe`, and put it into the `c:\make` directory.

8. Download the prebuilt FreeType libraries from the `openjdk-unofficial-builds` GitHub project (directory `7_64`) and put binaries into the `c:\freetype\lib` directory and header files into the `c:\freetype\include` directory.

9. Install the OpenJDK 7 binaries or Oracle Java 7 into `c:\jdk7`.

10. Download the official OpenJDK 8 source code archive (this archive was not available at the time of writing this book) and decompress it into the `c:\sources` directory.

11. Write the following command into the `build.bat` text file:

```
@echo off
set PATH=C:/path_prepend;C:/WINDOWS/system32;C:/WINDOWS;C:/
make;C:/cygwin/bin;C:/jdk7/bin
bash
echo Press any key to close window ...
pause > nul
```

12. Run `build.bat` from Windows Explorer. The `cmd.exe` window should appear with bash launched.

13. From the bash Command Prompt run the following commands:

```
cd /cygdrive/c/sources
bash ./configure \
    --with-boot-jdk=c:/jdk7 \
    --with-freetype=c:/freetype \
chmod -R 777 .
make > make.log 2>&1
```

14. Launch another Cygwin console and run the following commands:

```
cd /cygdrive/c/sources
tail -f make.log
```

15. Wait for the build to finish.

16. Run the following build binaries:

```
cd build/windows-x86_64-normal-server-release/images/j2sdk-image
./bin/java -version
    openjdk version "1.8.0-internal"
    OpenJDK Runtime Environment (build 1.8.0-internal-
      obf_2014_02_22_17_13-b00)
    OpenJDK 64-Bit Server VM (build 25.0-b69, mixed mode)
```

How it works...

Cygwin installation is covered in the recipe *Installing Cygwin for Windows builds* in *Chapter 2, Building OpenJDK 6*. Directories in the root of disk C are used here for brevity. Generally, arbitrary paths consisting of ASCII letters or numbers without spaces can be used. Newer version of DirectX SDK also can be used.

Different GNU make versions may have different problems on Windows. This particular version from the cmake project was tested on different Windows versions and works fine.

This recipe uses prebuilt FreeType 2.4.10 libraries from the `openjdk-unofficial-builds` `GitHub` project. FreeType may be built from sources using the same Windows SDK 7.1 toolchain.

The `make` output will be redirected to the `make.log` file. The `2>&1` statement ensures that both `stdout` and `stderr` will be redirected.

The `tail -f` command allows us to watch the contents of the `make.log` file as they are written during the build process.

The `pause > nul` command added at the end of the batch file prevents the `cmd.exe` window from disappearing in the case of runtime errors.

There's more...

The `--with-target-bits=32` configure option can be used to build i586 binaries on the amd64 operating system. In this case, the x86 version of the FreeType libraries should be specified by the `--with-freetype` option and Express Edition of Visual Studio 2010 should be installed.

The `tee` command may be used instead of `>` and `tail` to write the build log to the file and console simultaneously.

See also

- ▶ The *Working with GNU Autoconf* recipe from this chapter
- ▶ The *Preparing CA certificates* recipe from *Chapter 2, Building OpenJDK 6*
- ▶ The *Installing Cygwin for Windows builds* recipe from *Chapter 2, Building OpenJDK 6*
- ▶ The *Building 64-bit FreeType libraries for OpenJDK 7 on Windows* recipe from *Chapter 3, Building OpenJDK 7*
- ▶ Official instructions about building OpenJDK 8 at `http://hg.openjdk.java.net/jdk8u/jdk8u/raw-file/2f40422f564b/README-builds.html`

5
Building IcedTea

In this chapter, we will cover the following topics:

- ▶ Building IcedTea 6
- ▶ Building IcedTea 7
- ▶ Building OpenJDK 7 with IcedTea patches
- ▶ Building IcedTea 7 with NSS security provider
- ▶ Building IcedTea 6 with SystemTap support

Introduction

IcedTea is a build and integration project for OpenJDK launched by Red Hat in June 2007. It allows users to build OpenJDK using free software tools. It also provides alternative open source implementations of the Java browser plugin and Java Web Start as part of the IcedTea-Web subproject.

Given the current state of the OpenJDK project itself, it is not easy to understand the full value of the IcedTea project. Some features of OpenJDK, which seem standard now, like the absence of binary components and an advanced build system, were pioneered in the IcedTea project.

The IcedTea project was started by Red Hat and the GNU classpath in 2007, soon after the Sun Java source code was published under an open source license. The main goal was to create a free Java package to include in GNU/Linux distributions. Popular distributions (such as Fedora or Arch) have strict requirements for included software. Generally speaking, the full source code must be available under the open source license, and binaries must be built using the free software build tools. At the time of the release, some OpenJDK modules (for example, font- and sound-related modules) were available in binary form only, and only a proprietary Sun Java compiler could be used for the build.

IcedTea incorporated the GNU Autoconf build system. This made it possible to use the GNU Compiler for Java to compile OpenJDK code and replace the binary modules with open source implementations. In 2008, the `IcedTea 6` binaries in the Fedora 9 distribution passed the Java Technology Compatibility Kit test suite successfully and became a fully compatible Java 6 implementation.

One distinguishable feature of the IcedTea project is **bootstrap builds**. Bootstrap mode means that the build process runs twice. First, the OpenJDK with some patches is built using the **GNU Compiler for Java** (**GCJ**) and then, the newly built binaries are used as the compiler for the resulting production build. In the early days of IcedTea, this process was the only way to ensure that no non-free binary parts were included (or accidentally leaked) into the resulting binaries from the non-free Sun Java compiler. Such bootstrapping with another compiler is a common procedure for free software. Besides preventing binary leaks, such a procedure can also be used to prevent possible malicious compiler bookmarks. For recent IcedTea versions, GCJ is not required for the built and prebuilt OpenJDK binaries, and can be used as the boot JDK without the full bootstrap process.

IcedTea is more open to new and experimental features than OpenJDK. It allows you to use alternative virtual machine implementations (such as Zero, Shark, and JamVM) and also supports cross-compiling for additional architectures (such as ARM, MIPS), which are not supported by OpenJDK.

IcedTea also provides more tight integration with an operating system. Originally, Sun Java distributions for Linux were made to be as self-contained as possible. Implementation of many standard features such as image processing support (PNG, JPG, GIF), compressing (ZIP), and cryptographic algorithms (elliptic curve-based ones) were included in the OpenJDK code base. These allow better portability but restrict users with older and possibly less secure versions of the open source libraries. Modern Linux distributions have advanced package management tools to control and update the common dependencies between packages. IcedTea has introduced the support for using some libraries from the host operating system, instead of using the versions included with OpenJDK.

Building IcedTea 6

The IcedTea project, historically, had a lot of changes in it compared to vanilla OpenJDK 6 source code. The number of changes went down eventually, as some of them were included in the main OpenJDK 6 source tree. Some of the changes, such as NIO2 API support (taken from OpenJDK 7), were experimental and were removed.

The changes are stored in the IcedTea source tree in the form of patches (different files) and not as changesets in a separate branch. This can confuse users who are not experienced with class Unix/Linux patch techniques and tools. The different files are stored in the `patches` directory and are applied to the OpenJDK source tree during the `configure` build step.

Contrary to OpenJDK 8, the GNU Autoconf build system is not integrated tightly into the IcedTea build process. The Autoconf `configure` step prepares the environment for building the OpenJDK sources and the standard (slightly patched) OpenJDK makefiles are run on the Autoconf `make` step.

In this recipe, we will build IcedTea 6 on Ubuntu 12.04 LTS amd64.

Getting ready

For this recipe, we will need a clean Ubuntu 12.04 (server or desktop version) running.

How to do it...

The following procedures will help you to build IcedTea 6:

1. Install the prepackaged binaries of OpenJDK 6:

   ```
   sudo apt-get install openjdk-6-jdk
   ```

2. Install the GCC toolchain and build dependencies:

   ```
   sudo apt-get build-dep openjdk-6
   sudo apt-get install libmotif-dev
   ```

3. Download and decompress the appropriate `icedtea6*` source code tarball from `http://icedtea.wildebeest.org/download/source/`:

   ```
   wget http://icedtea.wildebeest.org/download/source/icedtea6-
   1.13.1.tar.xz

   tar xJvf icedtea6-1.13.1.tar.xz
   ```

4. Configure the build specifying the preinstalled OpenJDK path and disable the system's LCMS2 support:

   ```
   ./configure \
   --with-jdk-home=/usr/lib/jvm/java-6-openjdk-amd64 \
   --disable-system-lcms
   ```

5. Start the build:

   ```
   make
   ```

6. Wait for the build to finish.

How it works...

Prepackaged binaries of OpenJDK 6 are required because some of the build steps are run using the external Java runtime.

The `build-dep` command is used to install all the dependencies that are required to build the specified package. As Ubuntu-packaged OpenJDK 6 is quite close to the official OpenJDK 6, this command will install almost all the required dependencies.

The `libmotif-dev` package is the additional package that is required, and contains the Motif GUI toolkit header files.

In the configuration step, IcedTea checks the environment and prepares adjustments to the OpenJDK sources that are to be applied in build step.

In build step, the official OpenJDK 6 sources are downloaded and then adjusted in accordance with the build configuration. After that, the usual OpenJDK 6 build is run. Then, it is run for the second time using the results of the first build as a bootstrap JDK. The resulting binaries are produced by the second build.

Recent versions of IcedTea require the color management library LCMS Version 2.5 or higher. As such a version is not available in Ubuntu 12.04 repositories, we use LCMS bundled with OpenJDK sources.

There's more...

IcedTea has a much more flexible configuration compared to OpenJDK. Some of the options will be explored in later recipes in this chapter.

See also

- ▶ *Chapter 2, Building OpenJDK 6*
- ▶ The *Working with GNU Autoconf* recipe from *Chapter 4, Building OpenJDK 8*
- ▶ The IcedTea project website at `http://icedtea.classpath.org/wiki/Main_Page`
- ▶ The acceptance speech *Reflections on Trusting Trust* by Ken Thompson during the ACM A.M. Turing Award 1983, which can be found at `http://cm.bell-labs.com/who/ken/trust.html`.

Building IcedTea 7

During the long years of development of OpenJDK 7, the build process was cleaned up and improved significantly. Many changes (such as replacing the binary plugins with open source components) were included in the main OpenJDK source tree after "soaking" in between other experimental changes in IcedTea.

Due to these changes, the IcedTea 7 source tree contains much fewer patches for OpenJDK 7 compared to its predecessor. Similar to IcedTea 6, Autoconf `configure` step applies patches and prepares the environment, and the `make` step runs the original OpenJDK 7 makefiles.

Source patches are mostly used for compatibility with platform Linux libraries (`zlib`, `libpng`, and so on) instead of ones contained in the source tree. Makefile patches, besides this task, are also used to change the Java launcher—version switch output. Many applications use these outputs to determine the version of JRE they run on. Besides the version number format, one notable change is that in Oracle the Java version line starts with the `java version <version number>` string, whereas the vanilla OpenJDK version line starts with `openjdk version <version number>`. While the version number can be modified using environment variables, this prefix cannot be modified. To achieve better compatibility with existing applications, IcedTea uses the makefile patch to change this prefix from `openjdk` to `java`.

In this recipe, we will build IcedTea 7 on Ubuntu 12.04 LTS.

Getting ready

For this recipe, we will need a clean Ubuntu 12.04 (server or desktop version) running.

How to do it...

The following procedures will help you to build Iced Tea 7:

1. Install the prepackaged binaries of OpenJDK 6:

   ```
   sudo apt-get install openjdk-6-jdk
   ```

2. Install the GCC toolchain and build dependencies:

   ```
   sudo apt-get build-dep openjdk-6
   ```

3. Download and decompress the appropriate `icedtea-2*` source code tarball from `http://icedtea.wildebeest.org/download/source/`:

   ```
   http://icedtea.wildebeest.org/download/source/icedtea-2.4.5.tar.xz
   tar xJvf icedtea-2.4.5.tar.xz
   ```

4. Configure the build, specifying the preinstalled OpenJDK path, and disable the system's LCMS2 support:

    ```
    ./configure \
    --with-jdk-home=/usr/lib/jvm/java-6-openjdk-amd64 \
    --disable-system-lcms
    ```

5. Start the build:

    ```
    make
    ```

6. Wait for the build to finish.

How it works...

The prepackaged binaries of OpenJDK 6 are required because some of the build steps are run using the external Java runtime.

The `build-dep` command is used to install all the dependencies that are required to build the specified package.

In the build step, the official OpenJDK 6 sources are downloaded and then adjusted in accordance with the build configuration. After that, the usual OpenJDK 6 build is run. Then, the OpenJDK 6 build is run a second time using the results of the first build as a bootstrap JDK. The resulting binaries are produced by the second build.

Recent versions of IcedTea require the color management library LCMS Version 2.5 or higher. As such a version is not available in Ubuntu 12.04 repositories, we used the LCMS bundled with OpenJDK sources.

There's more...

IcedTea has a much more flexible configuration compared to OpenJDK. Some of the options will be explored in the later recipes in this chapter.

See also

▸ *Chapter 3, Building OpenJDK 7*

▸ The *Working with GNU Autoconf* recipe from *Chapter 4, Building OpenJDK 8*

▸ IcedTea project website at `http://icedtea.classpath.org/wiki/Main_Page`

Building OpenJDK 7 with IcedTea patches

IcedTea 7 has a much shorter release cycle compared to OpenJDK 7. IcedTea releases roughly correspond to Oracle Java security releases and contain the same security patches where applicable, so, IcedTea 7 can be used to build up-to-date OpenJDK 7 builds on Windows and Mac OS X platforms.

Performing full IcedTea 7 builds on a non-Linux platform might be difficult because the build configuration step expects Linux as a host platform. Instead of this, the IcedTea project can be used to patch OpenJDK sources on Linux, and then the patched sources can be built on other platforms using the usual OpenJDK 7 build steps.

Getting ready

For this recipe, we will need a clean Ubuntu 12.04 (server or desktop version) running.

How to do it...

The following procedures will help you to prepare the OpenJDK 7 source code with IcedTea patches:

1. Install the prepackaged binaries of OpenJDK 6:

   ```
   sudo apt-get install openjdk-6-jdk
   ```

2. Install the GCC toolchain and build dependencies:

   ```
   sudo apt-get build-dep openjdk-6
   ```

3. Download and decompress the appropriate `icedtea-2*` source code tarball from `http://icedtea.wildebeest.org/download/source/`:

   ```
   http://icedtea.wildebeest.org/download/source/icedtea-2.4.5.tar.xz
   ```

   ```
   tar xJvf icedtea-2.4.5.tar.xz
   ```

4. Run the configuration script to enable the use of the libraries bundled with OpenJDK sources:

   ```
   ./configure \
   --with-jdk-home=path/to/openjdk7 \
   --with-rhino=path/to/rhino-1.7.4.jar \
   --disable-bootstrap \
   --disable-system-zlib \
   --disable-system-jpeg \
   --disable-system-png \
   --disable-system-gif \
   ```

```
--disable-system-lcms \
--disable-system-pcsc \
--disable-compile-against-syscalls \
--disable-nss
```

5. Start the build process:

    make

6. During the build, the patched OpenJDK 7 source will be put into the `openjdk` directory. Copy this directory to a Windows or Mac OS X machine.

7. Build the patched sources using the usual OpenJDK 7 build process, with the additional environment variables:

    export FT2_CFLAGS='-I$(FREETYPE_HEADERS_PATH) -I$(FREETYPE_HEADERS_PATH)/freetype2'

    export DISABLE_INTREE_EC=true

How it works...

IcedTea 7 contains a set of patches that are applied (depending on configuration options) at the start of the build process. In this recipe, we do not want to build IcedTea itself, but we want to collect patched IcedTea sources to build them later, on another platform using the usual build process for OpenJDK 7, as described in *Chapter 3, Building OpenJDK 7*.

There's more...

Applying patches is performed in the early stages of the build. It is not necessary to wait for the IcedTea build to end: the build process can be interrupted after the patches are applied.

See also

▶ The *Building IcedTea 7* recipe in this chapter

▶ *Chapter 3, Building OpenJDK 7*

▶ The *Working with GNU Autoconf* recipe from *Chapter 4, Building OpenJDK 8*

▶ IcedTea project website at `http://icedtea.classpath.org/wiki/Main_Page`

Building IcedTea 7 with the NSS security provider

OpenJDK supports pluggable modules for cryptography service implementation. Widely used modern cryptographic algorithms (such as ciphers, paddings, and so on) are usually available on multiple platforms. Different platforms can have different native implementations of these algorithms. These implementations can be more performant than OpenJDK internal ones because they can rely on the details of the platform they run on. Also, platform implementations can be used as bridges to the facilities of hardware crypto-devices such as smartcards or eTokens. OpenJDK pluggable crypto-providers allow you to use a wide range of cryptographic implementations through a single Java API interface.

Network Security Services (**NSS**) is an open source cryptography library that was developed for the Netscape web browser and is currently maintained by the Mozilla Foundation. NSS provides implementation of a wide range of cryptographic algorithms that support **Transport Layer Security** (**TLS**) and S/MIME and is used in the Firefox web browser, besides other software. NSS also has support for hardware crypto-devices (smartcards/eTokens).

IcedTea 7 can be built with support for NSS as a crypto-provider.

Getting ready

For this recipe, we will need a clean Ubuntu 12.04 (server or desktop version) running.

How to do it...

The following procedures will help you to build IcedTea 7 with NSS:

1. Install the prepackaged binaries of OpenJDK 6:

   ```
   sudo apt-get install openjdk-6-jdk
   ```

2. Install the GCC toolchain and build dependencies:

   ```
   sudo apt-get build-dep openjdk-6
   ```

3. Download and decompress the appropriate `icedtea-2*` source code tarball from `http://icedtea.wildebeest.org/download/source/`:

   ```
   http://icedtea.wildebeest.org/download/source/icedtea-2.4.5.tar.xz
   tar xJvf icedtea-2.4.5.tar.xz
   ```

4. Run the configuration script and enable the NSS crypto-provider:

```
./configure --with-jdk-home=/usr/lib/jvm/java-6-openjdk-amd64
--disable-system-lcms
--enable-nss
```

5. Start the build:

```
make
```

6. Wait for the build to finish.

How it works...

OpenJDK supports pluggable cryptography implementations using unified service-provider interfaces. IcedTea 7 allows you to delegate cryptographic tasks to the platform NSS library.

See also

▸ The *Building IcedTea 7* recipe from this chapter

▸ *Chapter 3, Building OpenJDK 7*

▸ The *Working with GNU Autoconf* recipe from *Chapter 4, Building OpenJDK 8*

▸ The Mozilla NSS developer documentation at `https://developer.mozilla.org/en-US/docs/Mozilla/Projects/NSS`

Building IcedTea 6 with the SystemTap support

Applications running on modern operating systems usually communicate with the underlying OS kernel through **system calls** (**syscalls**) or through an intermediate platform API. Some operating systems provide advanced tracing tools to monitor the applications running, and for troubleshooting. Such tools (such as `dtrace` on Oracle Solaris) allow the user to intercept all application activity, syscalls, Unix signals processing, and so on, to diagnose performance and functional problems.

For proper support of tracing tools, applications should have *probe-points* (or *tracepoints*) compiled into their binaries.

SystemTap is a tracing tool and a scripting language for Linux-based operating systems. IcedTea 6 can be built with SystemTap support.

Getting ready

For this recipe, we will need a clean Ubuntu 12.04 (server or desktop version) running.

How to do it...

The following procedures will help you to build IcedTea 6 with SystemTap:

1. Install the prepackaged binaries of OpenJDK 6:

   ```
   sudo apt-get install openjdk-6-jdk
   ```

2. Install GCC toolchain and build dependencies:

   ```
   sudo apt-get build-dep openjdk-6
   sudo apt-get install libmotif-dev
   ```

3. Download and decompress the appropriate `icedtea6*` source code tarball from `http://icedtea.wildebeest.org/download/source/`:

   ```
   wget http://icedtea.wildebeest.org/download/source/icedtea6-
   1.13.1.tar.xz

   tar xJvf icedtea6-1.13.1.tar.xz
   ```

4. Configure the build, specifying the preinstalled OpenJDK path and disable the system's LCMS2 support:

   ```
   ./configure \
   --with-jdk-home=/usr/lib/jvm/java-6-openjdk-amd64 \
   --disable-system-lcms \
   --enable-systemtap
   ```

5. Start the build:

   ```
   make
   ```

6. Wait for the build to finish.

There's more...

We built IcedTea 6 with the support of JVM user space markers. These markers allow SystemTap to probe various JVM events including the loading of classes, just-in-time translation of method, and garbage collection.

See also

- The *Building IcedTea 6* recipe from this chapter
- *Chapter 2, Building OpenJDK 6*
- The *Working with GNU Autoconf* recipe from *Chapter 4, Building OpenJDK 8*
- The SystemTap project website at `https://sourceware.org/systemtap/`

6
Building IcedTea with Other VM Implementations

In this chapter, we will cover the following topics:

- ▸ Configuring cross-compilation between ARM and x86
- ▸ Building IcedTea for ARM with integrated CACAO VM
- ▸ Porting JamVM to use OpenJDK
- ▸ Configuring Zero assembler with the Shark compiler to use OpenJDK
- ▸ Building MIPS and other architectures using OpenEmbedded recipes

Introduction

Though various x86-compatible platforms are widespread and common to use, there are other architectures to think about. Java language itself is designed to be as cross-platform, as possible. In an x86-compatible world, it means that Java will work equally well and predictable for the vast majority of operating systems. Where more architectures are concerned, it should work on a great number of them.

The ARM architecture is the second architecture among the most popular ones. It gives a great balance between power saving and performance, and is used mostly in embedded and portable devices. There are several operating systems, supporting ARM, such as various Linux distributions, Android, Symbian, MeeGo, and many Windows releases.

In this chapter, we will speak about building IcedTea on ARM, using virtual Java machines, which are not official and aren't parts of the OpenJDK community. They are built for different purposes—academic, performance, and so on.

Unfortunately, these days, the only operating system that works with ARM and OpenJDK both, is Linux. Nuances of building IcedTea on Linux differ from distribution to distribution, though the main idea and philosophy is the same.

In this chapter, we will try to use as many different distribution-based examples and device nuances, as possible, though the most thoroughly tested ones will be the following pairs:

- Raspberry Pi and Raspbian
- Nexus 7 and Ubuntu touch

This chapter will also cover a topic of cross-compilation with an x86-based system, because one may probably need a faster compilation that ARM processors are capable of, especially in the case of small computers of the Raspberry Pi class.

We will have three VMs in this chapter: ZeroVM, CACAO VM, and Jam VM. However, only the Zero assembler is a member of an OpenJDK project. The Zero assembler is an effort to get rid of platform-specific assembler languages and to build an interpreter-only virtual machine. It will make porting any Java executable to any operating system a remarkably easy task, but with a significant performance impact because of the absence of JIT. However, there is Shark, a JIT-compiler for Zero, which uses LLVM to compile the Zero-assembler to the platform-specific code. It's obvious, though, that Shark works only for architectures that are supported by LLVM itself.

JamVM is also famous because of its really small size, which is, depending on architectures, between 200 and 250 kilobytes. In this space, it implements the full JVM specification, published by Oracle, known as **blue book**.

Configuring cross-compilation between ARM and x86

Though many of the recent ARM devices have great performance and the same core numbers, as their desktop fellows, there are always those whose performance is not sufficient enough to do complicated work in a reasonable amount of time. Don't want to be bored by endless hours of compilation? Use OpenEmbedded builds. **OpenEmbedded** is a build framework to create Linux distributions and can cross-compile for a large variety of architectures.

Getting ready

We will need a real or emulated ARM device with Linux installed on it. The following recipes are primarily for the deb-based distributions, but the general idea remains the same for any ARM-based device that runs Linux kernel with GNU-based tools.

Also, we will need another device with Linux, or Windows with Cygwin installed, to do the main compilation job.

This recipe also assumes that you will use the deb-based distributions. If you are using the ebuild-based distributions, use their own cross-compile tools. In the rpm-based distributions, the process is quite similar.

How to do it...

First, we need to make use of the OpenEmbedded project. OpenEmbedded is a project whose goal is to build a platform-specific environment and build various known packages. Take a look at the following procedure to build various packages using the OpenEmbedded project:

1. In order to use it, we will install some packages:

    ```
    sudo apt-get install git g++ gawk zip diffstat texi2html texinfo
    subversion chrpath libgl1-mesa-dev libglu1-mesa-dev libsdl1.2-dev
    ```

2. After that, we need to get an OpenEmbedded environment:

    ```
    git clone git://git.openembedded.org/openembedded-core oe-core
    ```

3. Then, we need to create three more projects in the oe-core directory:

    ```
    cd oe-core
    ```

4. Moving ahead, let's clone some layers into our root directory:

    ```
    git clone git://git.openembedded.org/bitbake bitbake
    ```

    ```
    git clone git://git.openembedded.org/meta-openembedded
    ```

    ```
    git clone https://github.com/woglinde/meta-java.git
    ```

5. Finally, initialize an OpenEmbedded environment:

    ```
    . ./oe-init-build-env
    ```

Now we have a fully operational OpenEmbedded environment. All we have to do is to configure our build. There are two ways to do it: by editing the config files manually or through the Hob GUI.

Configuring OpenEmbedded build manually

You will need to edit two configuration files: the first configuration file is for Java layer and the second is generic and easy to include this layer in the build, as shown in the following steps:

1. First, edit the `conf/local.conf` file.

2. We will set JamVM as a preferred virtual machine:

   ```
   PREFERRED_PROVIDER_virtual/java-native = "jamvm-native"
   ```

3. Set other versions as you wish (Version 1.8.11, for example):

   ```
   PREFERRED_PROVIDER_virtual/javac-native = "ecj-bootstrap-native"

   PREFERRED_VERSION_cacaoh-native = "<version_number>"

   PREFERRED_VERSION_icedtea6-native = "<version_number>"
   ```

4. We will need an ARM build, so we will select a qemu-arm machine as the target machine:

   ```
   MACHINE ?= "qemuarm"
   ```

5. We will also need to mention how many compilation processes can be in progress together:

   ```
   PARALLEL_MAKE = "-j 2"
   ```

6. Also, we can reconfigure a number of threads for one compiling package. For a Quad-core computer, it will be 2:

   ```
   BB_NUMBER_THREADS = "2"
   ```

7. Then, we will edit the `conf/bblayers.conf` file.

8. The following parameter is a version of the file format. It means that there was 3 incompatible formats before this:

   ```
   LCONF_VERSION = "4"
   ```

9. We will then set layers to command OpenEmbedded system on what exactly to build:

   ```
   BBFILES ?= ""

   BBLAYERS = " \
     /home/user/oe-core/meta \
     /home/user/oe-core/meta-openembedded/meta-oe \
     /home/user/oe-core/meta-java \
     "
   ```

Using the Hob utility to configure the OpenEmbedded build

Hob is a graphical UI for BitBake. Please take a look at the following procedures to use the Hob utility to configure the OpenEmbedded build:

1. Let's run a `hob` executable from a build directory:

    hob

    This can be done only after an environment initialization. You will have a command not found message otherwise.

    ```
    No command 'hob' found, did you mean:
     Command 'bob' from package 'python-sponge' (universe)
     Command 'hoz' from package 'hoz' (universe)
     Command 'tob' from package 'tob' (universe)
     Command 'hnb' from package 'hnb' (universe)
    hob: command not found
    ```

2. A starting screen will appear as shown:

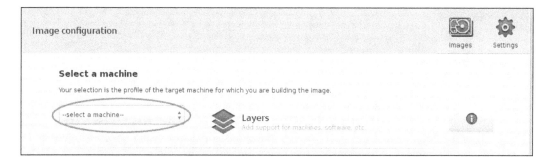

3. First, we will select a virtual machine. For ARM processors, the most convenient is the qemu-arm machine.

4. After that, we will need to select two additional layers. One is the **meta-oe** layer and the second is **meta-java**.

> While the `meta-java` folder is in the root folder of OpenEmbedded, the path to `meta-oe` is `meta-openembedded/meta-oe/`.

5. When a machine is chosen, the tool will parse all recipes and compute all dependencies needed. Then, the window should look like this:

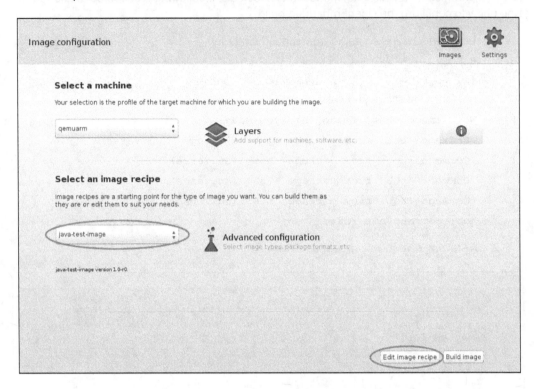

6. Then select a recipe. Here is one Java-related recipe: **java-test-image**. Although, it would be better not to choose it and choose **core-image-basic** instead.

    You can try to assemble your image from scratch. You can select the package you want and dependencies will be automatically calculated.

You can choose in an advanced configuration section, exactly what the output will be. You can even get it in a .deb form, as shown:

1. You need to edit recipes and add **openjdk-7-jre** to them as shown:

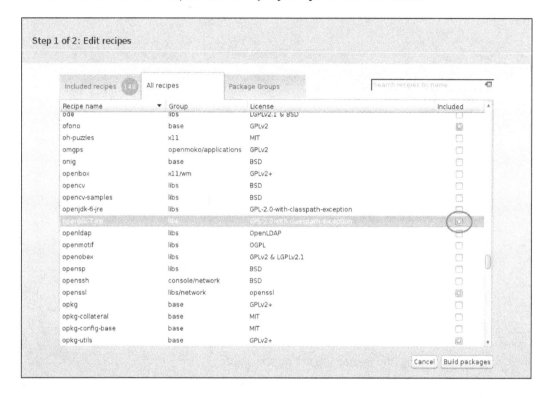

Also, you can add some dependencies that are necessary for the build.

2. When all is ready, press the **Build packages** button and the following screen will appear:

If something goes wrong, the **Issues** tab will not be empty.

After the build

You will need to copy the build output from the **tmp-eglibc** folder to your ARM device.

How it works...

OpenEmbedded is a stack of cross-compile recipes for various tools that needs a lot of time for compilation. OpenEmbedded will create a root filesystem from scratch. Then it will build the packages that you want to be built. OpenEmbedded provides a bunch of abstraction layers, from the developer to the core layer. These layers include recipes and tools to build an environment and a target project.

So, after a performed configuration, the tool will build an environment and then some projects in it.

There's more...

Building OpenEmbedded recipes is not a trivial task. It often needs some problem solving skills. It's not unusual when your build, that literally takes hours to pass, is interrupted with some errors even when you are trying to build a stock Java-test image.

Though the basics of recipe-building and correcting will be given in the following recipes, we can provide a roadmap to deal with some problems right here, in this section.

> Some cases, which were found and overcome by authors, will be found in *Chapter 8, Hacking OpenJDK*.

Configure problems – when a header file is not found

Though the building process is similar to creating a well-maintained Linux repository from scratch, it's not so simple. It's a task of building the whole thing from source, and some header movement in some minor package maybe a major problem that is fatal to your build, as shown:

1. So, it's a dependency problem. At first, try to find out, do you need the package, which header is not found, at all.

2. If so, find out whether you can disable it through the standard `./configure` properties (those which are specified before make).

3. If you can, you're lucky. Just find a recipe for your package and edit the `.bb` or `.inc` file. For OpenJDK, it's `openjdk-7-common.inc`.

4. Add (or remove) the desired `./configure` property to (or from) `EXTRA_OECONF`. Don't forget the screening \. If you need that dependency or cannot disable it, it's another matter.

5. First, consider switching to an older/newer version of the `.bb` files. It may solve some problems, but can easily add to them as well.

6. If this is impossible or will not help, try to find a patch to the source and apply it.

Fetch problems – where your package is not accessible through any mirror available

First, try to check whether all the mirrors that are used are permanently offline. If not, just wait for a bit while one of those becomes accessible.

Compile problems – where a compile error occurs

There is always a solution to this kind of problem, which is searchable through the Internet.

It may be a wrong dependency version or even a major compilation issue that slipped away from the maintainer's eye. The solution is to patch your build using some known patches or even your own patch, or change the source parameter of the package.

Parsing problems – where your recipes cannot be parsed

It is not a common problem but it was encountered, for example, in the `openjdk-7` branch of the `meta-java` repository. Often it doesn't mean that something is completely broken. Check the indicated lines of recipe files for missing \, partial comments, and other minor formatting issues. If the problem still appears, consider changing your current branch.

Building IcedTea for ARM with integrated CACAO VM

This recipe promises to be quite simple, because the integration of CACAO VM is already a part of IcedTea itself. It will not require any patching or other complicated things.

Getting ready

We may need a real or emulated ARM device, which has Linux and any Java environment installed. We need Java to perform a `javac` compilation, which is a necessary part of the IcedTea building process.

How to do it...

We will download IcedTea, unpack it, and build it with the specified parameters, that's all.

1. First, let's get the latest IcedTea source from the server:

   ```
   wget http://icedtea.wildebeest.org/download/source/icedtea-
   <icedtea_version>.tar.gz
   ```

   It will download an archive.

2. Perform a checksum check if required.

3. Let's unpack an archive and copy it into the `icedtea` directory:

   ```
   tar -xzf icedtea-XXXX

   cd icedtea-XXXX
   ```

4. Then, you might have to install some dependency packages needed to make your IcedTea.

5. The given packages are those that were missing on the authors' machine during the first build:

```
sudo apt-get install zip gawk xsltproc libjpeg8-dev libgif-dev
libpng-dev liblcms2-dev libgtk2-dev cups libcups2-dev libc6-dev
libattr1-dev alsa-ocaml-dev
```

6. Then, we will make a link for build configuration to find the Java home directory:

```
sudo ln -s /usr/lib/jvm/java-7-openjdk-armhf/ /usr/lib/jvm/java-
1.7.0-openjdk
```

> If you have a distribution-recommended way to change the default Java home directory, please follow it instead.

7. Then we will enable the CACAO VM in our configuration. Also, we will configure the newly built IcedTea to use the CACAO VM not only as the build configuration, but as a default:

```
./configure --enable-cacao --with-icedtea —with-icedtea-
home=<your_openjdk_home>
```

8. When running `configure`, you probably will encounter errors with messages indicating that some program or library is missing. It's okay, you just need to install them using your package manager.

9. After doing that, we will build IcedTea using just one simple command:

```
make
```

It is a long process, even using cross-compilation, so it's best to have a cup of tea or something.

How it works...

IcedTea is now supporting CACAO VM as a build configuration just out of the box. We will only need to enable this option to configure and add missing dependencies. Normally, IcedTea uses a ZeroVM on ARM, but without Shark JIT compilation. Under the hood, however, it literally applies hundreds of patches and uses an amount of memory that is not acceptable on embedded devices.

There's more...

Since you may experience some difficulties with building IcedTea on some devices, you may need to use cross-compiling the way we used it before.

You may need just to set a variable to the local configuration file:

```
PREFERRED_PROVIDER_virtual/java-native = "cacao-native"
```

Porting JamVM to use OpenJDK

Another Zero HotSpot alternative for non-JIT supported platforms is JamVM—an extremely small VM, which is the smallest among those supporting the blue book specification (one that was published in the book form) for Java VMs.

Getting ready

We may need a real or emulated ARM device that has Linux and any Java environment installed. We need Java to perform a `javac` compilation, which is a necessary part of IcedTea building process.

How to do it...

Though JamVM patches may be applied manually, we will use the more simple way:

1. First, let's clone the source from the repository:

   ```
   git clone git://git.berlios.de/jamvm
   ```

2. Then we configure it to use OpenJDK as Java runtime libraries:

   ```
   ./autogen.sh –with-java-runtime-library=openjdk
   ```

3. Then we will actually build it from source using the `make` command:

   ```
   make && make install
   ```

4. Next, we need to copy `libjvm` to `lib`:

   ```
   cp libjvm.so  /usr/local/jamvm/lib.
   ```

5. Then let's copy the OpenJDK contents:

   ```
   cd /usr/lib/jvm
   cp -r java-7-openjdk jamvm-openjdk
   cp /usr/local/jamvm/lib/libjvm.so jamvm-openjdk/jre/lib/armv6/
   server
   ```

6. Then, let's run our compiled Java:

   ```
   /usr/lib/jvm/jamvm-openjdk/jre/bin/java -version
   ```

7. We will see the output like this:

   ```
   java version "1.7.0_20"
   OpenJDK Runtime Environment (IcedTea7 1.9.5) (7b20-1.9.5-0ubuntu1)
   JamVM (build 1.7.0-devel, inline-threaded interpreter)
   ```

There's more

Also, the Jam M support is a part of an OpenEmbedded Java layer. In order to add it, you will remove the ZeroVM support and add a JamVM support. It's a simple task, though you may experience errors during configuration and building.

Also, you can run whatever Java program you choose with JamVM, even if your IcedTea build is not configured to use it.

Just type the following:

```
java  -jamvm <other parameters and program name>
```

Configuring Zero-assembler with the Shark compiler to use OpenJDK

Zero-assembler HotSpot port is the default Java VM for all newly-built OpenJDK instances on ARM prior to Java 8. It is the default Java VM for quite a few JIT-unsupported platforms. However, there is an effort to bring JIT power to it, named Shark.

Getting ready

We may need a real or emulated ARM device, which has Linux and any Java environment installed. We need Java to perform a `javac` compilation, which is a necessary part of the IcedTea building process.

How to do it...

1. Let's download an IcedTea source.

    ```
    wget http://icedtea.wildebeest.org/download/source/icedtea-
    <icedtea_version>.tar.gz
    ```

    It will download an archive.

2. Then, you can check a checksum.

3. Let's unpack it and copy it into the `icedtea` directory:

    ```
    tar -xzf icedtea-XXXX
    cd icedtea-XXXX
    ```

4. Then, you may need to install some dependency packages needed to make your IcedTea.

The following packages are those that were missing on my machine during my first build.

```
sudo apt-get install zip gawk xsltproc libjpeg8-dev libgif-dev
libpng-dev liblcms2-dev libgtk2-dev cups libcups2-dev libc6-dev
libattr1-dev alsa-ocaml-dev
```

5. Then, we will make a link for the build configuration to find the Java home directory:

```
sudo ln -s /usr/lib/jvm/java-7-openjdk-armhf/ /usr/lib/jvm/java-
1.7.0-openjdk
```

 If you have a distribution-recommended way to change the default Java home directory, please follow it instead.

6. Then we will enable Zero-Shark in our configuration. Also, we will configure the newly built IcedTea to use Shark VM not only as the build, but as the default:

```
./configure --enable-zero  --enable-shark --with-icedtea —with-
icedtea-home=<your_openjdk_home>
```

When running `configure`, you probably will encounter errors with messages indicating that some program or library is missing. It's okay, you just need to install them using your package manager.

7. After doing that, we will build IcedTea using just one simple command:

```
make
```

How it works...

Normally, IcedTea uses a ZeroVM on ARM but without Shark JIT-compilation. All we need to do is to command it to use ZeroVM and Shark JIT compiler.

Shark is a project that uses a famous list of LLVM-supported platforms to enable JIT support on all of them, which is quite impressive. It may not be as fast as native JIT but something is better than nothing.

 On ARM, there is a workable OpenJDK that uses JIT-compilation in HotSpot out of the box. However, it's only in the early-access mode and since it's JDK 8, this support will not be ported any prior to it.

The LLVM project's goal is to achieve the cross-platform compilation across as many languages and platforms as possible. It uses frontend and backend transforms to provide a flexibility of their tools as shown in the following figure:

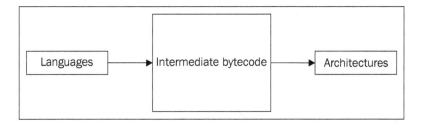

Because of this structure, LLVM can be used to compile the Java class methods' code to an intermediate language and then to a native code. It leaves the simplest features as reflection and so on to the VM.

There's more

Also, you could always cross-compile IcedTea with Zero-Shark support. In order to do so, refer to the last recipe in this chapter.

Building for MIPS and other architectures using OpenEmbedded recipes

When ARM-based devices are widespread and popular, there are always other architectures. The great power of Java is its cross-platformness, so let's try to have builds for some other architecture.

Getting ready

You will need an Internet connection and Linux or Windows with Cygwin installed on your computer. Also, from the author's experience, you will need at least 4GB RAM.

For a comfortable build, it's recommended to have a powerful hardware and a fast HDD.

Also, you may experience some lags or even OOM-kills during build, so make sure that all your data is saved.

Also, you will need an OpenEmbedded project configured, as described in the first recipe of this chapter.

How to do it...

First, we will see how to add architectures and software to OpenEmbedded:

1. Open your browser, and go to `http://layers.openembedded.org/layerindex/branch/master/layers/`.

    You will find a list of architectures supported and a list of software that you can install.

2. Do a Git clone of the repositories containing the code that you need (such as `meta-asus` or `meta-htc`).

3. Then prepare your build environment and open the Hob GUI as shown:

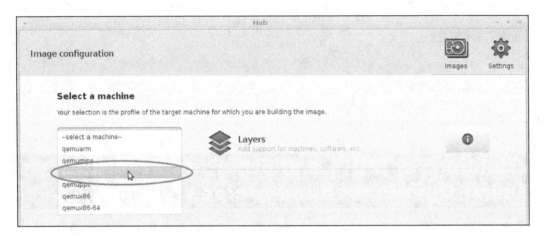

4. Select the machine from the drop-down list.

5. Then, you will probably need to set some architecture-specific `./configure` options. In order to do that, you will need to change a `bitbake` file, adding or correcting the `EXTRA_OECONF` variable. Don't forget to add trailing \s.

How it works...

The main goal of this project is to create the repository and distribution from scratch, with precompiled images and dependencies. It consists of metadata, called the `.bb` files, and many dependencies between them.

If this project is not running very smoothly, and you may need to make some changes in order to make your way through. A `.bb` file is a file of the following structure:

```
#A description of this recipe.
 DESCRIPTION = ""
#A homepage, if any
```

```
 HOMEPAGE = ""
#A license
 LICENSE = ""
#Dependecies
 DEPENDS = ""
#URI of the sources
 SRC_URI = " \
   "

 # SRC_URI could also point to a git repository, eg:
 # SRC_URI = "git://host:port/path/to/repo.git;branch=win;protocol=ssh
;user=username"

 # any .patch files included here will be auto-magically applied,
increasing the -p level until it sticks.
 # SRC_URI = "file://some.patch"

#package revision. This is a really important thing, you will change
it each time when you update the recipe.
 PR = "r0"

#checksums for tarball packages
 SRC_URI[md5sum] = ""
 SRC_URI[sha256sum] = ""
 S = "${WORKDIR}/CHANGEME-${PV}"

#Action which will be performed on oe_configure stage
 do_configure () {
    ./configure --prefix=${prefix}
 }

#Action which will be performed on oe_make stage
 do_compile () {
    make
 }


 #Action which will be performed on install stage
do_install () {
    DESTDIR=${D} oe_runmake install
 }
```

This is a plain recipe template and you can add whatever dependency you want through it. Also, you can add patches into the recipe directory or even add sources to it.

There's more...

You always can build OpenJDK on other architectures using a standard HotSpot Zero port. It is fully interpretable and it can make your programs run very slowly, but it's better than nothing. Just follow the standard procedure:

```
./configure
```

```
make
```

This approach has its downsides, because most of the architectures aside from Intel and ARM are embedded, so you will not be able to make something fast, or even make it at all. For example, on Raspberry Pi with a newly-built Raspbian and 512 Mb RAM, building IcedTea will randomly crash because of lack of memory, even with large swapfiles.

7
Working with WebStart and the Browser Plugin

In this chapter, we will cover the following topics:

- ▶ Building the IcedTea browser plugin on Linux
- ▶ Using the IcedTea Java WebStart implementation on Linux
- ▶ Preparing the IcedTea Java WebStart implementation for Mac OS X
- ▶ Preparing the IcedTea Java WebStart implementation for Windows

Introduction

For a long time, for end users, the Java applets technology was the face of the whole Java world. For a lot of non-developers, the word Java itself is a synonym for the Java browser plugin that allows running Java applets inside web browsers. The **Java WebStart** technology is similar to the Java browser plugin but runs remotely on loaded Java applications as separate applications outside of web browsers.

The OpenJDK open source project does not contain the implementations for the browser plugin nor for the WebStart technologies. The Oracle Java distribution, otherwise matching closely to OpenJDK codebases, provided its own closed source implementation for these technologies.

The IcedTea-Web project contains free and open source implementations of the browser plugin and WebStart technologies. The IcedTea-Web browser plugin supports only GNU/Linux operating systems and the WebStart implementation is cross-platform.

While the IcedTea implementation of WebStart is well-tested and production-ready, it has numerous incompatibilities with the Oracle WebStart implementation. These differences can be seen as corner cases; some of them are:

- **Different behavior when parsing not well-formed JNLP descriptor files**: The Oracle implementation is generally more lenient for malformed descriptors.

- **Differences in JAR (re)downloading and caching behavior**: The Oracle implementation uses caching more aggressively.

- **Differences in sound support**: This is due to differences in sound support between Oracle Java and IcedTea on Linux. Linux historically has multiple different sound providers (ALSA, PulseAudio, and so on) and IcedTea has more wide support for different providers, which can lead to sound misconfiguration.

The IcedTea-Web browser plugin (as it is built on WebStart) has these incompatibilities too. On top of them, it can have more incompatibilities in relation to browser integration. User interface forms and general browser-related operations such as access from/to JavaScript code should work fine with both implementations. But historically, the browser plugin was widely used for security-critical applications like online bank clients. Such applications usually require security facilities from browsers, such as access to certificate stores or hardware crypto-devices that can differ from browser to browser, depending on the OS (for example, supports only Windows), browser version, Java version, and so on. Because of that, many real-world applications can have problems running the IcedTea-Web browser plugin on Linux.

Both WebStart and the browser plugin are built on the idea of downloading (possibly untrusted) code from remote locations, and proper privilege checking and sandboxed execution of that code is a notoriously complex task. Usually reported security issues in the Oracle browser plugin (most widely known are issues during the year 2012) are also fixed separately in IcedTea-Web.

Building the IcedTea browser plugin on Linux

The IcedTea-Web project is not inherently cross-platform; it is developed on Linux and for Linux, and so it can be built quite easily on popular Linux distributions. The two main parts of it (stored in corresponding directories in the source code repository) are `netx` and `plugin`.

NetX is a pure Java implementation of the WebStart technology. We will look at it more thoroughly in the following recipes of this chapter.

Plugin is an implementation of the browser plugin using the NPAPI plugin architecture that is supported by multiple browsers. Plugin is written partly in Java and partly in native code (C++), and it officially supports only Linux-based operating systems. There exists an opinion about NPAPI that this architecture is dated, overcomplicated, and insecure, and that modern web browsers have enough built-in capabilities to not require external plugins. And browsers have gradually reduced support for NPAPI. Despite that, at the time of writing this book, the IcedTea-Web browser plugin worked on all major Linux browsers (Firefox and derivatives, Chromium and derivatives, and Konqueror).

We will build the IcedTea-Web browser plugin from sources using Ubuntu 12.04 LTS amd64.

Getting ready

For this recipe, we will need a clean Ubuntu 12.04 running with the Firefox web browser installed.

How to do it...

The following procedure will help you to build the IcedTea-Web browser plugin:

1. Install prepackaged binaries of OpenJDK 7:

   ```
   sudo apt-get install openjdk-7-jdk
   ```

2. Install the GCC toolchain and build dependencies:

   ```
   sudo apt-get build-dep openjdk-7
   ```

3. Install the specific dependency for the browser plugin:

   ```
   sudo apt-get install firefox-dev
   ```

4. Download and decompress the IcedTea-Web source code tarball:

   ```
   wget http://icedtea.wildebeest.org/download/source/icedtea-web-1.4.2.tar.gz

   tar xzvf icedtea-web-1.4.2.tar.gz
   ```

5. Run the configure script to set up the build environment:

   ```
   ./configure
   ```

6. Run the build process:

   ```
   make
   ```

7. Install the newly built plugin into the /usr/local directory:

   ```
   sudo make install
   ```

8. Configure the Firefox web browser to use the newly built plugin library:

```
mkdir ~/.mozilla/plugins
cd ~/.mozilla/plugins
ln -s /usr/local/IcedTeaPlugin.so libjavaplugin.so
```

9. Check whether the IcedTea-Web plugin has appeared under **Tools** | **Add-ons** | **Plugins**.

10. Open the `http://java.com/en/download/installed.jsp` web page to verify that the browser plugin works.

How it works...

The IcedTea browser plugin requires the IcedTea Java implementation to be compiled successfully. The prepackaged OpenJDK 7 binaries in Ubuntu 12.04 are based on IcedTea, so we installed them first. The plugin uses the GNU Autoconf build system that is common between free software tools. The `xulrunner-dev` package is required to access the `NPAPI` headers.

The built plugin may be installed into Firefox for the current user only without requiring administrator privileges. For that, we created a symbolic link to our plugin in the place where Firefox expects to find the `libjavaplugin.so` plugin library.

There's more...

The plugin can also be installed into other browsers with `NPAPI` support, but installation instructions can be different for different browsers and different Linux distributions.

As the `NPAPI` architecture does not depend on the operating system, in theory, a plugin can be built for non-Linux operating systems. But currently, no such ports are planned.

See also

- ▸ The *Using the IcedTea Java WebStart implementation on Linux* recipe
- ▸ The *Preparing the IcedTea Java WebStart implementation for Mac OS X* recipe
- ▸ The *Preparing the IcedTea Java WebStart implementation for Windows* recipe
- ▸ *Chapter 5, Building IcedTea*
- ▸ The *Working with GNU Autoconf* recipe from *Chapter 4, Building OpenJDK 8*
- ▸ The IcedTea-Web project website at `http://icedtea.classpath.org/wiki/IcedTea-Web`
- ▸ The NetX project website at `http://jnlp.sourceforge.net/netx/`
- ▸ The Java WebStart developers guide at `http://docs.oracle.com/javase/6/docs/technotes/guides/javaws/`

- The NPAPI project site at `https://wiki.mozilla.org/NPAPI`
- Details on NPAPI support in different browsers at `http://www.firebreath.org/display/documentation/Browser+Plugins+in+a+post-NPAPI+world`

Using the IcedTea Java WebStart implementation on Linux

On the Java platform, the JVM needs to perform the class load process for each class it wants to use. This process is opaque for the JVM and actual bytecode for loaded classes may come from one of many sources. For example, this method allows the Java Applet classes to be loaded from a remote server to the Java process inside the web browser. Remote class loading also may be used to run remotely loaded Java applications in standalone mode without integration with the web browser. This technique is called Java WebStart and was developed under **Java Specification Request (JSR)** number 56.

To run the Java application remotely, WebStart requires an application descriptor file that should be written using the **Java Network Launching Protocol (JNLP)** syntax. This file is used to define the remote server to load the application form along with some metainformation. The WebStart application may be launched from the web page by clicking on the JNLP link, or without the web browser using the JNLP file obtained beforehand. In either case, running the application is completely separate from the web browser, but uses a sandboxed security model similar to Java Applets.

The OpenJDK project does not contain the WebStart implementation; the Oracle Java distribution provides its own closed-source WebStart implementation. The open source WebStart implementation exists as part of the IcedTea-Web project. It was initially based on the **NETwork eXecute (NetX)** project. Contrary to the Applet technology, WebStart does not require any web browser integration. This allowed developers to implement the NetX module using pure Java without native code. For integration with Linux-based operating systems, IcedTea-Web implements the `javaws` command as shell script that launches the `netx.jar` file with proper arguments.

In this recipe, we will build the NetX module from the official IcedTea-Web source tarball.

Getting ready

For this recipe, we will need a clean Ubuntu 12.04 running with the Firefox web browser installed.

How to do it...

The following procedure will help you to build a NetX module:

1. Install prepackaged binaries of OpenJDK 7:

   ```
   sudo apt-get install openjdk-7-jdk
   ```

2. Install the GCC toolchain and build dependencies:

   ```
   sudo apt-get build-dep openjdk-7
   ```

3. Download and decompress the IcedTea-Web source code tarball:

   ```
   wget http://icedtea.wildebeest.org/download/source/icedtea-web-
   1.4.2.tar.gz
   ```

   ```
   tar xzvf icedtea-web-1.4.2.tar.gz
   ```

4. Run the `configure` script to set up a build environment excluding the browser plugin from the build:

   ```
   ./configure –disable-plugin
   ```

5. Run the build process:

   ```
   make
   ```

6. Install the newly-built plugin into the `/usr/local` directory:

   ```
   sudo make install
   ```

7. Run the WebStart application example from the Java tutorial:

   ```
   javaws http://docs.oracle.com/javase/tutorialJWS/samples/
   deployment/dynamictree_webstartJWSProject/dynamictree_webstart.
   jnlp
   ```

How it works...

The `javaws` shell script is installed into the `/usr/local/*` directory. When launched with a path or a link to the JNLP file, `javaws` launches the `netx.jar` file, adding it to the boot classpath (for security reasons) and providing the JNLP link as an argument.

See also

- The *Preparing the IcedTea Java WebStart implementation for Mac OS X* recipe
- The *Preparing the IcedTea Java WebStart implementation for Windows* recipe
- The *Building the IcedTea browser plugin on Linux* recipe
- The *Working with GNU Autoconf* recipe from *Chapter 4, Building OpenJDK 8*

- ► The IcedTea-Web project website at `http://icedtea.classpath.org/wiki/IcedTea-Web`

- ► The NetX project website at `http://jnlp.sourceforge.net/netx/`

- ► The Java WebStart developers guide at `http://docs.oracle.com/javase/6/docs/technotes/guides/javaws/`

Preparing the IcedTea Java WebStart implementation for Mac OS X

The NetX WebStart implementation from the IcedTea-Web project is written in pure Java, so it can also be used on Mac OS X. IcedTea-Web provides the `javaws` launcher implementation only for Linux-based operating systems. In this recipe, we will create a simple implementation of the WebStart launcher script for Mac OS X.

Getting ready

For this recipe, we will need Mac OS X Lion with Java 7 (the prebuilt OpenJDK or Oracle one) installed. We will also need the `netx.jar` module from the IcedTea-Web project, which can be built using instructions from the previous recipe.

How to do it...

The following procedure will help you to run WebStart applications on Mac OS X:

1. Download the JNLP descriptor example from the Java tutorials at `http://docs.oracle.com/javase/tutorialJWS/samples/deployment/dynamictree_webstartJWSProject/dynamictree_webstart.jnlp`.

2. Test that this application can be run from the terminal using `netx.jar`:

   ```
   java -Xbootclasspath/a:netx.jar net.sourceforge.jnlp.runtime.Boot
   dynamictree_webstart.jnlp
   ```

3. Create the `wslauncher.sh` bash script with the following contents:

   ```bash
   #!/bin/bash
   if [ "x$JAVA_HOME" = "x" ] ; then
       JAVA="$( which java 2>/dev/null )"
   else
       JAVA="$JAVA_HOME"/bin/java
   fi
   if [ "x$JAVA" = "x" ] ; then
       echo "Java executable not found"
   ```

```
        exit 1
    fi

    if [ "x$1" = "x" ] ; then
        echo "Please provide JNLP file as first argument"
        exit 1
    fi

    $JAVA -Xbootclasspath/a:netx.jar net.sourceforge.jnlp.runtime.Boot
    $1
```

4. Mark the launcher script as executable:

   ```
   chmod 755 wslauncher.sh
   ```

5. Run the application using the launcher script:

   ```
   ./wslauncher.sh dynamictree_webstart.jnlp
   ```

How it works...

The `next.jar` file contains a Java application that can read JNLP files and download and run classes described in JNLP. But for security reasons, `next.jar` cannot be launched directly as an application (using the `java -jar netx.jar` syntax). Instead, `netx.jar` is added to the privileged boot classpath and is run specifying the main class directly. This allows us to download applications in sandbox mode.

The `wslauncher.sh` script tries to find the Java executable file using the PATH and JAVA_ HOME environment variables and then launches specified JNLP through `netx.jar`.

There's more...

The `wslauncher.sh` script provides a basic solution to run WebStart applications from the terminal. To integrate `netx.jar` into your operating system environment properly (to be able to launch WebStart apps using JNLP links from the web browser), a native launcher or custom platform scripting solution may be used. Such solutions lay down the scope of this book.

See also

- The *Using the IcedTea Java WebStart implementation on Linux* recipe
- The *Building OpenJDK 7 on Mac OS X* recipe from *Chapter 3, Building OpenJDK 7*
- The IcedTea-Web project website at `http://icedtea.classpath.org/wiki/IcedTea-Web`
- The NetX project website at `http://jnlp.sourceforge.net/netx/`

▶ The Java WebStart developers guide at `http://docs.oracle.com/javase/6/docs/technotes/guides/javaws/`

▶ Apple Inc. support article about enabling WebStart on Apple Java at `http://support.apple.com/kb/HT5559`

Preparing the IcedTea Java WebStart implementation for Windows

The NetX WebStart implementation from the IcedTea-Web project is written in pure Java, so it can also be used on Windows; we also used it on Linux and Mac OS X in previous recipes in this chapter. In this recipe, we will create a simple implementation of the WebStart launcher script for Windows.

Getting ready

For this recipe, we will need a version of Windows running with Java 7 (the prebuilt OpenJDK or Oracle one) installed. We will also need the `netx.jar` module from the IcedTea-Web project, which can be built using instructions from the previous recipe in this chapter.

How to do it...

The following procedure will help you to run WebStart applications on Windows:

1. Download the JNLP descriptor example from the Java tutorials:

    `http://docs.oracle.com/javase/tutorialJWS/samples/deployment/dynamictree_webstartJWSProject/dynamictree_webstart.jnlp`

2. Test that this application can be run from the Command Prompt using `netx.jar`:

    `java -Xbootclasspath/a:netx.jar net.sourceforge.jnlp.runtime.Boot dynamictree_webstart.jnlp`

3. Create a batch file, `wslauncher.bat`, with the following contents:

    ```
    @echo off

    if "%JAVA_HOME%" == "" goto noJavaHome

    if not exist "%JAVA_HOME%\bin\javaw.exe" goto noJavaHome

    set "JAVA=%JAVA_HOME%\bin\javaw.exe"

    if "%1" == "" goto noJnlp

    start %JAVA% -Xbootclasspath/a:netx.jar net.sourceforge.jnlp.
    runtime.Boot %1

    exit /b 0

    :noJavaHome
    ```

```
echo The JAVA_HOME environment variable is not defined correctly
exit /b 1
:noJnlp
echo Please provide JNLP file as first argument
exit /b 1
```

4. Run the application using the launcher script:

    ```
    wslauncher.bat dynamictree_webstart.jnlp
    ```

How it works...

The `netx.jar` module must be added to the boot classpath as it cannot be run directly because of security reasons.

The `wslauncher.bat` script tries to find the Java executable using the `JAVA_HOME` environment variable and then launches specified JNLP through `netx.jar`.

There's more...

The `wslauncher.bat` script may be registered as a default application to run the JNLP files. This will allow you to run WebStart applications from the web browser. But the current script will show the batch window for a short period of time before launching the application. It also does not support looking for Java executables in the Windows Registry. A more advanced script without those problems may be written using Visual Basic script (or any other native scripting solution) or as a native executable launcher. Such solutions lay down the scope of this book.

See also

- The *Preparing the IcedTea Java WebStart implementation for Mac OS X* recipe
- The *Building 64-bit OpenJDK 7 on Windows 7 x64 SP1* recipe from *Chapter 3, Building OpenJDK 7*
- The IcedTea-Web project website at `http://icedtea.classpath.org/wiki/IcedTea-Web`
- The NetX project website at `http://jnlp.sourceforge.net/netx/`
- The Java WebStart developers guide at `http://docs.oracle.com/javase/6/docs/technotes/guides/javaws/`
- Articles on ActiveX technology from Microsoft that is similar to NPAPI at `http://msdn.microsoft.com/en-us/library/aa751968%28v=vs.85%29.aspx`

8
Hacking OpenJDK

In this chapter we will cover:

- ▶ Setting up the development environment with NetBeans
- ▶ Working with Mercurial forests
- ▶ Understanding OpenJDK 6 and 7 incremental builds
- ▶ Debugging Java code using NetBeans
- ▶ Debugging C++ code using NetBeans
- ▶ Using NetBeans to compile HotSpot
- ▶ Using HotSpot dev parameters
- ▶ Adding new intrinsic to HotSpot
- ▶ Building VisualVM from the source code
- ▶ Creating a plugin for VisualVM
- ▶ Getting benefits from the AdoptOpenJDK project

Introduction

The real beauty of OpenJDK is its open nature, which means that developers can not only use it to run an application, but also change it to their needs or contribute to its development. The availability of the source code and ease of access to it opens huge opportunities to individuals who have special requirements, or just want to learn more about the way JVM works internally and want to adapt it for any special requirements. This chapter will help you to get into it and provide some recipes to make the process of setting up the required development environment as easy as possible.

At first, it will cover how to set up the development environment and which tools are required to get started. It will cover the IDE setup, and some tweaks required to launch JVM and start debugging. The next step is to make changes and rebuild the code, and the latter is going to be slightly different from the normal build described in *Chapter 5, Building IcedTea, Chapter 6, Building IcedTea with Other VM Implementations*, and *Chapter 7, Working with WebStart and the Browser Plugin*. The rest of that section dedicated to will be useful techniques which can be used to debug changes.

This chapter assumes that the reader has a reasonable knowledge of C++ and Java. Any knowledge of JVM is ideal, as the reader should know what JIT is and how it works.

Most of the recipes in the JIT section are independent and can be executed separately, so the reader just can pick what he/she needs and proceed with it.

Setting up the development environment with NetBeans

This recipe will cover the steps required to install, run, and set up the project in NetBeans IDE. NetBeans is an open source IDE for developing, primarily in Java. It also has rich support for C++ and that makes it a good tool for OpenJDK development which uses both languages. This recipe uses NetBeans IDE v.7.

Getting ready

Download the latest version of the NetBeans `All` bundle for your platform from `http://www.netbeans.org/downloads`. The `All` bundle must have C/C++ and Java support in the same IDE. It is also necessary to have the OpenJDK code checked out and available on the machine.

Make sure that everything is set up for the OpenJDK build and it can be executed without errors. How to do that is described in *Chapter 2, Building OpenJDK 6, Chapter 3, Building OpenJDK 7*, and *Chapter 4, Building OpenJDK 8*.

How to do it...

We will install and configure the NetBeans IDE that is used in the OpenJDK project as the standard one.

1. First we need to install the NetBeans IDE. This is a very simple process which consists of a few simple steps. Run the downloaded executable and at the bottom of the first screen, select the **Customize** button. This will show following window:

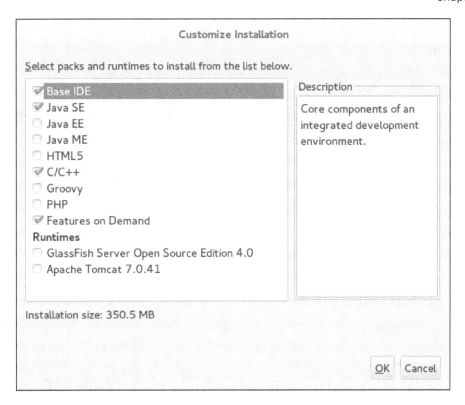

Ensure that **Base IDE**, **Java SE**, **C/C++**, and **Features on Demand** are selected. The rest are optional and not required to run and debug OpenJDK, but there is no harm in installing that functionality.

2. After the setup, all plugins you should update to the latest version. Updates are available via the **Help/Check for updates** menu item.

3. When NetBeans is set up, it is required to make a slight change to its configuration.

   OpenJDK is a big project and its memory requirements are bigger than the ones defined in the default settings. To increase the memory available for IDE:

   1. Go to the $HOME/.netbeans/NETBEANS_VERSION/etc folder (on Windows $HOME is %HOMEPATH%).

   2. If the folder doesn't exist, create it.

3. Then, if that folder doesn't have the `netbeans.conf` file, copy it from the Netbeans installation directory, which is located in the `etc` folder.

4. Open the file with any text editor and locate the `netbeans_default_options` parameter which it should look similar to this:

```
netbeans_default_options="-J-client -J-Xss2m -J-Xms32m
-J-XX:PermSize=32m -J-Dapple.laf.useScreenMenuBar=true
-J-Dapple.awt.graphics.UseQuartz=true -J-Dsun.java2d.
noddraw=true -J-Dsun.java2d.dpiaware=true -J-Dsun.zip.
disableMemoryMapping=true"
```

4. When the parameter is located, add `-J-Xmx2g`, or, if that option is already present, update it to a value not less than 2G (2 gigabytes). This will increase the memory available to JDK to 2G. Restart your IDE if it was running before in order to apply that change.

> It is worth adding that, because of the large memory requirement of Netbeans IDE, It's recommended to run it on a system that is capable of providing nothing less than 2 GB of memory to the process. Basically, it means that it should be a machine with a 64-bit OS and about 4 to 6 GB of RAM.

5. Now Netbeans IDE is ready for the project to be set up. Run it and go to **File | New Project** on the dialog box and select **C/C++ Project with Existing Sources**:

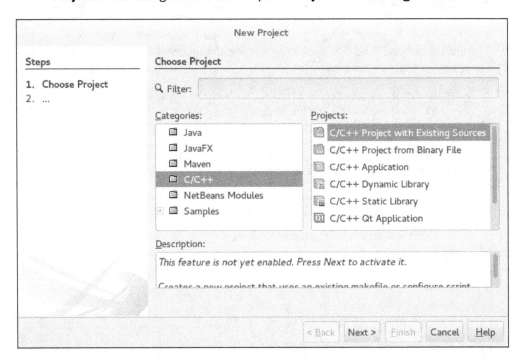

6. Then press **Next** and, on the following dialog box, select the folder with the root of OpenJDK sources:

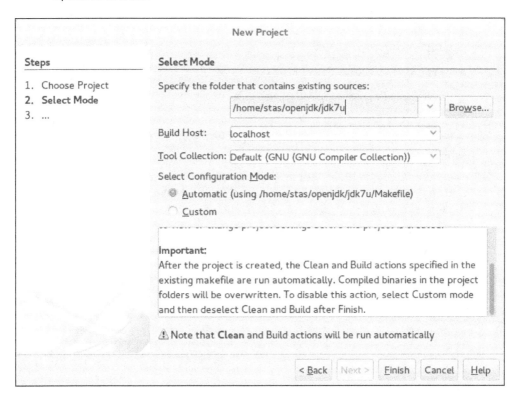

 You can always obtain your OpenJDK code by typing `hg clone http://hg.openjdk.java.net/jdk6/jdk6 && ./get_source.sh`

7. Press **Finish** and Netbeans will attempt to clean and build the project. Clean, most probably, will execute without problems, but build will not work because it requires some environment setup, which we will do later on.

After trying to build the project, Netbeans will spend a fair bit of time (minutes) scanning sources and building indexes. This would be a good time to have some coffee.

8. The next step is to configure Netbeans to build the project. As already mentioned, the build script requires some environment setup. The following is a simple bash script which can be used to create an appropriate environment:

```
#!/bin/sh
export LANG=C
export ALT_BOOTDIR=/usr/lib/jvm/java
./jdk/make/jdk_generic_profile.sh
make $*
```

9. In the root folder of the OpenJDK source tree, create a file `build.sh` and save this script in that folder.

10. Then navigate to the **Run | Set project configuration | Customize** menu item and, in the tree on the left-hand side, select **Build | Make**. There you will see the following dialog:

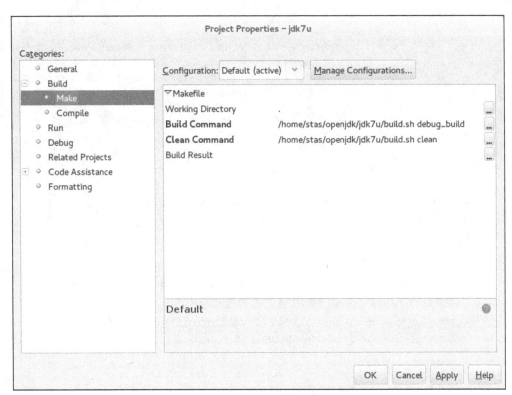

11. As shown in the screenshot, set the **Build Command** and **Clean Command** variables to execute your `./build.sh` with the `debug_build` and `clean` commands, respectively.

12. If the `product` version of OpenJDK is required, then just create another configuration with `product_build` and the parameter for `build.sh`.

See also

Netbeans is not the only available IDE which supports both Java and C++. There are other IDEs which are similarly capable. One example is the Eclipse IDE which is also a powerful multiplatform IDE written in Java, and has similar functionality.

Working with Mercurial forest

Mercurial is a cross-platform version control system. It was designed to work with big projects and large amounts of code, which undoubtedly are present in the OpenJDK project. The OpenJDK official repository is a Mercurial.

The Forest plugin is the one used for various OpenJDK subprojects to merge and coexist. It works with nested Mercurial repositories, which normally are regarded as isolated. The main idea is to propagate changes from the root repository to the nested ones.

The main purpose of it is to allow a developer to work with the code, which is a minor part of a full OpenJDK project repository, without needing to make any changes to the whole repository (change a revision number, for example).

Getting ready

First of all, we will need to install Mercurial itself. On Windows it can be done by going to the official Mercurial site and downloading it from `http://mercurial.selenic.com/wiki/Download`.

For Linux distributions, there are, usually, Mercurial versions in their official repositories.

For example, on Debian and Debian-inherited distributions, Mercurial installs as follows:

```
sudo apt-get install mercurial
```

If you have any problems with a Mercurial installation, refer to the official site or to your Linux distribution resources.

How to do it...

Let's explain it with a simple, non Java-related example. We will assume that a Mercurial instance already exists in the OS. Since Mercurial has a command line tool, we will use a command line for everything.

1. Let's create two repositories:

   ```
   mkdir repo-one
   cd repo-one
   hg init
   echo "hello" > hello.txt
   hg ci -m"init one"
   cd ..


   mkdir repo-two
   cd repo-two
   hg init
   echo "hello" > hello.txt
   hg ci -m"init two"
   cd ..
   ```

2. We will need to locate the `.hgrc` file:

   ```
   locate hgrc
   ```

3. Let's copy the `forest.py` file from `https://bitbucket.org/gxti/hgforest/src`.

4. Then let's edit your `.hgrc` file:

   ```
   [extensions]
   forest = patch/to/forest.py
   ```

We now have a brand new `fclone` command in our repository.

1. Let's copy the first repository into the second one:

   ```
   hg clone repo-one repo-two/one
   ```

   The `repo-two` repository isn't an integral part of `repo-one`, it only lays inside it.

2. Let's clone a `repo-two` repository and attach `repo-one to it`, using the `fclone` command:

   ```
   hg fclone repo-two wc-two
   ```

   We've just copied `repo-two`, including `repo-two/one`.

3. Let's make some changes to `repo-two/hello.txt` and `repo-two/one/hello.txt`:

   ```
   echo some >> repo-two/hello.txt  &&  echo some1 >> repo-two/hello.txt
   ```

4. We will commit each change using a separate command:

   ```
   cd wc-two/ && ls
   hg ci -m"edited hello.txt"
   cd one/
   hg ci -m"edited hello.txt"
   cd ..
   ```

5. Let's push a result back to `repo-two`:

   ```
   hg fpush
   ```

   We will have two changed files in repo-one.

6. Let's push one of them further to `repo-two`:

   ```
   cd ../repo-two
   hg fpush
   ```

7. Now, the changes from `repo-two/one` are propagated to `repo-one`.

How it works...

Mercurial is a relatively simple control system. It is vastly extendable with different plugins, which are configured through the `.hgrc` file.

The Mercurial `forest` plugin propagates changes in nested repositories to the root ones, and synchronizes the parent repository content with a nested one.

Understanding OpenJDK 6 and 7 incremental builds

The process of OpenJDK compilation is very time consuming. It is very boring, especially when one is developing a small part of the whole project, which needs full recompilation for testing purposes. To do it in a simple way and to compile only the necessary parts, there are incremental builds.

Getting ready

We need to download the OpenJDK (6 or 7) source code. You may need `libmotif` installed. Windows users may need to install Cygwin.

How to do it...

We will see how OpenJDK is built incrementally, avoiding adding any nasty bugs.

1. First, let's build OpenJDK for the first time:

   ```
   make all
   ```

2. This will take some time, so have a cup of tea.

3. Then, we will build it for the second time:

   ```
   make all
   ```

4. You can see from the input that nothing was actually built.

5. Then, let's insignificantly change some source file (for example, `cardTableModRefBS.cpp`).

6. Let's `make` OpenJDK again, but this time we will `grep` the output:

   ```
   make all | grep -i .cpp
   ```

7. We see that, in the output, only two files are actually compiled, `hotspot/src/share/vm/memory/cardTableModRefBS.cpp` and `hotspot/src/share/vm/runtime/vm_version.cpp`.

How it works...

The build program checks the files that were updated and compiles only those which were updated after the last compiler run. However, if any `.hpp` files are modified, the build will be performed in clean mode, for example, no optimization will be performed.

There's more...

Weird things tend to happen while using incremental builds. The probability of such things is increased proportionally with build times.

There are, basically, two ways to perform a clean build:

- ▶ One cleans all files, and compilation from scratch becomes necessary:

    ```
    make clean && make all
    ```

- ▶ The second is to specify parameters, which will force the clean mode of the build.

Debugging Java code using NetBeans

Obviously, when someone is writing any code, some debugging is required. It is no surprise that NetBeans, as a high-standard IDE, provides some tools to do that. This recipe will show how to debug the Java code using NetBeans.

Getting ready

You will need to install NetBeans and set up a development environment, as described previously in the chapter.

How to do it...

We will use NetBeans to debug our own OpenJDK Java code. We will need to rebuild OpenJDK with debug symbols, and configure NetBeans to make debugging possible:

1. First, let's make our OpenJDK instance with debug symbols:

    ```
    bash ./configure --enable-debug
    make all CONF=linux-x86_64-normal-server-fastdebug
    ```

2. Let's ensure that a debuggable version is built:

    ```
    ./build/linux-x86_64-normal-server-fastdebug/jdk/bin/java -version
    openjdk version "1.8.0-internal-fastdebug"
    OpenJDK Runtime Environment (build 1.8.0-internal-fastdebug-
    dsmd_2014_03_27_05_34-b00)
    OpenJDK 64-Bit Server VM (build 25.0-b70-fastdebug, mixed mode)
    ```

3. Now we have a debuggable OpenJDK. Let's set it as the default for NetBeans.

4. Let's open the `etc/netbeans.conf` file in your NetBeans installation path.

5. We will change one line:

    ```
    netbeans_jdkhome="<path_to_jdkhome>"
    ```

6. After that, we will launch NetBeans and ensure that our JDK is loaded correctly.

7. We will select **Tools | Java Platforms**, and the following screen will appear:

8. Let's try to debug the `java.lang.String` class. We will set our breakpoints to an unavoidable part of this class—to one of the constructors, as shown in the following screenshot:

```
188              *        characters outside the bounds of the {@code value} array
189              */
190   ⊟    public String(char value[], int offset, int count) {
191              if (offset < 0) {
192                  throw new StringIndexOutOfBoundsException(offset);
193              }
              if (count < 0) {
                  throw new StringIndexOutOfBoundsException(count);
196              }
197              // Note: offset or count might be near -1>>>1.
              if (offset > value.length - count) {
                  throw new StringIndexOutOfBoundsException(offset + count);
200              }
201              this.value = Arrays.copyOfRange(value, offset, offset+count);
202          }
203
204   ⊟    /**
205           * Allocates a new {@code String} that contains characters from a subarray
206           * of the <a href="Character.html#unicode">Unicode code point</a> array
```

9. This set of breakpoints is sufficient to hook up virtually every Java executable ever launched. But, if we decide to push things forward and attach a debugger, we will get an error message:

```
Not able to submit breakpoint LineBreakpoint String.java
: 138, reason: No source root found for URL 'file:/home/
dsmd/00experimental/java_build/jdk8intr/jdk8/jdk/src/share/
classes/java/lang/String.java'. Verify the setup of project
sources.

Invalid LineBreakpoint String.java : 138
```

10. To avoid this, we need to specify our Java sources directly to NetBeans. Our project is a C++ project, and it tends to ignore the Java files.

11. The result for the `String` class will be as shown in the following screenshot:

12. Then, just launch some Java executable, that uses strings:

```
build/linux-x86_64-normal-server-fastdebug/jdk/bin/java -Xdebug
-Xrunjdwp:transport=dt_socket,address=8998,server=y -jar /path/to/
jar.jar
```

13. Attach the Java debugger, as shown:

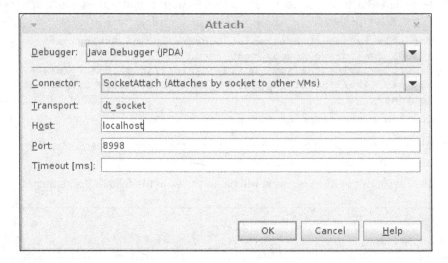

14. Enjoy, you can now see OpenJDK from the inside, in motion:

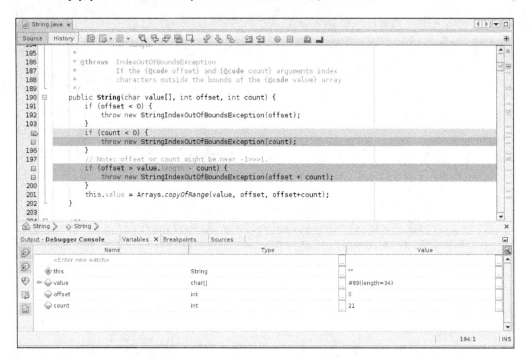

How it works...

It's just a debugger with a few simple nuances.

In some Linux distributions, you can install debug versions of OpenJDK with sources provided in a ZIP file. These sources are automatically picked up by NetBeans.

Debugging C++ code using NetBeans

If you plan to make changes to HotSpot or any other C++ part of OpenJDK, then it is certain that you will need to do some step-by-step debugging of the code. This recipe will explain how to set up NetBeans IDE for that purpose.

Getting ready

To get started, there are only a few things required—downloaded Open JDK sources and installed NetBeans IDE. It is assumed that the OpenJDK project is already set up and can build sources.

How to do it...

1. The first step is to set up an executable that will run. Go to **Run | Set project configuration / Customize** and then **Build | Make**, and set **build/linux-amd64-debug/hotspot/outputdir/linux_amd64_compiler2/jvmg/gamma** as the build result, as shown in the following screenshot:

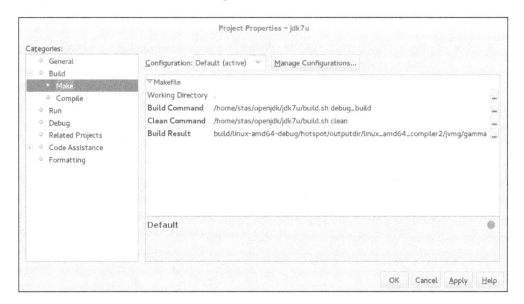

2. Then select the **Run** option on the tree on the left had side and set **Run Command** as **"${OUTPUT_PATH}" –version**:

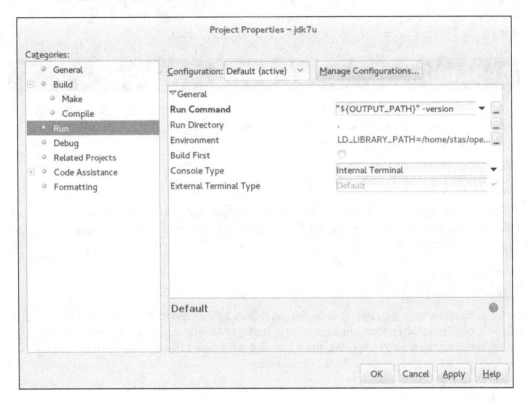

3. The –version flag here is just the simplest thing you can run—get the Java version. You can later change it to whatever you want, for example, to run a Java program.

4. The next step is to set up some environment variables required for Java to run. This can be done by setting them up in the **Environment** section as shown in the following dialog. Set LD_LIBRARY_PATH to build/linux-amd64-debug/hotspot/ outputdir/linux_amd64_compiler2/jvmg and JAVA_HOME to build/linux-amd64-debug/j2sdk-server-image.

5. Now it's all ready to debug. To check that it works, set a breakpoint in hotspot/ src/share/tools/launcher/java.c somewhere at the beginning of the main function and go to **Debug | Debug Main Project** or use the shortcut *Ctrl + F5*.

How it works...

Careful readers may have noticed that **Debug** used `gamma` JVM launcher, instead of `java`, which is used when you run Java normally. This is to simplify things; `gamma` is the lightweight version of `java`, it doesn't perform checks which are not necessary for debugging purposes.

Using NetBeans to compile HotSpot

When doing HotSpot development, it is very annoying to wait for a complete OpenJDK build to be executed. So, it makes sense to exclude other parts and compile just what we are interested in, that is, the HotSpot part. This recipe will explain how to do that.

Getting ready

The only prerequisite for this recipe is the availability of source code on the machine, and Netbeans installed, with an OpenJDK project created.

How to do it...

This is a very simple recipe to follow. If you have already completed *Setting up development environment with NetBeans*, the only thing which is required to be done is to change the argument `hotspot_build` and add another argument `DEBUG_NAME=debug`, the whole build command line should look like this:

build.sh hotspot-build DEBUG_NAME=debug

The **Build/Make** screen of the **Project Properties** dialog in that case will look like this:

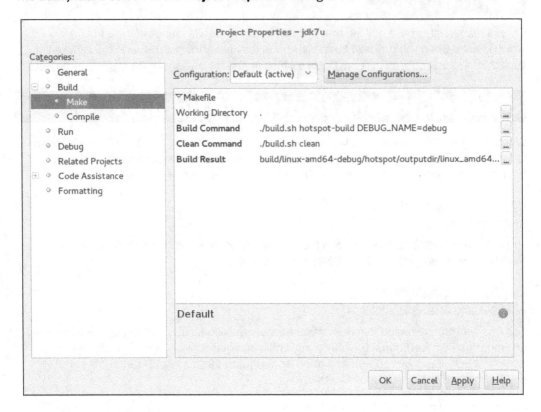

How it works...

Luckily, there are targets created in the `make` configuration which only built the HotSpot bit. These targets can be located in the `./make/hotspot-rules.gmk` file.

The `debug` command which creates the non-optimized version or the HotSpot, is not the only option for the `DEBUG_NAME` variable. The `fastdebug` command is the other option in which build will create an optimized version with assertions. When `DEBUG_NAME` is not set, the product version of HotSpot is built.

Using HotSpot dev parameters

HotSpot has other options, which may significantly change its behavior. Here we will make use of some of these options, which are used only on the dev versions of OpenJDK.

Getting ready

We will need to compile a dev OpenJDK version, in order to use the dev options.

How to do it...

We will use parameters that are available in the developer version of OpenJDK. In the production builds, they are disabled or set as constant values.

To make use of these parameters, we will run Java as follows:

```
java -  -XX:<optionName>
```

Here is a list of some usable dev options:

- `InlineUnsafeOps`: This option will, if enabled, inline native memory operations from `sun.misc.Unsafe`. It may offer some performance improvements in some cases.

- `DieOnSafepointTimeout`: This option will kill the process if the safepoint is not reached, but the timeout is exceeded. It is disabled by default.

- `ZapResourceArea`: This option will zap freed resource / arena space with `0xABABABAB`. It is true in debug mode, but is deselected in production VMs. It may be used for really paranoid security reasons, though it has some performance impact.

- `ZapJNIHandleArea`: This option will zap freed JNI handle space with `0xFEFEFEFE`. It only has a debug value.

- `ZapUnusedHeapArea`: This option will zap unused heap space with `0xBAADBABE`. It may be used for security reasons.

- `Verbose`: This option prints additional debugging information from other modes. It is the main logging option of the dev HotSpot.

- `UsePrivilegedStack`: This option enables the security JVM functions. It is `true` by default, but in dev mode, you still have the opportunity to run HotSpot with disabled security.

- `MemProfiling`: This option writes memory usage profiling to logfile. It is `false` by default, and can be run for some memory profiling issues.

- `VerifyParallelOldWithMarkSweep`: This option will use the `MarkSweep` GC code to verify phases of the parallel old. It may be used for debugging purposes when changing the JVM memory handling mechanism.

- `ScavengeWithObjectsInToSpace`: This option is really interesting. Java uses two-space GC, where survivor space is concerned, and this options allows scavenges to occur when `to_space` contains objects. Also, when doing so, it clears an unused area, if `ZapUnusedHeapArea` is enabled.

- ▶ `FullGCALot`: This option forces full GC at every *Nth* exit from the runtime system (N=`FullGCALotInterval`). It may be a very expensive operation, but some developers may build it into JDKs for desktop use. It may be cheaper than to use swap space to absorb endless megabytes from the overgrown heap.

- ▶ `AdaptiveSizePolicyReadyThreshold`: This option is the number of collections before adaptive sizing is started. The default is 5, but it may make sense to make it 1 on desktop systems since the biggest bottleneck of those is the swap space, especially if several Java programs are running simultaneously on one machine.

- ▶ `EagerInitialization`: This option eagerly initializes classes if possible. It is `false` by default, so maybe it is unsafe to turn it on. But the idea seems good, especially on server machines.

- ▶ `GuaranteedSafepointInterval`: This option guarantees a safepoint (at least) every few milliseconds (0 means none). The default is 1000. It may be used to tweak the stop-the-world state problem. The bigger the option value, the longer these stops will be; and if we make the value too small, we will have too many unnecessary stops.

- ▶ `MaxTrivialSize`: This option is the maximum bytecode size of a trivial method to be inline. It is 6 by default. It is similar to the C++ compiler inline options, but for the bytecode compiler.

- ▶ `MinInliningThreshold`: This option is the minimal invocation count a method needs to have to be inline. It is 250 by default.

- ▶ `SharedOptimizeColdStartPolicy`: This option is the reordering policy for `SharedOptimizeColdStart`. The 0 value favors the classload-time locality, 1 uses a balanced policy, and 2 favors runtime locality.

The default is 2 and it is rarely necessary to change it, but in some cases it will make sense to make it 1 if your application has too many classes that may load after the application starts.

Adding new intrinsic to HotSpot

Intrinsic is a function whose implementation is handled specially by a compiler. Typically, it means that the function call is replaced by automatically generated instructions. This is very similar to the inline functions, but the compiler knows more about intrinsics as they are part of the compiler itself, so it can use them more wisely.

Intrinsics are usually more performance-oriented than native functions because there is no JNI overhead.

Getting ready

To get started, all we need is an installed NetBeans IDE for code editing and OpenJDK sources. The user should be able to read C++ code and a little knowledge of assembly would be beneficial.

It would be worth checking that SSE4.2 (an extended instruction set with six new commands, mostly for character searching and comparison) is supported by the CPU (the CRC32 command used in our example is from that command set). It was introduced with Core i7 Intel chips back in 2009, so if you are using an Intel CPU, it should be present. The first time it was introduced for AMD was as Bulldozer chips back in 2011, so you should have relatively recent chips to support it. If your CPU is not compatible with that command, do not worry. The recipe is applicable to any intrinsics you may want to introduce; there is no difference, apart from the actual implementation of the code you want to intrinsify.

How to do it...

Adding new intrinsics is not a simple process. Follow these instructions carefully. Ensure you compile the code after every step; doing so may save some time.

The instruction which we are going to intrinsify is the CRC32 calculation, which is implemented by `java.util.zip.CRC32`.

To start, let's make a small amendment to the Java class that is responsible for the CRC32 calculation. We are going to add a method which will be intrinsified by HotSpot. Open the `jdk/src/share/classes/java/util/zip/CRC32.java` file and add a new method `doUpdateBytes`:

```
private static int doUpdateBytes(int crc, byte[] b, int off, int len)
{
    return updateBytes(crc, b, off, len);
}
```

That implementation just makes a call to the currently used `updateBytes` native method. That's the only change in Java. The rest is going to be the C++ internals of the HotSpot.

Open the `hotspot/src/share/vm/precompiled/precompiled.hpp` file and add the following line into it:

```
#include "smmintrin.h"
```

The `smmintrin.h` file contains GCC intrinsics, which are going to be used by our implementation of the CRC32 function.

Then, as we are using SSE4.2 instructions, we need to inform the compiler. To do so, open the `hotspot/make/linux/makefiles/gcc.make` file (assuming you are making the build on Linux), and locate the line consisting of `CFLAGS += -fno-rtti`. Just after that line, add the `-msse4.2` flag, so it will look like this:

```
CFLAGS += -fno-rtti # locate that line
CFLAGS += -msse4.2  # add this new line here
```

Now we are ready to implement our CRC32 function in C++. In the `hotspot/src/cpu/x86/vm/` folder, create the `CRC32Calc` class and the `static_calcCrc32` static method. Here is the `CRC32Calc.hpp` file with the class declaration:

```
#ifndef CRC32CALC_HPP
#define  CRC32CALC_HPP

class CRC32Calc {
public:
    CRC32Calc() {};
    virtual ~CRC32Calc() {};

    static int static_calcCrc32(int crc, const char* data, int
dataOffset, int dataLen);
};
#endif  /* CRC32CALC_HPP */
```

The `CRC32Calc.cpp` file with its implementation is as shown:

```
#include "CRC32Calc.hpp"
#include "precompiled.hpp"
int CRC32Calc::static_calcCrc32(int crc, const char* data, int
dataOffset, int dataLen) {
    const int dataSize = dataLen - dataOffset;
    int result = crc;
    int uints32 = (int)(dataSize / sizeof(int));
    int units8 = dataSize % sizeof(int);

    const int* pUint32 = (const int*)data;
    while (uints32--) {
        result = ::_mm_crc32_u32(result, *pUint32);
        pUint32++;
    }

    const char* pUnit8 = (const char*)pUint32;
    while (units8--) {
```

```
        result = ::_mm_crc32_u8(result, *pUnit8);
        pUnit8++;
    }

    return result;
}
```

The following instructs HotSpot how to intrinsify our method.

Locate `hotspot/src/share/vm/classfile/vmSymbols.hpp`. That is the file which contains the declaration of all intrinsics and add the following definition to it:

```
do_class(java_util_zip_crc32,        "java/util/zip/CRC32")
\
do_intrinsic(_crc32_doUpdateBytes, java_util_zip_crc32, doUpdateBytes_
name, int_byteArray_int_int_signature, F_R)   \
do_name(     doUpdateBytes_name,
"doUpdateBytes")                                            \
do_signature(int_byteArray_int_int_signature,           "(I[BII)I"
)                                                           \
```

This is the declaration of intrinsics which maps the Java method with the code which will replace it in the runtime. Be careful when adding it. It is based on macros, which means, if there is a typo or any other mistake, it will be very hard to figure out where the problem is.

The next step is to define which code we are going to generate for the intrinsic. We are not going to be very smart here, as this is just an exercise to see how the functionality works. So all our assembler is going to do is generate a call to the C function. Add the following into `hotspot/src/cpu/x86/vm/stubGenerator_x86_64.cpp` and `hotspot/src/cpu/x86/vm/stubGenerator_x86_32.cpp`:

```
#include "CRC32Calc.hpp"
```

Now it's a bit tricky and requires some low-level code. We are going to tell HotSpot how to generate the assembly for our method. To do so, add the `generator` method into the `StubGenerator` class which is declared in both `hotspot/src/cpu/x86/vm/stubGenerator_x86_64.cpp` and `hotspot/src/cpu/x86/vm/stubGenerator_x86_32.cpp` for x86_64 and x86 architectures respectively. The code for the method is as follows:

```
// Arguments:
//
// Inputs:
//    c_rarg0    - input crc
//    c_rarg1    - byte array with data for calculation
//    c_rarg2    - offset in the input array
```

```
    //   c_rarg3    - number of data bytes after offset
    //
    // Output:
    //    eax - result crc
    address generate_crc32_doUpdateBytes() {
       __ align(CodeEntryAlignment);
       StubCodeMark mark(this, "StubRoutines", "crc32_doUpdateBytes");
       address start = __ pc();

       __ enter(); // required for proper stackwalking of RuntimeStub
 frame
       __ pusha();
       // no need to put params in regr - they are already there
       // after this call rax should already have required return value
       __ call_VM_leaf(CAST_FROM_FN_PTR(address, CRC32Calc::static_
 calcCrc32), 4);
       __ popa();

       __ leave(); // required for proper stackwalking of RuntimeStub
 frame
       return start;
    }
```

Now we need a variable which will contain the address of the generated method. To do so, add the following static member declaration to `hotspot/src/share/vm/runtime/stubRoutines.hpp`:

```
    static address _crc32_doUpdateBytes;
```

To the same file, add the following method, which just returns the value of the declared variable:

```
    static address crc32_doUpdateBytes() { return _crc32_doUpdateBytes; }
```

Then, in `hotspot/src/share/vm/runtime/stubRoutines.cpp`, assign a default value to `_crc32_doUpdateBytes`:

```
    address StubRoutines::_crc32_doUpdateBytes = NULL;
```

Then, in both `hotspot/src/cpu/x86/vm/stubGenerator_x86_64.cpp` and `hotspot/src/cpu/x86/vm/stubGenerator_x86_32.cpp`, locate the `generate_all` method and assign the following value to the variable `_crc32_doUpdateBytes`:

```
    StubRoutines::_crc32_doUpdateBytes = generate_crc32_doUpdateBytes();
```

The next step is to add the method which creates a descriptor. The descriptor is the definition of our function—how many arguments it takes, which types of arguments it accepts, and so on. The first step is to add the method declaration into the `OptoRuntime` class in the `hotspot/src/share/vm/opto/runtime.hpp` file:

```
static const TypeFunc* crc32_Type();
```

This will be the function which creates the type information for our method call—it describes the arguments and returns the parameters. After implementation it creates an array of types of input parameters and the type of the return value. Place it in the `hotspot/src/share/vm/opto/runtime.cpp` file:

```
const TypeFunc* OptoRuntime::crc32_Type() {
   // create input type (domain): int, pointer, int, int
   int num_args      = 4;
   int argcnt = num_args;
   const Type** fields = TypeTuple::fields(argcnt);
   int argp = TypeFunc::Parms;
   fields[argp++] = TypeInt::INT;        // crc
   fields[argp++] = TypePtr::NOTNULL;    // data
   fields[argp++] = TypeInt::INT;        // offset
   fields[argp++] = TypeInt::INT;        // len
   const TypeTuple* domain = TypeTuple::make(TypeFunc::Parms+argcnt,
fields);

   // create return value
   fields = TypeTuple::fields(1);
   fields[TypeFunc::Parms+0] = TypeInt::INT;

   const TypeTuple* range = TypeTuple::make(TypeFunc::Parms+1, fields);

   return TypeFunc::make(domain, range);
}
```

Now we will implement the method that will inline the code in the runtime. In the `hotspot/src/share/vm/opto/library_call.cpp` file, locate the definition of the `LibraryCallKit` class, and add the following method declaration:

```
bool inline_crc32();
```

Also, in the same file, add the implementation:

```
bool LibraryCallKit::inline_crc32() {
   address stubAddr = StubRoutines::crc32_doUpdateBytes();
   const char *stubName = "crc32_doUpdateBytes";
```

```
        Node* inputCrc = argument(0);
        Node* in_data  = argument(1);
        Node* offset   = argument(2);
        Node* len      = argument(3);

        // Call the stub.
        make_runtime_call(RC_LEAF|RC_NO_FP, OptoRuntime::crc32_Type(),
                          stubAddr, stubName, TypePtr::BOTTOM,
                          inputCrc, in_data, offset, len);

        return true;
    }
```

Finally tell HotSpot that we indeed want to intrinsify our method call and make a call to the inlining method `inline_crc32`.

To tell HotSpot that we want to intrinsify the method, `Compile::make_vm_intrinsic` method in the file `hotspot/src/share/vm/opto/library_call.cpp` has to return a non-null pointer to `CallGenerator`. To do so, add the following line into the `switch(id)` switch statement in that method:

```
    case vmIntrinsics::_crc32_doUpdateBytes:
        break;
```

It is not strictly required to have that case and break, the default works just well; but it makes it more explicit that we are using intrinsics for the CRC32 calculation method.

Then, to make a call to the inlining method, in the same `hotspot/src/share/vm/opto/library_call.cpp` file, locate `LibraryCallKit::try_to_inline`, find `switch (intrinsic_id())`, and add the following line of code:

```
    case vmIntrinsics:: _crc32_doUpdateBytes: return inline_crc32();
    new line.
```

How it works...

To check whether the method was intrinsified, use the `-XX:+PrintCompilation` and `-XX:+PrintInlining` Java arguments. To see what the intrinsics are compiled into, use `-XX:+PrintAssembly` (this should be prepended by `-XX:+UnlockDiagnosticsVMOptions` when running on the product build).

There's more...

To see if SSE4.2 is supported, just compile and run the following code:

```
// This is Linux version
#include <cpuid.h>T
#include <stdio.h>
void main () {
    unsigned int eax, ebx, ecx, edx;
    __get_cpuid(1, &eax, &ebx, &ecx, &edx);
    if (ecx & bit_SSE4_2)
        printf ("SSE4.2 is supported\n");
    return;
}


// And this is the version for windows
#include <intrin.h>
int _tmain(int argc, _TCHAR* argv[])
{
  int cpuInfo[4] = { -1 };
  __cpuid(cpuInfo, 1);
  bool bSSE42Extensions = (cpuInfo[2] & 0x100000) || false;
  if (bSSE42Extensions) {
    printf("SSE4.2 is supported\n");
  }
  return 0;
}
```

There are lots of intrinsic methods. See `library_call.cpp` and `vmSymbols.hpp`:

▸ `Object.getClass` gives one or two instructions.

▸ `Class.isInstance` and `Class.isAssignableFrom` are as cheap as instances of bytecodes when the operands are constants, and otherwise no more expensive than aastore type checks.

▸ Most single-bit class queries are cheap and even constant-foldable.

▸ Reflective array creation is about as cheap as the `newarray` or `anewarray` instructions.

▸ `Object.clone` is cheap and shares code with `Arrays.copyOf` (after Java6).

Java is not the only language which uses intrinsics they are also widely used in C++ for SSE operations.

Interestingly, _mm_crc32_u32 and _mm_crc32_u8 are intrinsics themselves, known by the GCC or MS compiler, which are directly replaced by assembly instructions in the compiled code.

Building VisualVM from the source code

VisualVM is an open source project which is not a part of OpenJDK. It is a powerful tool which is helpful to anyone who uses applications based on JDK. It allows us to monitor parameters of the system, browse heap dumps, create thread dumps, and so on. As the tool is open source, it is possible to get the source code and customize it as required, or simply just to see how it works. This recipe will go through the steps which are required to download the source code and build VisualVM from it.

Getting ready

This recipe requires a machine with Subversion and Ant installed. Also, as VisualVM is a graphical application, a graphical environment is required to run it. It is possible to perform a build without launching the application.

How to do it...

The first step is to get the source code:

1. Create a folder for the sources, for example, `/home/user/visualvm`.

2. Go to the newly created folder and, assuming you need sources from the `trunk`, run the following command:

   ```
   svn checkout https://svn.java.net/svn/visualvm~svn/trunk
   ```

3. This will create the `trunk` folder with sources in the current directory.

To start, we need to download the NetBeans Platform binaries. The version needed depends on the version of VisualVM we are going to build. In this example, we will use `trunk`, the current development version which requires NetBeans Platform v.8; but as that may change, it is recommended to consult the page for the appropriate version using the link `http://visualvm.java.net/build.html`. These binaries are available directly from the VisualVM website, not from the NetBeans website. For this example, the URL is `https://java.net/projects/visualvm/downloads/download/dev/nb80_visualvm_27062014.zip`. When the file is downloaded, unpack it into the `trunk/visualvm` folder, as shown:

1. Now, execute Ant to run the build.

   ```
   ant build-zip
   ```

2. When the build is complete, we should see something similar to the following output in the command prompt:

   ```
   BUILD SUCCESSFUL
   Total time: 34 seconds
   ```

This indicates that the build was successful. This step is not required if we just need to run VisualVM, as Ant will also run the build target; but if there is no need to run, and just build is required, this step can be useful.

3. To run VisualVM, run the following command:

   ant run

4. If the application is not built yet, then Ant will build it first and then run it. As VisualVM is a GUI application, we will see the following screen:

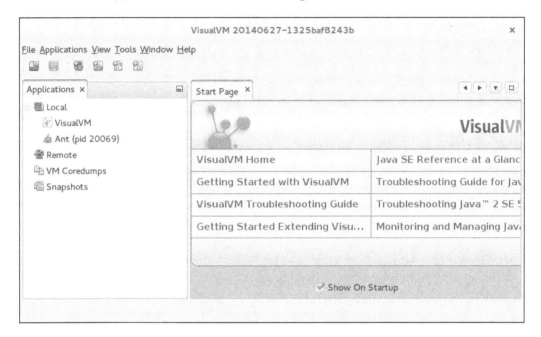

This is the landing screen of VisualVM. The fact that we can see it means that the application is built and works properly. The zipped archive file with the distribution can be found in the `visualvm/dist` folder.

See also

▶ More information about VisualVM build is available on the home page `http://visualvm.java.net/build.html`. Each version has a different page, as build instructions vary from version to version. For example, each build may require a slightly different version of the Netbeans platform.

Creating a plugin for VisualVM

VisualVM is just an application which has a predefined and limited set of features. It is a framework, which means that it is possible to extend it. The way in which VisualVM provides for extension is via the plugin API which allows us to create new plugins which are then available through the application. Such plugins can do various things, but are mostly used to provide new ways of monitoring or controlling the JVM applications.

Getting ready

The current (at the time of writing) trunk version of VisualVM requires the NetBeans platform and IDE v.8. So we need to ensure that the current version of the platform is available on the machine. If there is any doubt, check the page with VisualVM trunk build instructions at `http://visualvm.java.net/build/build.html`.

How to do it...

Let's start with what we are going to monitor. It seems like the simplest thing we can do is to build a component which will tick the data that we can read. For example, look at the following class:

```
package org.openjdk.cookbook;

import javax.management.MBeanServer;
import javax.management.ObjectName;
import java.lang.management.ManagementFactory;

public class SleepProbe implements SleepProbeMBean {
    private volatile long lastSleepSampleMs = 100;

    public static void main(String[] args) throws Exception {
        MBeanServer mbs = ManagementFactory.getPlatformMBeanServer();
        ObjectName name = new ObjectName("org.openjdk.
cookbook:type=SleepProbe");
        SleepProbe mbean = new SleepProbe();
        mbean.start();
        mbs.registerMBean(mbean, name);
        System.out.println("Started MBean");
        Thread.sleep(Long.MAX_VALUE);
    }

    @Override
```

```
    public long getActualSleepTime() {
        return lastSleepSample;
    }

    public void start() {
        new Thread(new Runnable() {
            @Override
            public void run() {
                while ( !Thread.currentThread().isInterrupted() ) {
                    try {
                        final long start = System.nanoTime();
                        Thread.sleep(100);
                        final long end = System.nanoTime();
                        lastSleepSampleMs = (long)((double)(end-
start))/1000000;
                    } catch (InterruptedException e) {
                        Thread.currentThread().interrupt();
                        break;
                    }
                }
            }
        }).start();
    }
}
```

This code sleeps for 100 ms and measures how long it actually slept. The value is not going to be exact, but will be about `100`. It publishes the last measurement of the sleep time via the `lastSleepSample` variable which is available via the `SleepProbeMBean` interface:

```
package org.openjdk.cookbook;
public interface SleepProbeMBean {
    public long getActualSleepTime();
}
```

This class and interface should be put into a separate project, so you can run them independently of the VirtualVM plugin project:

1. To start, we need to create a plugin project in IDE. Launch the IDE, go to **File | New Project** and select **NetBeans Platform Application** from the project type:

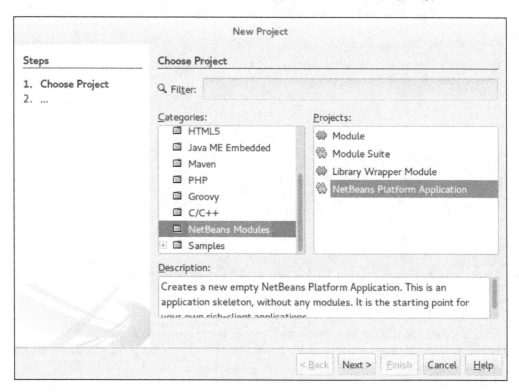

2. On the next screen, select **VisualVM** as the **NetBeans Platform** (if it is not available, see further instructions), the project name, and the location, as shown:

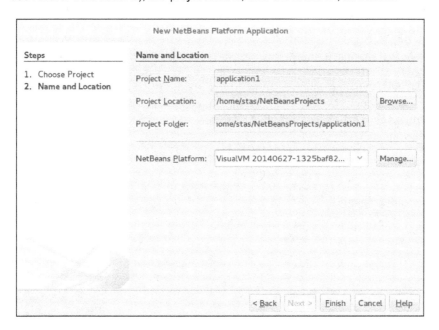

3. If **VisualVM** is not available in the list of platforms, then click on the Manage icon and, in the displayed dialog, add a new platform by pointing it to the folder with the VisualVM distribution, as shown in the following screenshot:

4. In this example, the distribution was built from source (see the *Building VisualVM from the source code* recipe). Press **Next** and then **Finish**.

5. Now just complete the wizard and you will have a new empty project with some properties and build script.

6. Note that there is a known bug in some versions of NetBeans (`https://netbeans.org/bugzilla/show_bug.cgi?id=242564`), which is causing problem with dependencies and which will not allow us to add the required dependencies later. To work around this, right click on the project and then click on **Properties**. On the **Project Properties** dialog, select **Libraries**:

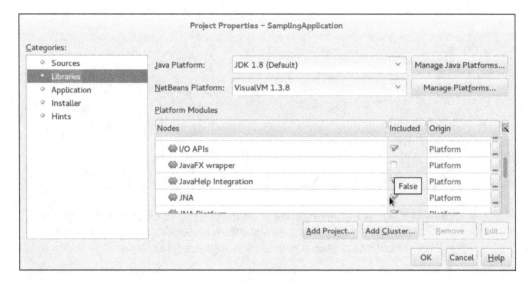

7. Uncheck **JavaFX wrapper** under the platform component. Ensure that all the other checkboxes are checked, including **profiles** and **visualvm** nodes.

8. Now we need to create a module for our plugin. Right click on the **Modules** item in the project tree and select **Add New...**:

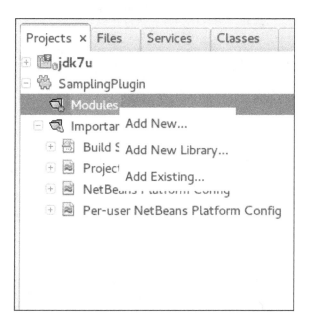

9. Name it as SamplingModule and press **Next**. On the next screen, put net . cookbook.openjdk as Code Name Base and press on **Finish**. This will create an empty module where we will need to add some components.

10. The next step is to add the dependencies to the module. Right click on the module and select **Properties**, then go to **Libraries | Module Dependencies**, and click on **Add Dependency**. On the **Add Module Dependency** dialog, put `VisualVM` into the **Filter** field as shown:

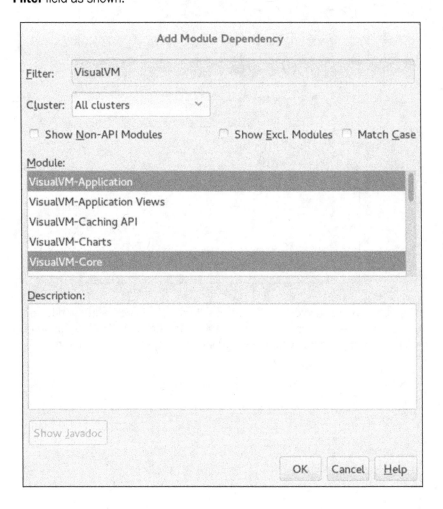

11. Select **VisualVM-Application**, **VisualVM-Core**, and **VisualVM-Tools** (not visible on the screenshot), then click on **OK**.

12. The next step is to add the installer and some source code. To do so, right click on the newly created module and go to **New | Other**. This will show the dialog with the option to select the file type. Click on **Installer/Activator** and click on **Next**, as shown:

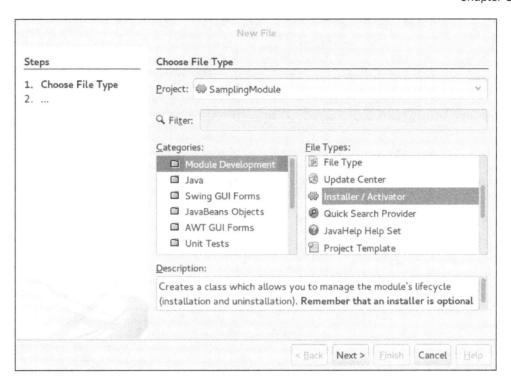

13. Then just complete the wizard by clicking on **Finish**. This will create a class with the name `Installer` in the package `net.cookbook.openjdk`. For now, leave that class as it is, we will update it later in the recipe.

14. The next step is to create a component which will draw a graph for us. To do so, we will create a simple panel which will refresh itself every half a second with a new sample from the sampler `MBean`. In the `net.cookbook.openjdk` package, create a new class and name it as `SamplingGraphPanel`:

```
package net.cookbook.openjdk;

import com.sun.tools.visualvm.application.Application;
import com.sun.tools.visualvm.tools.jmx.*;
import java.awt.*;
import java.util.LinkedList;
import javax.management.*;
import javax.swing.JPanel;
import org.openide.util.Exceptions;

public class SamplingGraphPanel extends JPanel implements Runnable
{
    private static final int MAX_DATA_POINTS = 20;
```

```java
        private static final int MAX_VALUE = 110;
        private static final int GAP = 30;

        private final LinkedList<Long> samples = new
LinkedList<Long>();
        private final Application application;
        private Thread refreshThread;

        public SamplingGraphPanel(Application application) {
            this.application = application;
            this.setBackground(Color.black);
        }

        @Override
        public void paintComponent(Graphics gr) {
            super.paintComponent(gr);

            Graphics2D g2 = (Graphics2D)gr;
            g2.setRenderingHint(RenderingHints.KEY_ANTIALIASING,
RenderingHints.VALUE_ANTIALIAS_ON);

            final double xScale = ((double) getWidth()-2*GAP)/
(samples.size()-1);
            final double yScale = ((double) getHeight()-2*GAP)/(MAX_
VALUE-1);

            Stroke oldStroke = g2.getStroke();
            g2.setColor(Color.green);
            g2.setStroke(new BasicStroke(3f));
            for (int i = 0; i < samples.size()-1; ++i) {
                final int x1 = (int) (i * xScale + GAP);
                final int y1 = (int) ((MAX_VALUE-samples.
get(i))*yScale+GAP);
                final int x2 = (int) ((i+1) * xScale + GAP);
                final int y2 = (int) ((MAX_VALUE - samples.get(i+1)) *
yScale + GAP);
                g2.drawLine(x1, y1, x2, y2);
            }
        }

    public void start() {
        refreshThread = new Thread(this);
        refreshThread.start();
```

```
        }

    public void stop() {
        if ( refreshThread != null ) {
            refreshThread.interrupt();
            refreshThread = null;
        }
    }


    @Override
    public void run() {
        JmxModel jmx = JmxModelFactory.
getJmxModelFor(application);
        MBeanServerConnection mbsc = null;
        if (jmx != null && jmx.getConnectionState() == JmxModel.
ConnectionState.CONNECTED) {
            mbsc = jmx.getMBeanServerConnection();
        }

        try {
            while ( mbsc != null && !Thread.currentThread().
isInterrupted() ) {
                if ( samples.size() == MAX_DATA_POINTS ) {
                    samples.remove();
                }
                Long val = (Long)mbsc.getAttribute(new
ObjectName("org.openjdk.cookbook:type=SleepProbe"),
"ActualSleepTime");
                samples.add(val);
                repaint();
                try {
                    Thread.sleep(500);
                } catch (InterruptedException e) { break; }
            }
        } catch (Exception e) {
            Exceptions.printStackTrace(e);
        }
    }
}
```

15. This class will read a value from the `MBean` implements on the first step of this receipt every 500ms, and add the value to the list with samples. Then it refreshes the graph, which gets repainted. Fundamentally, that code is just a Java Swing code, which can be run in any application. The only VisualVM-specific bit here is some helper classes used to get `MBean` from the `Application` object.

16. Now, in `SamplingModule`, create a class which will be responsible for showing the data. Name it `SamplingView` and put it into the `net.cookbook.openjdk` package, as shown below:

```java
package net.cookbook.openjdk;

import com.sun.tools.visualvm.application.Application;
import com.sun.tools.visualvm.core.ui.DataSourceView;
import com.sun.tools.visualvm.core.ui.components.
DataViewComponent;
import javax.swing.*;
import org.openide.util.Utilities;

public class SamplingView extends DataSourceView {
    private DataViewComponent dvc;
    private SamplingGraphPanel panel;
    public static final String IMAGE_PATH = "net/cookbook/openjdk/
icon.png";

    public SamplingView(Application application) {
        super(application,"Sampling Application", new
ImageIcon(Utilities.loadImage(IMAGE_PATH, true)).getImage(), 60,
false);
    }

    protected DataViewComponent createComponent() {
        //Data area for master view:
        JEditorPane generalDataArea = new JEditorPane();
        generalDataArea.setBorder(BorderFactory.
createEmptyBorder(14, 8, 14, 8));

        panel = new SamplingGraphPanel(SamplingProvider.
getSleepProbeInstance((Application)getDataSource()));
DataViewComponent.MasterView masterView = new DataViewComponent.
MasterView("Sampling Overview", null, generalDataArea);
        DataViewComponent.MasterViewConfiguration
masterConfiguration = new DataViewComponent.
MasterViewConfiguration(false);
        dvc = new DataViewComponent(masterView,
masterConfiguration);
        //Add detail views to the component:
```

```
           dvc.addDetailsView(new DataViewComponent.
DetailsView("Sampling Graph", null, 10, panel, null),
DataViewComponent.TOP_LEFT);

           return dvc;
    }

    @Override
    protected void removed() {
        super.removed();
        panel.stop();
    }
}
```

17. It is important that the file referenced by IMAGE_PATH actually exists, otherwise the plugin will not start and will fail with an exception. The simplest way you can do this is to download any of available free icons from the Internet, for example at `https://www.iconfinder.com/icons/131715/download/png/32` and put it into the same package folder as the `SamplingView` class.

18. The next step is to create a provider which will create the view instance and identify that the application we are connected to is supported by the plugin. In the `net.cookbook.openjdk` package, create a class with the name `SamplingProvider` and with the following implementation:

```
package net.cookbook.openjdk;

import com.sun.tools.visualvm.application.Application;
import com.sun.tools.visualvm.core.ui.*;
import com.sun.tools.visualvm.tools.jmx.*;
import javax.management.*;
import org.openide.util.Exceptions;

public class SamplingProvider extends DataSourceViewProvider<Appli
cation> {
    private static DataSourceViewProvider instance = new
SamplingProvider();
    @Override
    public boolean supportsViewFor(Application application) {
        boolean result = false;
        JmxModel jmx = JmxModelFactory.
getJmxModelFor(application);
        if (jmx != null && jmx.getConnectionState() == JmxModel.
ConnectionState.CONNECTED) {
            MBeanServerConnection mbsc = jmx.
getMBeanServerConnection();
            if (mbsc != null) {
```

```
                        try {
                            mbsc.getObjectInstance(new ObjectName("org.
    openjdk.cookbook:type=SleepProbe"));
                            result = true; // no exception - bean found
                        }catch (InstanceNotFoundException e) {
                            // bean not found, ignore
                        } catch (Exception e1) {
                            Exceptions.printStackTrace(e1);
                        }
                    }
                }
            return result;
        }


        @Override
        protected DataSourceView createView(Application application) {
            return new SamplingView(application);
        }

        static void initialize() {
            DataSourceViewsManager.sharedInstance().
    addViewProvider(instance, Application.class);
        }

        static void unregister() {
            DataSourceViewsManager.sharedInstance()
                        .removeViewProvider(instance);
        }

        public static Object getSleepProbeInstance(Application
    application) {
            ObjectInstance instance = null;
            JmxModel jmx = JmxModelFactory.
    getJmxModelFor(application);
            if (jmx != null && jmx.getConnectionState() == JmxModel.
    ConnectionState.CONNECTED) {
                MBeanServerConnection mbsc = jmx.
    getMBeanServerConnection();
                if (mbsc != null) {
                    try {
                        instance = mbsc.getObjectInstance(new
    ObjectName("org.openjdk.cookbook:type=SleepProbe"));
                    } catch (InstanceNotFoundException e) {
                        // bean not found, ignore
                    } catch (Exception e) {
```

```
                    Exceptions.printStackTrace(e);
                }
            }
        }
        return instance;
    }
}
```

19. The main methods of this class are `supportsViewFor` and `createView`.
    The `createView` method is small and easy, it just creates a view instance
    and passes through the application so that the view can get data out of it. The
    `supportsViewFor` class is slightly bigger, but it doesn't really match. It connects to
    the given application via JMX and tries to get the instance of `MBean` which our plugin
    is interested in. If `MBean` is not there, it means that the application is not supported
    and the method returns `false`.

20. Now it is time to see how the plugin works. To do this, first start the application created
    on the first step of this receipt. Then right-click on **SamplingModule** and select **Run**.
    This will start VisualVM with our plugin. From the list of processes in VisualVM, select
    our process and click on the **Sampling Application** tab. There you will see our graph
    showing slight changes in the sleep time as shown in the following screenshot:

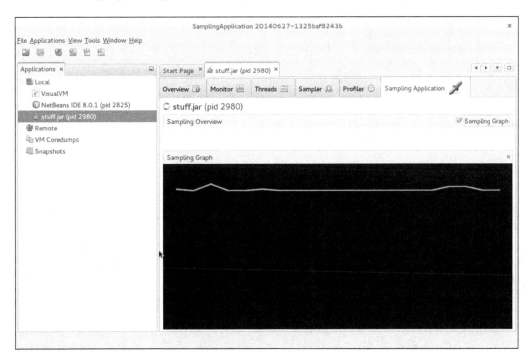

After following these steps, it should not be a problem for the reader to extend this example
and use it for any kind of monitoring applications that he/she wants in VisualVM.

See also

There is some documentation available on the VisualVM website, which helps with creating the plugin for VisualVM and which covers, in more detail, some classes which are used in this receipt, at `http://visualvm.java.net/api-quickstart.html`.

It is also worth having a look at existing plugins source code and some samples available. These can be found in `<code_root>/plugins` and `<code_root>/samples` respectively. For instructions on how to download the source code, please see the *Building VisualVM from the source code* recipe.

Getting benefits from the AdoptOpenJDK project

AdoptOpenJDK is a program, initially developed by a small group of enthusiasts, but which became part of an official OpenJDK community. Some of the purposes are to clarify and simplify OpenJDK building, installation, and usage, but there is still more. It provides build automation, a report generator, build testing, and more. We will cover some basic features that will be useful for everyone.

Getting ready

To follow this recipe, we will need an OpenJDK instance installed, and an Internet connection established.

How to do it...

AdoptOpenJDK is a very helpful and a very sophisticated project set with quite a few different subprojects. Many of them concern testing and evangelism, so we could not include them here as recipes.

Visualizing JIT logs

There is a project named Jitwatch in AdoptOpenJDK. Its purpose is to visualize JIT compiler logs. It helps to find some of our project's performance deficiencies and inspect a native assembly output, as it's just fun after all. Have a look at the following points:

1. First, let's download an executable jar `http://www.chrisnewland.com/images/jitwatch.jar`.

2. In order to analyze an executable, we will need to run it with the following switches:

    ```
    -XX:+UnlockDiagnosticVMOptions -XX:+TraceClassLoading
    -XX:+LogCompilation -XX:+PrintAssembly
    ```

The UnlockDiagnosticVMOptions parameter gives access to other diagnostic options, such as SharedOptimizeColdStart, PauseAtStartup, and so on.

The LogCompilation logs compilation activity in detail to hotspot.log or LogFile, which is yet another VM option.

The TraceClassLoading parameter lets JVM ensure that all loaded classes are visible, even the ones without any JIT-compiled code related to them.

The PrintAssembly parameter lets us see the assembler output of the JIT compilation. It uses hsdis, a HotSpot disassembler, which is a part of OpenJDK.

3. Start the analyzer:

```
java -jar ./jitwatch.jar
```

You will see the following screen:

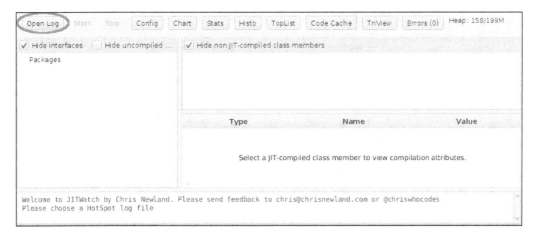

4. Open your hotspot.log and, then press **Start**.

Enjoy the experience.

Securing your javadocs

1. We will try to eliminate a javadoc vulnerability (CVE-2013-1571) that seems to exist in Java releases before 7u22.

2. To do that, we will need to clone a repository, such as:

```
git clone https://github.com/AdoptOpenJDK/JavadocUpdaterTool.git
&& cd JavadocUpdaterTool
```

Build the project

```
mvn clean install
```

3. We will try to scan a directory for potential vulnerabilities. We will run the following command from the directory in which the `JavadocPatchTool.jar` file is located:

```
java -jar JavadocPatchTool.jar -R -C <directory>
```

If the tool finds any applicable HTML files, it will print out a list of such files.

4. To fix a single applicable file, we will run the following command:

java -jar JavadocPatchTool.jar <path>

Here, <path> is the path to the directory which contains the applicable file.

5. To fix all the applicable files in the tree, run the following command:

```
java -jar JavadocPatchTool.jar -R <path_to_tree>
```

> To learn about more benefits from the AdoptOpenJDK
> project, visit the appropriate page at `https://java.net/`
> `projects/adoptopenjdk/pages/Benefits`.

How it works...

JIT log visualizer is no more than a tool to process logs generated by OpenJDK. But it is a very useful tool that may significantly improve performance.

Java is used in various projects that need security, so the vulnerability in javadocs has an impact on those who still use Java 6 and are unable to change it to Java 7. So the tool that fixes it with no transitions in the technology is really invaluable.

There's more...

There are many more projects in AdoptOpenJDK. Most of them are evangelist or testing ones; thus, they are slightly beyond the scope of this book.

However, you can always find them on various AdoptOpenJDK sites. There is no need to mention all of them in this book, they are tightly linked. In order to find them, it is sufficient to just look around.

9

Testing OpenJDK

In this chapter, we will cover the following topics:

- ► Running tests using the downloaded or the built version of jtreg
- ► Building jtreg from the source
- ► Running the standard set of OpenJDK tests
- ► Writing your own test for jtreg
- ► Using jtreg in GUI mode
- ► Writing TestNG tests for jtreg
- ► Compiling JT Harness from the source code
- ► Building and running jcstress
- ► Writing tests for jcstress
- ► Creating a benchmark project using JMH
- ► Downloading the source and compiling JMH

Introduction

Back in 1997, when JDK 1.1 was completed and JDK 1.2 had just started, there was an obvious problem—JDK had to be tested somehow and there had to be a tool for it. This is the moment when **jtreg** appeared as the regression test harness. At that time, there were not many testing frameworks for Java. In fact, there was not even much software written in Java. So choices were very limited and the only reasonable option was the framework that was being used at that time for the **Java Compatibility Kit** (**JCK**). Its name was **JavaTest**. But, as JCK tests were very different from what a JDK regression test is supposed to do, the framework required some adaptation and that is when jtreg appeared. At the moment, even though many years have passed since 1997, jtreg still remains the primary tool for running unit and regression tests in OpenJDK. Since its introduction in OpenJDK, more than 10,000 tests have been created that run using the jtreg framework.

As a testing tool, jtreg might look a little unusual for modern developers who are used to tools such as jUnit and TestNG. The main reason jtreg looks different is because it has a long history. It appeared before jUnit in 1997, which appeared sometime around 2000. At that time, especially when technology was so young, three years was a long period. It seems possible that the other contributing factor was that jtreg for a long time remained a proprietary tool and, as it was doing its job, there was no need to change it. Also, it was not open to the wide open source community, who could have changed its shape over time. The other reason that contributes to its difference when compared to the current *classical* tools is that it provides some special features that are not usually available in testing frameworks, but are required to do testing on JDK. These features include running a test in a separate instance (or for some tests, even several instances) of JVM with a specific set of parameters, testing Java applets (remember them?), running shell scripts as tests, running GUI tests which require user interaction, and so on. This is a pretty big set of additional features, which is enough to justify building a separate framework for it.

Having said all that, it would not be fair to say that jtreg is some old-fashioned tool that is stuck in the 1990s and does not attempt to change itself to be closer to the modern way of building frameworks for software testing. It has been integrated with testing frameworks such as **TestNG** and provides a way to create tests that are based on that framework. However, the majority of tests in JDK are still just classes with a main method that are executed by the framework. Though, to be fair, such an approach has its benefits since it allows one to run individual tests without any framework. There are also some tests that are just batch files and there is an ongoing effort to get rid of them.

As a tool that evolved from JavaTest, jtreg inherited compatibility with its framework. This compatibility has been now isolated into a separate project called **Java Test Harness** (**JT Harness**). This is a framework for running, building, and deploying tests suites. It also provides a GUI to manage and execute the test suites.

In this chapter, you will learn enough to be a confident jtreg user and know how to use JT Harness. You will find out how to build jtreg and JT Harness from the source code, how to run tests, and how to write your own tests. The chapter covers only plain Java and TestNG tests, as they are the most useful ones for OpenJDK developers. This chapter does not cover the usage of shell tests, as their usage is not considered a good practice and they were created to work around JVM limitations that existed a few years back. At the current moment, all OpenJDK contributors are encouraged to replace the shell tests with the Java version, wherever possible.

Running tests using the downloaded or the built version of jtreg

The simplest way to get started with jtreg is to just download it, unpack it, and run some tests. In this recipe, we will do exactly that, without doing any additional things such as building it from the source code or trying to create our own tests.

Getting ready

For this recipe, nothing much is really required—just the Internet connection, a machine with an installed or built OpenJDK, and the OpenJDK source code. In a Windows environment, Cygwin has to be installed in your machine.

How to do it...

The following are a few simple steps to get a set of tests executed by jtreg:

1. If jtreg is not yet available on the machine, go to the official page of jtreg (`https://adopt-openjdk.ci.cloudbees.com/job/jtreg/lastSuccessfulBuild/artifact/`) and download the latest available version of jtreg. The other option is to build it from the source code. To do this, follow the instructions in the *Building Jtreg from the source* recipe that is covered later in this chapter. After you have either downloaded jtreg or built it using the source code, proceed to the next step.

2. Unpack the downloaded archive to a folder.

3. In the root folder of the OpenJDK source tree, create a shell script with the name, `run_test.sh`. This script will be used to run jtreg:

   ```
   #!/bin/sh
   export JT_JAVA=/etc/alternatives/java_sdk_1.7.0_openjdk/
   /home/user/openjdk/jtreg/bin/jtreg -jdk:$JT_JAVA -agentvm
   -automatic -verbose:summary -w build/jtreg/work -r build/jtreg/
   report hotspot/test/compiler/5091921
   ```

   The only thing here that needs to be changed is the `JT_JAVA` environment variable that has to point to the version of OpenJDK that is higher or equal to 1.5.

4. After running the script, you will see the output as shown:

   ```
   [user@localhost jdk7u_clean]$ ./run_test.sh
   Passed: compiler/5091921/Test5091921.java
   Passed: compiler/5091921/Test6186134.java
   Passed: compiler/5091921/Test6196102.java
   ```

```
Passed: compiler/5091921/Test6357214.java
Passed: compiler/5091921/Test6559156.java
Passed: compiler/5091921/Test6753639.java
Passed: compiler/5091921/Test6850611.java
Passed: compiler/5091921/Test6890943.java
Passed: compiler/5091921/Test6897150.java
Passed: compiler/5091921/Test6905845.java
Passed: compiler/5091921/Test6931567.java
Passed: compiler/5091921/Test6935022.java
Passed: compiler/5091921/Test6959129.java
Passed: compiler/5091921/Test6985295.java
Passed: compiler/5091921/Test6992759.java
Passed: compiler/5091921/Test7005594.java
Passed: compiler/5091921/Test7020614.java
Test results: passed: 17
```

5. After the test, run the HTML report that is generated by jtreg. This is available in the folder specified by the `-r` parameter.

How it works...

As you can see, the shell script that is used to run jtreg is simple and there are only a few points that need to be clarified. These are the `JT_JAVA` environment variables and the command line arguments of jtreg.

`JT_JAVA` is one of the two environment variables used by the jtreg shell script. `JT_JAVA` specifies the version of Java that will be used to run the framework, but not the tests. In this recipe, for the sake of simplicity, we used the same version of Java to run jtreg and the tests.

The jtreg command line arguments are all described in detail on the jtreg webpage (`http://openjdk.java.net/jtreg/command-help.html`), so we will cover just a few of them that are used in this recipe:

- ► `-jdk`: This argument will generate the JDK that will be used to run tests. Basically, it is the version of Java which is tested by the test run. In our example, we used the version that was installed on the machine. If you want to use the version that was built from the source, the variable should be changed appropriately to point to the output of the build.

- ▶ `-agentvm`: This is the mode when jtreg uses the pool of reusable JVMs to run the tests. When a test requires a separate JVM for the run, that JVM is not created, but it is borrowed from the pool of reusable instances. If any parameter is not specified, jtreg will recreate a JVM for each test and this will significantly slow down the test run.

- ▶ `-verbose:summary`: This argument specifies the output mode. The `summary` parameter means that it will print just the status and the test name.

- ▶ `-automatic`: This argument means that only the automatic tests that do not require user intervention will be run.

- ▶ `-w`: This argument provides the location of the working directory. This will be used to store class files, and so on.

- ▶ `-r`: This argument provides the reporting directory in which reports are to be stored. To see the report, open the `<reporting directory>/html/report.html` file in any browser.

See also

- ▶ The complete list of command line options is available at `http://openjdk.java.net/jtreg/command-help.html`.

- ▶ Some might find it useful to run tests only for a specific bug and, for that, the `bug:<bug_id>` command-line option can be used. The tests' logfiles can be found in the working directory (specified by the `-w` parameter or in `JTwork` if that parameter is not defined). Logfiles are in text format with a `.jtr` extension. These files contain the test output along with the command line and an exception, if thrown, and are very useful for troubleshooting.

Building jtreg from the source

Apart from downloading jtreg as a binary package, there is also an option to download the source code and build jtreg from the source. This can be beneficial for developers who might want to make changes in the source code or get the latest fix that has not yet been released as a binary package.

Getting ready

You will need an Internet connection, a machine capable of running make and batch files (Linux or Cygwin), and an installed Mercurial.

How to do it...

The following simple steps will show you how to get the jtreg source code and make the build:

1. Download the sources from `http://hg.openjdk.java.net/code-tools/jtreg`. To do this, just execute the following command that will clone the jtreg source tree in the local folder, `jtreg`:

   ```
   [user@localhost tmp]$ hg clone http://hg.openjdk.java.net/code-tools/jtreg

   destination directory: jtreg

   requesting all changes

   adding changesets

   adding manifests

   adding file changes

   added 85 changesets with 1239 changes to 602 files

   updating to branch default

   586 files updated, 0 files merged, 0 files removed, 0 files unresolved
   ```

   After the execution of the command, the current directory can be found in the new `jtreg` folder with all the jtreg sources.

2. If there is no Ant software installed on the machine, install it using `yum` (or any other packaging tool), or simply download it from `http://ant.apache.org/` and then unpack it. If you are using a Linux machine, you also have an option to install it by running `yum` or any other similar tool that can be found at `http://ant.apache.org/` and then unpack it.

3. Download the latest available version of JT Harness, which is available at `https://jtharness.java.net/`. Unpack it in the `jtreg/lib` folder.

4. jtreg requires JUnit, but not the latest version. The version has to be earlier than 4.11. The simplest way to get it would be to download the version from Maven central at `http://mvnrepository.com/artifact/junit/junit/4.5`. A jtreg build requires just the JAR file. Put this file in the `jtreg/lib` folder.

5. To make things slightly more exciting, a jtreg build also requires another testing framework—**TestNG v.6.8**. This can be downloaded from `http://testng.org/doc/download.html`.

   Note that the required version is the version for Ant users. To make things simpler, just use the link, `http://testng.org/testng-6.8.zip`. Unpack the downloaded archive in the `jtreg/lib` folder.

6. The next dependency is `JavaHelp`. This seems to be available only via a direct link at `http://download.java.net/javadesktop/javahelp/javahelp2_0_05.zip`. Unpack it in the `jtreg/lib` folder.

7. And then, finally, the last dependency, that is `Xalan`, the XML transformation library. The required version is 2.7.1, which can be downloaded from one of the websites listed at `http://www.apache.org/dyn/closer.cgi/xml/xalan-j`. Follow the same procedure that you did with the other libraries and unpack it in the `jtreg/lib` folder.

8. Now, it is time to write the script that will execute the build. Put the following script code into the `make.sh` file of the `jtreg` folder, created in the first step:

```
#!/bin/sh
export JDK15HOME= /etc/alternatives/java_sdk_1.7.0_openjdk/
export JAVAHELP_HOME=/home/user/openjdk/jtreg/lib/jh2.0/javahelp
export ANTHOME=/usr/share/ant
export JTHARNESS_HOME=/home/user/openjdk/jtreg/lib/jharness4.4.1
export JUNIT_JAR=/home/user/openjdk/jtreg/lib/junit4.5/junit-
4.5.jar
export TESTNG_HOME=/home/user/openjdk/jtreg/lib/testng-6.8
export TESTNG_JAR=/home/user/openjdk/jtreg/lib/testng-6.8/testng-
6.8.jar
export XALANHOME=/home/user/openjdk/jtreg/lib/xalan-j_2_7_1
make -C make
```

As you can see, the script is simple and it is only required to set the environment variables. Not much explanation is required, as all the variable names are pretty self-explanatory. So, just assign appropriate values that are relevant for your machine setup. All the variables are mandatory and have to be defined to run the framework.

9. The final step is to just run that script:

```
[user@localhost jtreg]$ ./make.sh
```

After the build, which should take just a few seconds, the resulting JAR file can be found in the `build/images/jtreg/` folder. This folder will contain a fully workable and self-sufficient jtreg distribution:

```
[user@localhost jtreg]$ ls -l build/images/jtreg/
total 60
drwxrwxr-x. 2 user user 4096 May  3 21:27 bin
-rw-rw-r--. 1 user user  994 May  3 21:23 COPYRIGHT
drwxrwxr-x. 3 user user 4096 May  3 21:23 doc
```

```
drwxrwxr-x. 4 user user  4096 May   3 21:27 legal
drwxrwxr-x. 2 user user  4096 May   3 21:27 lib
-rw-rw-r--. 1 user user 19241 May   3 21:27 LICENSE
drwxrwxr-x. 3 user user  4096 May   3 21:23 linux
-rw-rw-r--. 1 user user  3790 May   3 21:27 README
-rw-rw-r--. 1 user user    72 May   3 21:27 release
drwxrwxr-x. 3 user user  4096 May   3 21:23 solaris
drwxrwxr-x. 3 user user  4096 May   3 21:23 win32
```

Running the standard set of OpenJDK tests

This recipe is not much different from the one that describes a simple test execution. However, it will focus on how to run JDK tests. This knowledge might be required if someone is making changes to HotSpot or to any other part of OpenJDK.

Standard tests are available only in three root folders for JDK7 and in four folders for JDK8. These are `hotspot`, `jdk`, `langtools`, and `nashorn` (for jdk8 only). Although tests are not available for other areas such as CORBA, JDBC, JAXP, and so on, it doesn't mean that they are not tested at all. It just means that tests for them are not part of OpenJDK, that is, they are not provided by vendors.

The way tests are organized varies with the dependency of the area they are testing, for example, `hotspot` and `langtools` are mostly grouped by functional areas they are testing and, then, by bugs (by their numbers). The `jdk` folder is mostly organized by the package name, as this set of tests covers the Java APIs.

Keep in mind that some tests might fail, but it does not mean that something is particularly wrong with OpenJDK. It just means that there are some situations when it is rather hard to create a test that can pass in any environment. For example, there can be tests that need a special network configuration or some other sort of special environment, which might not be set up on the machine.

There is a set of tests that are known to fail and there is usually a good reason for that. The most obvious example is a test that covers some known problem, but whose fix is not going to happen soon. These tests are listed in `jdk/test/ProblemList.txt` or marked with a `@ignore` tag. These tests should usually be excluded from the standard test run.

Getting ready

As we will be running tests for OpenJDK, it is required to have relevant sources available on the machine. The machine should also be set up for the OpenJDK build, as we will be using OpenJDK make files to execute the test run.

jtreg should be downloaded and unpacked in a folder on the machine so that it is ready for the test run.

Some OpenJDK tests are shell scripts, so you will need to use either a Linux machine or, in the case of a Windows machine, Cygwin with support for the Bourne shell, even though Cygwin is not recommended, as there is a chance that some shell tests will not run properly on it.

How to do it...

One of the most convenient ways to run tests is to run them separately for each area, such as hotspot, jdk, and so on. As the aim of this recipe is to just explain the concept, we will be using the jdk tests, which are just a subset of all the tests available in OpenJDK, but the same pattern can be applied to all the other areas as well. Follow the given steps:

1. In the OpenJDK source root folder, create a file with the name, run_jdk_lang_tests.sh and the following content:

   ```
   #!/bin/sh
   export JTREG_HOME=/home/user/openjdk/jtreg/build/images/jtreg/
   export JT_HOME=/home/user/openjdk/jtreg/build/images/jtreg/
   export PRODUCT_HOME=/home/stas/openjdk/jdk7u_clean/build/linux-amd64/j2sdk-image/
   cd jdk/test
   make TESTDIRS=java/lang
   ```

   The JTREG_HOME and JT_HOME environment variables are both the same and should point to a folder with jtreg. Unfortunately, there are places in make files where both these variables are used.

   PRODUCT_HOME points to a JDK in the test. It is not strictly required to point it to a version of JDK that was just built from the source, but there is also no sense in executing tests on a version that one can't change.

   TESTDIRS points to a subset of tests to run. Obviously, the wider that subset, the more tests will be executed and the longer it will take to run. So usually it makes sense to limit this subset to something reasonable, unless there is a need to do a regression test after making big changes.

2. Now let's run the script. It will execute tests in the jdk folder and output hundreds of lines like these:

   ```
   TEST: java/lang/StringBuilder/Insert.java
     build: 1.112 seconds
     compile: 1.112 seconds
   ```

```
    main: 0.161 seconds

  TEST RESULT: Passed. Execution successful

  - - - - - - - - - - - - - - - - - - - - - - - - - - - - - - - - - - - - - - - - - - - - - -
```

3. When it's all finished, the make script will report something as shown:

```
Summary:

TEST STATS: name=  run=383  pass=383  fail=0  excluded=4

EXIT CODE: 0

EXIT CODE: 0

Testing completed successfully
```

The preceding output tells us how many tests were executed, how many failed, how many passed, and so on. Now, when all the tests that we were interested in are run, the results can be found in the `jdk/build/linux-amd64/testoutput/JTreport` folder. There will be standard jtreg text and HTML report files that can be viewed using any web browser.

There's more...

If someone came to a point where there was a need to run an OpenJDK test, there is a good chance that there would be a situation when the tests had to be updated or extended. In that case, it is important to have a good understanding of what is going on inside these tests and what is the exact reason for each of them to exist. Mostly, that information is available in the `@bug` and `@summary` tags. It is highly recommended to pay attention to their content and put in some effort to see how they correlate with actual test code.

Most of the tests contain additional information in the `@bug` and `@summary` tags. It is important to refer to these tags to understand the reason for the test. For example, when you run tests, it is not uncommon to see an output like the following:

```
- - - - - - - - - - - - - - - - - - - - - - - - - - - - - - - - - - - - - - - - - - - - - -
TEST: java/lang/invoke/7157574/Test7157574.java
  build: 1.194 seconds
  compile: 1.193 seconds
  main: 0.199 seconds
TEST RESULT: Passed. Execution successful
```

It means that this is the test for the bug with ID `7157574`, which can actually be found in the JDK bug tracking system at `https://bugs.openjdk.java.net/browse/JDK-7157574`. And, when one takes a look at the test, the following information will be in the header:

```
/* @test
 * @bug 7157574
```

```
 * @summary method handles returned by reflective lookup API sometimes
have wrong receiver type
 *
 * @run main Test7157574
 */
```

This header has a reference to the bug that this test is testing and, in the summary section, it explains exactly what this test is doing. Also, when you look at the source of a test, it is quite common to see that it contains a very detailed explanation of the problem and the way that the problem is being tested.

Writing your own test for jtreg

If you are going to add a new feature to OpenJDK or fix a bug, it is really a good idea to have a test case to cover the change in functionality and to ensure that the implementation change doesn't break anything. This recipe will help you to get some understanding of the process and create a simple test. You will find that writing your own test case for jtreg is not a complicated task, but it can be slightly unusual in some respects.

Getting ready

All that is required for this recipe is an installed jtreg and the OpenJDK sources. The latter is required only because this recipe assumes that the newly created test is for OpenJDK.

How to do it...

Writing tests for jtreg can be a little unusual, but when you get used to the pattern it is actually quite easy. To begin, just follow the steps. Keep in mind that all the paths are given relative to the OpenJDK source root:

1. Go to the root folder of OpenJDK and create the `jdk/test/demo/SampleTest.java` file first:

    ```
    /* @test
     * @summary Test to ensure that computer wasn't moved to the past
     * @compile SampleTimeProvider.java
     * @run main SampleTest
     * @run main/othervm SampleTest
     */
    public class SampleTest {
        public static void main(String[] args) {
            long currentTime = new SampleTimeProvider().
    getCurrentTime();
    ```

```
        if ( currentTime < 0 ) {
            throw new RuntimeException("It can't be 1969!");
        }
    }
}
```

2. Then, create the `jdk/test/demo/SampleTimeProvider.java` file as follows:

```
public class SampleTimeProvider {
    public long getCurrentTime() {
        return System.currentTimeMillis();
    }
}
```

3. Now, create a script file with the name, `run_jtreg.sh` in the source root folder of JDK and run it:

   #!/bin/sh

   export JT_JAVA=/usr/lib/jvm/java-1.7.0-openjdk-1.7.0.60-2.4.7.0.fc20.x86_64

   /home/user/openjdk/jtreg/build/images/jtreg/bin/jtreg -jdk:$JT_JAVA -agentvm -automatic -verbose:summary -w build/jtreg/work -r build/jtreg/report -exclude:./jdk/test/ProblemList.txt jdk/test/demo/SampleTest.java

4. The output should be as follows:

   [user@localhost jdk7u]$ ./run_jtreg.sh

   Directory "build/jtreg/work" not found: creating

   Directory "build/jtreg/report" not found: creating

   Passed: demo/SampleTest.java

   Test results: passed: 1

   Report written to /home/user/openjdk/jdk7u/build/jtreg/report/html/report.html

   Results written to /home/user/openjdk/jdk7u/build/jtreg/work

   As you can see, only one test was run and the run was successful. So, writing a simple test case is a very simple task.

5. Now, the final step. After all the tests have been run, let's look at the test result whose path was provided in the output of jtreg. Let's open `report/html/repost.html` in a web browser and take a look at what's there:

Here, we can see that only one test, **demo/SampleTest.java**, was executed and it was the one that passed.

How it works...

Some explanation is required to find out what actually happened. The test itself is in the `SampleTest.java` file. jtreg knows that the file contains the test by the presence of the `@test` tag in the class header comments. Without that tag, jtreg will not consider it as a test.

The only purpose of the `@summary` tag is to give a summary description for the test. This description will also be used in logs and reports. It is very important to have a good, readable description for that tag. Also, if a test is for a bug, it is necessary to have the `@bug` tag populated with an appropriate bug number.

The next tag, `@compile`, has a reference to another file, which is required to be compiled to run the test. The only reason for the existence of `SampleTimeProvider.java` is to show how to use the `@compile` tag. It is very unusual for Java to do things like this. Usually, everything is compiled and then things are picked from the classpath, but this is the way Java works.

The `@run` tag tells the harness how to run the test. As can be seen from the test class, this parameter can be defined several times, which means that the test will also be executed several times and each time it will be run with a configuration defined by the associated run tag. In our example, there are two runs, one in the same VM and the other in a new instance of VM, which is specified by the `othervm` parameter. If this tag is not defined, then, by default, jtreg assumes that it is `@run main ClassName`.

Note that a test fails if it runs for longer than 2 minutes (120 seconds) and can be overwritten by `@run main/timeout=xxx`.

Usually, a test indicates its failure by throwing an exception. A test from this recipe will throw `RuntimeException` when its conditions are not met.

jtreg requires the `TEST.ROOT` file to be created in the tests' root folder. Without that file, it will not execute any test. Luckily for us, JDK already has the required file with the appropriate content, so there is no need for us to worry about it.

See also

jtreg test cases are defined by the Javadoc tags and it is useful to be familiar with all of them. The complete list of tags and information about each tag is available either in the help file that can be accessed by running the jtreg command, `-onlineHelp`, or online at `http://openjdk.java.net/jtreg/tag-spec.txt`.

Using jtreg in GUI mode

jtreg is not only a command-line tool, but it also provides a relatively sophisticated graphical interface that allows you to run an individual set of tests, prepare test runs, see results of the run, and so on. This recipe will cover some basic features of UI that are enough for the user to start using the tool.

Getting ready

All that is required for this recipe is an installed jtreg and the OpenJDK sources.

How to do it...

1. Create the following script that will launch jtreg with a graphical UI:

    ```
    #!/bin/sh
    export JT_JAVA=/usr/lib/jvm/java-1.7.0-openjdk-1.7.0.60-
    2.4.7.0.fc20.x86_64

    /home/user/openjdk/jtreg/build/images/jtreg/bin/jtreg -g -jdk:$JT_
    JAVA -agentvm -automatic -verbose:summary -w build/jtreg/work -r
    build/jtreg/report -exclude:./jdk/test/ProblemList.txt jdk/test/
    ```

    The parameter that tells jtreg to launch JT Harness UI is -g. After it is launched, jtreg displays a window similar to the following one:

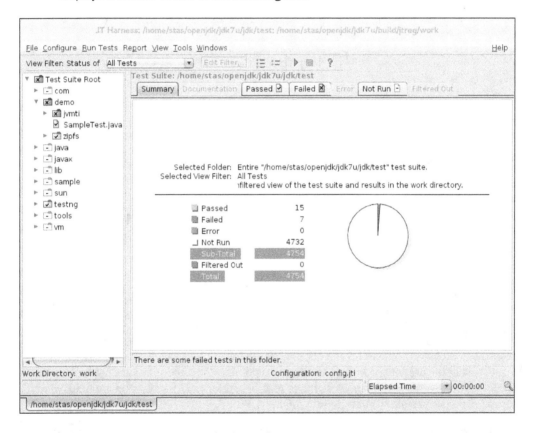

2. On the right-hand side of the preceding screenshot, you can see the results of the latest test run. It knows where to pick them up from the -r parameter. In this screenshot, you can also see the number of successful and failed tests, the total number of executed tests, and some other stats.

3. On the left-hand side of the preceding screenshot, there is a tree with all the available tests. This shows all the tests from the root of the test bundle, which is the folder with the `TEST.ROOT` configuration file. The green folder icon indicates the tests that ran successfully and the red one indicates the ones that failed.

4. To run a specific test from a set of tests, right-click on the individual test folder and select the **Execute these test** item from the pop-up menu. This will trigger the test run and a new report will be generated. For long running tests, there is a status window, which is available via the **Run Tests | Monitor Progress** menu item:

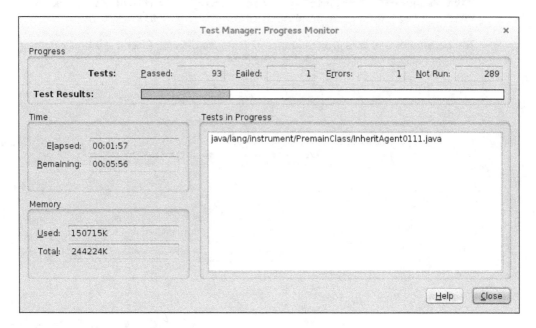

How it works...

The UI that is used by jtreg does not actually belong to jtreg. It is provided by JT Harness and jtreg just integrates it using the provided plugin system.

JT Harness provides a rich interface not only to run tests, but it also has a set of wizards to create test configurations, various report conversion tools, an agent monitoring tool, and so on. To get more information about all these features, refer to JT Harness online help, which is available via the **Help/Online Help** menu item.

Writing TestNG tests for jtreg

jtreg also provides support to run TestNG test cases, which might be a more familiar technique for many developers. There are some steps that need to be performed to make it happen and this recipe will go through them.

Getting ready

This recipe will require the OpenJDK source code and an installed version of jtreg. On a Windows machine, it is also required to have Cygwin installed.

How to do it...

The following procedure should be more familiar to Java developers than writing a native jtreg test, as TestNG is what most developers have heard of and used. Now, let's get to the practical part and create a test. The paths are relative to the OpenJDK source root.

1. Relative to the OpenJDK root folder, create a folder with the name, `jdk/test/testng/org/demo`. This is the folder where we are going to create our tests.

2. Create the file, `jdk/test/testng/TEST.properties`, relative to the OpenJDK source root. Add the following line there:

   `TestNG.dirs=.`

   It is not strictly required to create the file, and it is also possible to define the property in `jdk/test/TEST.ROOT`, which will work in the same way as our previous property. However, in most cases, it is practical to have that file so that it can contain some additional configuration that is specific to the set of TestNG tests, for example, the `lib.dirs` property.

3. In the `jdk/test/testng/org/mydemo` folder, create the following file with the name, `MyTestNGTest.java`:

```java
package org.mydemo;

import org.testng.Assert;
import org.testng.annotations.Test;

public class MyTestNGTest {
    @Test
    public void testMoreNanosThanMillis() {
        final long nanos = System.nanoTime();
        final long millis = System.currentTimeMillis();
        Assert.assertTrue(nanos > millis);
    }
}
```

4. Now, in OpenJDK's source root folder, create the following bash script (fix the paths as required to match the machine environment):

```
#!/bin/sh
```

```
export JT_JAVA=/usr/lib/jvm/java-1.7.0-openjdk-1.7.0.60-
2.4.7.0.fc20.x86_64
```

```
/home/user/openjdk/jtreg/build/images/jtreg/bin/jtreg -jdk:$JT_
JAVA -agentvm -automatic -verbose:summary -w build/jtreg/work -r
build/jtreg/report -exclude:./jdk/test/ProblemList.txt jdk/test/
testng
```

5. Then, give it a name, `./run_jtreg.sh`, and make it executable (running `chmod +x` `./run_jterg.sh` will do the job) and run it. The resulting output of the script should look similar to the following:

```
[user@localhost jdk7u]$ ./run_jtreg.sh
```

```
Passed: testng/org/mydemo/MyTestNGTest.java
```

```
Test results: passed: 1
```

```
Report written to /home/user/openjdk/jdk7u/build/jtreg/report/
html/report.html
```

```
Results written to /home/user/openjdk/jdk7u/build/jtreg/work
```

And that's it. The test has been run and, as can be seen from the output, it has passed. The result of the run can be seen by opening `/home/user/openjdk/jdk7u/build/jtreg/report/html/report.html` in the browser application.

How it works...

The file named `TEST.properties` that is created in the folder with the tests root package, requires a bit of explanation. This is the file that contains sets of configurations specific to the TestNG tests in the folder where the file is located. For example, it can have a reference to folders with libraries via the `lib.dirs` property. That is the `path` type property, which is the same as `TestNG.dirs`, and such properties are space-separated lists of paths to some of the folders or files. If the path in the list starts with `/`, then it is evaluated relative to a folder with `TEST.ROOT`, otherwise it is evaluated from the directory containing `TEST.properties`.

See also

As it is possible to use the TestNG annotations within the test classes, it is worth checking the TestNG website, which contains some documentation on this topic at `http://testng.org/doc/documentation-main.html`.

It is also possible to use the jtreg style tags and the TestNG style test together. In that case, the test should be created as a normal jtreg test (see the *Writing your own test for jtreg* recipe), using `testng` as the argument for `@run`, for example, `@run testng SampleTest`. In this scenario, there is no need for `TEST.properties` and things like `lib.dirs` are defined in the test source file via the jtreg tags, rather than in a separate configuration file.

Compiling JT Harness from the source code

JT Harness is a framework that allows you to execute different sets of tests. It is not necessary to use it only with jtreg. Other testing frameworks can be integrated with it as well. This means that it could be useful to have its source code to be able to build it from the source. This is exactly what this recipe is going to explain.

Getting ready

You will need Internet access to download the source code and install the additional software that is required for the build.

Ensure that Ant version 1.6.1 or later is installed on the machine. If not, then install it. The *How to do it...* section depends on the OS you are using. For example, on Fedora, that will be:

yum install ant

On Windows, the simplest way would be to just download the distribution and add Ant's `bin` folder to the `PATH` environment variable. The Ant distribution can be found at `http://ant.apache.org/`. Keep in mind that, to make it work, the `JAVA_HOME` environment variable has to contain the correct path of the Java distribution.

Ensure that Subversion is installed on the machine. In contrast to other tools, JT Harness doesn't use the Mercurial repository for its source code. On Fedora, Subversion can be installed by running `yum`:

yum install svn

On any other OS, it really depends on the OS. Check `http://subversion.apache.org/` to find out what is available.

How to do it...

Run the following command to check the source code:

```
svn checkout https://svn.java.net/svn/jtharness~svn/trunk jtharness
```

This command will create a folder with the name, `jtharness`, and download the source code. In that folder, create another folder and name it, `lib`. Here we will put the libraries required to build JT Harness.

Now download the following software (all paths are given relative to the `jtharness` folder):

1. JavaHelp seems to be available only via a direct link from `http://download.java.net/javadesktop/javahelp/javahelp2_0_05.zip`. Unpack it into `lib/jh2.0`.

2. Go to `http://asm.ow2.org/` and download the ASM Java bytecode manipulation library binaries version 3.1. Unpack the archive into `lib/asm-3.1`. This is required only for compilation.

3. Next, the required library is `Java Communications API`. Go to `http://www.oracle.com/technetwork/java/javasebusiness/downloads/java-archive-downloads-misc-419423.html` and download `Java Communications API 3.0u1` or any other higher version that is available. Unpack the archive into `lib/commapi`. This is required only for compilation.

4. Java Servlet APIs are only required for compilation. Probably the simplest way to download them is to get the JAR from Maven Central. Go to `http://search.maven.org/` and search for `javax.servlet servlet-api`. Download the JAR v.3.1.0 and put it directly into the `lib` folder.

5. The last one is JUnit, which is also only required for compilation. The recommended version is 4.4. Go to `http://junit.org/` and click on the **Download** link to download the appropriate version of the JAR file. Place it directly into the `lib` folder.

6. The next step is to get the sources. To do this, run the following command that will get the latest sources from the trunk:

   svn checkout https://svn.java.net/svn/jtharness~svn/trunk jtharness

   This will create the folder, `jtharness`, with two subfolders: `www` and `code`. The `www` folder contains pages with links to the documentation and other useful information, but we are really interested in the folder with the name `code`. It is actually not strictly necessary to download `www` at all, but it doesn't do any harm either.

7. Go to the folder, `jtharness/code/build`, locate the file `local.properties`, and edit it to set the following properties to point to the appropriate locations:

   - `jhalljar`: This provides the path to the JavaHelp `jhalljar.jar` file
   - `jhjar`: This property provides the path to the JavaHelp `jhjar.jar` file
   - `jcommjar`: This provides the path to `comm.jar` from the `Java Communications API`
   - `servletjar`: This provides the path to the `servlet-api.jar` file from `Java Servlet API`
   - `bytecodelib`: This provides a colon-separated path to the `asm-3.1.jar` and `asm-commons-3.1.jar` files
   - `junitlib`: This provides the path to `junit-4.4.jar` from jUnit

After the editing, the file should look similar to this:

```
#Please specify location of jhall.jar here - for compilation
jhalljar = /home/user/openjdk/jtharness/lib/jh2.0/javahelp/lib/
jhall.jar
# needed only at runtime
jhjar = /home/user/openjdk/jtharness/lib/jh2.0/javahelp/lib/jh.jar
# location of jar with implementation of java serial
communications API
jcommjar = /home/user/openjdk/jtharness/lib/commapi/jar/comm.jar
# location of jar with servlet API implementation
servletjar = /home/user/openjdk/jtharness/lib/javax.servlet-api-
3.1.0.jar
# bytecode library (BCEL or ASM)
# these are not interchangable
bytecodelib = /home/user/openjdk/jtharness/lib/asm-3.1/lib/asm-
3.1.jar:/home/stas/openjdk/jtharness/lib/asm-3.1/lib/asm-commons-
3.1.jar
# JUnit Library - Version 4 currently used to compile 3 and 4
support
junitlib = /home/user/openjdk/jtharness/lib/junit-4.4.jar
# Please specify location where the build distribution (output)
will be created
BUILD_DIR = ../JTHarness-build
```

If it is required, the BUILD_DIR variable can be changed to a different folder but, usually it is not necessary.

8. Now ensure that the current folder is jtharness/code/build and run Ant:

```
[stas@localhost build]$ ant
Buildfile: /home/user/openjdk/jtharness/code/build/build.xml
 ...skipped...
BUILD SUCCESSFUL
Total time: 45 seconds
When build is finished
```

When the build is finished, the folder, jtharness/JTHarness-build/binaries, contains the distribution of JT Harness.

See also

There are other targets available in the JT Harness build file that you may find useful:

- ▶ `run`: This builds and runs JT Harness. This is not the only way to launch the application. The other option is to run the following command from the source root folder after the build:

  ```
  java -jar JTHarness-build/binaries/lib/javatest.jar
  ```

- ▶ `clean`: This just builds the distribution directory.

- ▶ `build`: This builds JT Harness and then runs all the tests.

- ▶ `test`: This just runs the test.

- ▶ `Javadoc`: This generates the Javadoc API documentation.

- ▶ `build-examples`: This builds the example test suites packaged with the source. This target also automatically builds the core harness first.

Building and running jcstress

The **Java Concurrency Stress Test** (**jcstress**) is a set of tests for testing the correctness of the Java concurrency support. This is a new tool that is mostly targeted to Java 8, which means that not all the tests will run on previous versions of Java. As a new tool, jcstress is in its alpha phase and changes for fixes and improvements are common, which means that whoever is working with it is expected to update the source code and rebuild the tool relatively often.

Testing concurrency is not an easy task and it may or may not be easy to make such tests fail even with incorrect code. This happens due to the nature of concurrent code, which might work differently on different hardware configurations. Such variations arise from the number of CPUs or the CPU architecture. Overall, this means that many tests in jcstress are uncertain and they might require a long time before exposing potential problems.

Getting ready

You will need Internet access and the Mercurial repository to download the source code. As jcstress requires Java 8 for compilation and to run the full set of tests, it has to be installed on the machine and set as the current version. This means that the following commands should, as illustrated next, show Java 1.8 as the major version:

```
[user@localhost]$ java -version
openjdk version "1.8.0_11"
OpenJDK Runtime Environment (build 1.8.0_11-b12)
```

```
OpenJDK 64-Bit Server VM (build 25.11-b02, mixed mode)
[user@localhost jcstress]$ javac -version
javac 1.8.0_11
```

The build will also require Maven (one of the Java build tools) to be installed on the machine. The installation of this tool depends on the OS. For example, on Fedora, this can be done by running the following command as root:

```
[root@localhost ~]# yum install maven
```

On other OSs, the simplest way might be to download the binary from `http://maven. apache.org/download.cgi`, unpack the archive, point `M2_HOME` to the root of the unpacked folder and add `M2_HOME/bin` to the path.

How to do it...

Now it's time for action. The first few steps of this recipe will cover the build process and then it will switch to run the actual tests:

1. The first step is to download the sources. Go to the folder where you want to store the source code and run the following command:

   ```
   [user@localhost ~]$ hg clone http://hg.openjdk.java.net/code-
   tools/jcstress/ jcstress
   ```

   When this command is run, Mercurial is downloaded along with the source code from the remote repository and it is stored in the folder, `jcstress`.

2. Now, to build the tool, move to the folder `jcstress` and run the following command:

   ```
   [user@localhost jcstress]$ mvn clean install -pl tests-custom -am
   ```

   If successful, it should display something like this as the end:

   ```
   [INFO] BUILD SUCCESS
   [INFO] ------------------------------------------------------
   [INFO] Total time: 1:31.300s
   [INFO] Finished at: Tue Jul 29 22:23:19 BST 2014
   [INFO] Final Memory: 37M/410M
   [INFO] ------------------------------------------------------
   ```

   This means that the build has done what it was supposed to do and the tests are ready to be run.

3. To run all the tests, use the following command:

```
java -jar tests-custom/target/jcstress.jar
```

This will output thousands of lines like these:

```
(ETA:    00:39:58)  (R: 1.36E+07)  (T:  46/898)  (F: 1/1)  (I: 3/5)
[OK] o.o.j.t.atomicity.primitives.plain.VolatileCharAtomicityTest

(ETA:    00:40:05)  (R: 1.36E+07)  (T:  46/898)  (F: 1/1)
(I: 3/5)          [OK] o.o.j.t.atomicity.primitives.plain.
VolatileDoubleAtomicityTest
```

ETA is the estimated completion time, R is the runtime in nanoseconds, T is the test number, F is the fork number, and I is the test iteration number. This is all followed by the result (OK in this example) and the full name of the test class.

As you can see, the full standard set of tests run for approximately 40 minutes, and this might be too much, so there is an option to select which test to run using the -t parameter. This is a regular expression selected for the tests, for example:

```
[user@localhost jcstress]$ java -jar tests-custom/target/jcstress.jar -t
".*ByteBufferAtomicityTests.*"
```

This will only run tests which have ByteBufferAtomicityTests anywhere in their name.

When the tests are completed, it is time to have a look at the reports that are generated and, by default, they are put into the ./results/ folder. There you can find the file, index. html, which can be opened with any browser. The result will list all the tests and, if you click on the tests, all the observer outputs. These outputs can be something that is expected, not expected, or expected but somehow surprising to the user. This can result in the following outcomes for a test:

- FAILED: The test failed and the outcomes were not what was expected
- ERROR: The test crashed
- ACCEPTABLE: The test results matched the specifications
- ACCEPTABLE_INTERESTING: This is the same as ACCEPTABLE, but it has something to highlight
- ACCEPTABLE_SPEC: This is the same as ACCEPTABLE, but some interesting behavior is also observed that might not be otherwise expected

There's more...

It is recommended that you have a look at the other command-line options that are available for jcstress. This information can be retrieved by running the following command:

```
[user@localhost jcstress]$ java -jar tests-custom/target/jcstress.jar -h
```

jcstress has its own page at http://openjdk.java.net/, which has some very useful information and links to the source and mailing list at http://openjdk.java.net/projects/code-tools/jcstress/.

Writing tests for jcstress

The **Java Concurrency Stress test** is a wonderful tool that is used by JDK authors to ensure that their concurrent code works correctly with regards to concurrency. Concurrent code is hard to write and even harder to test. Most of their tests are probabilistic, require a lot of skill to write, and might take many days running time and the appropriate hardware to exhibit the fail behavior. Considering all this complexity, having a framework that can help with correct test execution is a big advantage. This recipe will go through the steps that are required to write your own tests for jcstress.

Getting ready

To follow this recipe, the only requirement is to have an environment that is capable of compiling and running jcstress (see the *Building and running jcstress* recipe).

How to do it...

The following steps will lead you through the process of creating a test and running it using jcstress:

1. To start, we will need a code to test. Let's pick the problem which, arguably, is the most common cause of headaches in concurrency and is very easy to reproduce. Data race sounds like a good candidate. We will make a class called CASValue and implement it:

```
package org.openjdk.jcstress.tests;

public class CASValue {
    private int i = 0;
    public boolean cas(int expected, int newValue) {
        boolean res = false;
        if (i == expected) {
            i = newValue;
            res = true;
        }
        return res;
    }
}
```

This class implements a single operation which is supposed to perform the compare-and-swap operation (see `http://en.wikipedia.org/wiki/Compare-and-swap`). Without synchronization, it will not work correctly in a multithreaded environment and should fail the test that we will create in the next steps of this recipe.

2. In the source root folder of jcstress, create the file, `tests-custom/src/main/java/org/openjdk/jcstress/tests/CASValue.java`, and put the source code of the `CASValue` class in it.

3. Now it's time to write a test to see whether our implementation is wrong. The test class will look like this:

```java
package org.openjdk.jcstress.tests;

import org.openjdk.jcstress.annotations.*;
import org.openjdk.jcstress.infra.results.LongResult2;

public class CASValueTests {
    @State
    public static class S extends CASValue { }

    @JCStressTest
    @Description("Tests correctness of CASValue CAS operations.")
    @Outcome(id = "[5,2]", expect = Expect.ACCEPTABLE, desc = "T1
-> T2 execution.")
    @Outcome(id = "[1,10]", expect = Expect.ACCEPTABLE, desc = "T1
-> T2 execution.")
    public static class ValCas_ValCas {
        @Actor public void actor1(S s, LongResult2 r) {
            r.r1 = s.cas(0, 5) ? 5 : 1;
        }
        @Actor public void actor2(S s, LongResult2 r) {
            r.r2 = s.cas(0, 10) ? 10 : 2;
        }
    }
}
```

4. Save this file in the same folder as `CASValue.java`, that is, in `tests-custom/src/main/java/org/openjdk/jcstress/tests/`, and give it the name, `CASValueTests.java`.

5. The `CASValueTests` class is the container class for other classes within the test. This is not strictly required, but it helps to keep the code clean. The `ValCas_ValCas` class, which is annotated with `@JCStressTest`, is the test case class that contains two actors—methods annotated with `@Actor`. These are the methods that will be run in parallel by the test framework.

6. The subclass S, annotated with @State, is the state that was shared among the actors and, in this case, is the class under test. It extends our class, CASValue, and is created solely to avoid adding the @State annotation on CASValue.

7. The @Outcome annotations specify the outcomes of the test. The outcomes can be ACCEPTABLE, FORBIDDEN, ACCEPTABLE_INTERESTING, and ACCEPTABLE_SPEC. These are defined by the expect attribute. The id attribute provides the list of outcomes, whereas desc is just a description of the outcome. This test case specifies that, for our test, the only valid outcomes for the values in LongResul2 are 5 and 2 and 1 and 10, which are the only expected ones if CAS works as expected. Any other outcomes are forbidden and will cause the test case to fail, which is exactly what we want.

8. Now it's time to compile the test. To do this, run the following command from the source root directory of jcstress:

```
[user@localhost jcstress] mvn clean install -pl tests-custom -am
```

This will just run the build for the tests-custom project, which will compile the classes that we have just created.

9. The next step is to run our test and see if it works:

```
[user@localhost jcstress] java -jar tests-custom/target/jcstress.jar -t ".*CASValueTests.*"
```

The -t parameter in this command specifies that we only want to run the tests that satisfy the .*CASValueTests.* regular expression.

As expected, the tests should fail, as the provided implementation does implement the CAS operation correctly. The output should have several test outcomes similar to this one:

```
(ETA:        n/a) (R: 5.95E+08) (T:    1/1) (F: 1/1) (I: 1/5)
[FAILED] o.o.j.t.CASValueTests$ValCas_ValCas

Observed state  Occurrences Expectation Interpretation

[5, 2]   (3,230,666)         ACCEPTABLE T1 -> T2 execution.

[1, 10]  (2,613,825)         ACCEPTABLE T2 -> T1 execution.

[5, 10]  (7,609,449)         FORBIDDEN Other cases are not expected.
```

It shows how many outputs of each outcome were observed. So far, the incorrect outcome [5, 10] is the leader with 7,609,449 occurrences. This shows that the test worked correctly and helped us to identify that we need to fix our implementation on the CAS class.

10. Now let's fix our class and run the test again. The easiest, though not the most efficient, way to fix the problem is to simply add the `synchronized` modifier to our CAS method:

```
public class CASValue {
    private int i = 0;
    public synchronized boolean cas(int expected, int newValue) {
        boolean res = false;
        if (i == expected) {
            i = newValue;
            res = true;
        }
        return res;
    }
}
```

11. After changing the implementation, run the build again:

```
mvn clean install -pl tests-custom -am
```

12. Then, rerun the test:

```
java -jar tests-custom/target/jcstress.jar -t ".*CASValueTests.*"
```

13. Now, the test should not show any failures and report that the test runs were successful:

```
(ETA: n/a) (R: 3.35E+08) (T:    1/1) (F: 1/1) (I: 1/5) [OK]
o.o.j.t.CASValueTests$ValCas_ValCas

(ETA: 00:00:02) (R: 1.69E+07) (T:    1/1) (F: 1/1) (I: 2/5) [OK]
o.o.j.t.CASValueTests$ValCas_ValCas

(ETA: 00:00:01) (R: 1.22E+07) (T:    1/1) (F: 1/1) (I: 3/5) [OK]
o.o.j.t.CASValueTests$ValCas_ValCas

(ETA: 00:00:00) (R: 1.07E+07) (T:    1/1) (F: 1/1) (I: 4/5) [OK]
o.o.j.t.CASValueTests$ValCas_ValCas

(ETA: now) (R: 1.00E+07) (T:    1/1) (F: 1/1) (I: 5/5) [OK]
o.o.j.t.CASValueTests$ValCas_ValCas
```

This shows that the change in the implementation worked and the implementation is correct according to the test case.

By following these steps, a developer can ensure that a concurrent code works as expected according to the specification, as long as the tests and test cases are implemented and defined correctly. However, keep in mind that concurrency is something that is hard to test, and an implementation that works on one hardware can easily fail on other hardware. It means that it is recommended to run these test on the widest possible range of configurations.

See also

This framework is built and maintained by Aleksey Shipilëv who has his own blog and also delivers lectures in various conferences. We recommend that you visit his home page (`http://shipilev.net/`), watch his videos on YouTube (for example, `https://www.youtube.com/watch?v=4p4vL6EhzOk`), and read some of his papers. This will help you to get tons of information on correct concurrency testing, concurrency in general, support for concurrency in Java, and other related topics.

Creating a benchmark project using JMH

Micro benchmarking itself is not an easy topic, and doing it correctly using languages like Java is a very difficult task. These difficulties arise from the way Java executes the code and the infrastructure required by JVM. Just as things like JIT and GC may affect the results of micro benchmarking heavily, to ensure that the result of each run is consistent and correct might not be an easy task to accomplish. To help with this problem, there are several frameworks that can help to ensure that the benchmark test runs properly. One of these frameworks is **Java Microbenchmark Harness** (**JMH**), which is a part of OpenJDK. This recipe will explain how developers can use this framework to benchmark his/her own code.

Getting ready

This recipe requires a machine with an Internet connection, Maven, Java SDK, and your favorite IDE that has support for Maven projects.

How to do it...

The following steps will take you through the process of creating a benchmark project and writing the benchmark, which can be used to analyze the performance of the code:

1. In the command line, run the following Maven command:

   ```
   [user@localhost ~] mvn archetype:generate -DinteractiveMode=false
   -DarchetypeGroupId=org.openjdk.jmh -DarchetypeArtifactId=jmh-
   java-benchmark-archetype -DgroupId=org.benchmark
   -DartifactId=mybenchmark -Dversion=1.0
   ```

2. After running this command, in the current directory, Maven will create a folder with the name, `mybenchmark`, which will have the skeleton of the project. If all goes well, the build should end with an output that is similar to the following:

```
[INFO] project created from Archetype in dir: /home/user/openjdk/
mybenchmark
[INFO] ------------------------------------------------------------
[INFO] BUILD SUCCESS
[INFO] ------------------------------------------------------------
[INFO] Total time: 9.188s
[INFO] Finished at: Sat Aug 02 20:16:01 BST 2014
[INFO] Final Memory: 11M/129M
[INFO] ------------------------------------------------------------
```

3. Now, when the project is generated, we can start working with it and create our first microbenchmark test. Open the generated project file (`/home/user/openjdk/mybenchmark/pom.xml`) with your favorite IDE. Ensure that Maven is correctly configured and all dependencies are downloaded correctly. Notice that there is already a class created for the benchmark whose name is `org.benchmark.MyBenchmark`. At the beginning, all it has is a single method where we will later put the code we are going to test.

4. As an example, let's test something that is relatively simple but has some room for improvement. A binary search is a good choice for this purpose. So, let's draft a simple implementation and put it into the `org.benchmark.BinarySearch1` class as shown next:

```
package org.benchmark;
public class BinarySearch1 {
    public static int search(long[] arr, long value) {
        return search(arr, value, 0, arr.length-1);
    }

    private static int search(long[] arr, long value, int start,
int end) {
        if (end < start)
            return -1;

        int imid = start + ((end - start) / 2);
        if (arr[imid] > value)
            return search(arr, value, start, imid-1);
        else if (arr[imid] < value)
            return search(arr, value, imid+1, end);
```

```
        else
            return imid;
    }
```

This is a very basic implementation, which will be fine for our experiment. If you are not familiar with binary search or where to get more information about this algorithm, visit the Wikipedia page at http://en.wikipedia.org/wiki/Binary_search_algorithm.

5. Now, when the first draft of the implementation is ready, we will create a microbenchmark for it. Put the following code into the `org.benchmark`. `MyBenchmark` class:

```
package org.benchmark;

import org.openjdk.jmh.annotations.*;
import java.util.Arrays;
import java.util.concurrent.TimeUnit;

@State(value = Scope.Thread)
@BenchmarkMode(Mode.AverageTime)
@OutputTimeUnit(TimeUnit.NANOSECONDS)
public class MyBenchmark {
    private long[] data = new long[5000];

    @Setup
    public void setup() {
        for (int i = 0; i != data.length; ++i) {
            data[i]=(long)(Math.random()*Long.MAX_VALUE-1);
        }
        Arrays.sort(data);
    }

    @Benchmark
    public int testBinarySearch1 () {
        return BinarySearch1.search(data, Long.MAX_VALUE);
    }
}
```

This code requires some clarification. The `@State` annotation is required to tell JMH that this class contains some data that is used by the tests, and that data in the `Scope.Thread` scope means that it will not be shared between several threads.

The `@BenchmarkMode(Mode.AverageTime)` annotation says that what we want to measure is the average time required to execute our test, which, by default, measures throughput. The `@OutputTimeUnit(TimeUnit.MICROSECONDS)` annotation sets `timeunit`. We need to define it, as the default is in seconds, which is a very big scale for the benchmark.

The setup method is annotated with the `@Setup` annotation, which means that it does some preparation for the tests and it will be called to initialize the data for the test. It is similar to the `@Before` annotation from JUnit. Keep in mind that this method is executed only once before running the test in the fork on JVM. It is not executed before each test method is called. This means that the same test method will work with the same data after each iteration.

The actual test is in the method annotated with `@Benchmark` that executes the code that we are testing.

6. Now that everything is set up, run a test and find out how fast our code is. First, let's build the project with our code and test it. To do this, go to the folder with the project and run the following command:

   ```
   [user@localhost mybenchmark] mvn clean install
   ```

7. Then, run the benchmark:

   ```
   [user@localhost mybenchmark] java -jar target/benchmarks.jar
   --wi=10 --i=5 --f=1 --jvmArgs=-server
   ```

   Here `wi` defines the number of `warmup` iterations, `i` the number of test run iterations, `f` says how many JVM forks to use, and `jvmArgs` are the parameters for forked JVM.

   The output for each of our test methods should look like this:

   ```
   # VM invoker: C:\Usres\User\jdk1.7.0\jre\bin\java.exe
   # VM options: -server
   # Warmup: 10 iterations, 1 s each
   # Measurement: 5 iterations, 1 s each
   # Threads: 1 thread, will synchronize iterations
   # Benchmark mode: Average time, time/op
   # Benchmark: org.benchmark.MyBenchmark.testBinarySearch1

   # Run progress: 0.00% complete, ETA 00:00:15
   # Fork: 1 of 1
   # Warmup Iteration   1: 74.562 ns/op
   # Warmup Iteration   2: 75.657 ns/op
   # Warmup Iteration   3: 79.575 ns/op
   ```

```
# Warmup Iteration    4: 75.718 ns/op
# Warmup Iteration    5: 76.432 ns/op
# Warmup Iteration    6: 75.965 ns/op
# Warmup Iteration    7: 73.987 ns/op
# Warmup Iteration    8: 75.677 ns/op
# Warmup Iteration    9: 76.326 ns/op
# Warmup Iteration   10: 77.050 ns/op
Iteration    1: 77.027 ns/op
Iteration    2: 75.870 ns/op
Iteration    3: 77.674 ns/op
Iteration    4: 81.460 ns/op
Iteration    5: 73.858 ns/op


Result: 77.178 ±(99.9%) 10.778 ns/op [Average]
  Statistics: (min, avg, max) = (73.858, 77.178, 81.460), stdev =
2.799
  Confidence interval (99.9%): [66.400, 87.956]


# Run complete. Total time: 00:00:18
Benchmark                          Mode   Samples   Score   Score
error   Units

o.b.MyBenchmark.testBinarySearch1     avgt         5   77.178
10.778   ns/op
```

The output shows the runs executed for each fork and the final result. Here we can see that, on average, our method takes `77.178` nanoseconds to run.

8. Now that we have the results, what to do with them? Generally, these results make sense only when they are compared with something else. Let's try to make some changes to the code and see whether it helps our implementation of binary search to work faster. We can try to remove recursion and see how it's going to work. Create another class with the name, `org.benchmark.BinarySearch2`, and put the following implementation there:

```
package org.benchmark;
public class BinarySearch2 {
    public static int search(long[] arr, long value) {
        return search(arr, value, 0, arr.length-1);
    }
    private static int search(long[] arr, long value, int start,
int end) {
```

```
        while (end >= start) {
            int imid = start + ((end - start) / 2);
            if(arr[imid] == value)
                return imid;
            else if (arr[imid] < value)
                start = imid + 1;
            else
                end = imid - 1;
        }
        return -1;
    }
}
```

This is the iterative implementation, which doesn't use recursive calls.

9. Now let's update the benchmark class so that we can compare recursive and iterative implementations:

```java
package org.benchmark;

import org.openjdk.jmh.annotations.*;
import java.util.Arrays;
import java.util.concurrent.TimeUnit;

@State(value = Scope.Group)
@BenchmarkMode(Mode.AverageTime)
@OutputTimeUnit(TimeUnit.NANOSECONDS)
public class MyBenchmark {
    private long[] data = new long[500000];

    @Setup
    public void setup() {
        for (int i = 0; i != data.length; ++i) {
            data[i] = (long)(Math.random() * (Long.MAX_VALUE-1));
        }
        Arrays.sort(data);
    }

    @Benchmark
    @Group(value = "bsearch")
    public int testBinarySearch1() {
        return BinarySearch1.search(data, Long.MAX_VALUE);
    }

    @Benchmark
```

```
    @Group(value = "bsearch")
    public int testBinarySearch2() {
        return BinarySearch2.search(data, Long.MAX_VALUE);
    }
}
```

The difference between this benchmark and the previous version is that this uses the benchmarking groups that give us a simple comparison of our implementations. The `@State` annotation now has to have the `Group` scope, otherwise the tests will be using different data instances, which is not what we would want, as we want algorithms to work in exactly the same conditions.

10. Now, rebuild the project:

    ```
    [user@localhost mybenchmark] mvn clean install
    ```

11. Then, run the test again:

    ```
    [user@localhost mybenchmark] java -jar target/benchmarks.jar
    --wi=10 --i=5 --f=1 --jvmArgs=-server
    ```

    The output is going to be slightly different from the previous one, because of the use of groups. The main difference in which we are interested is going to be at the end of the report:

    ```
    # Run complete. Total time: 00:00:18
    ```

Benchmark	Mode	Samples	Score
Score error Units			
o.b.MyBenchmark.bsearch	avgt	5	66.929
1.663 ns/op			
o.b.MyBenchmark.bsearch:testBinarySearch1	avgt	5	79.717
2.289 ns/op			
o.b.MyBenchmark.bsearch:testBinarySearch2	avgt	5	54.141
1.209 ns/op			

    What we can see here is that, for this particular configuration (which includes machine spec, version of JDK, OS, and so on), iterative implementation, which is implemented by the method, `testBinarySearch2()`, is on average faster than the recursive one, implemented by `testBinarySearch1()` (54.141 < 79.717).

After going through this recipe, you have learned how to run microbenchmark tests, how to interpret results, and how to compare the performance of different implementations. Ensure that you microbenchmark each hard task properly and remember that the results can vary significantly on different machines, JVM versions, and so on.

There's more...

JMH is a flexible framework that provides flexibility to the way it can be used. For example, if someone wants to run tests via the main method, without using `benchmarks.jar`, this can be easily achieved. To do this, just add the following main method to `MyBenchmark` and run it:

```
public static void main(String[] args) throws RunnerException {
    Options opt = new OptionsBuilder()
            .include(".*" + MyBenchmark.class.getSimpleName() + ".*")
            .warmupIterations(3)
            .measurementIterations(3)
            .forks(2)
            .build();
    new Runner(opt).run();
}
```

This example will give the same result as running the following command:

```
[user@localhost mybenchmark] java -jar target/benchmarks.jar --wi=3 --i=3
--f=2
```

We also recommend that you download the source code (see the *Downloading source and compiling JHM* recipe). Have a look at the recipe and JavaDocs, as the JavaDocs are well written and explain a lot about the framework.

See also

Similar to jcstress, this framework is also built and maintained by Aleksey Shipilëv who has his own blog and also delivers lectures in various conferences. We recommend you visit his home page (`http://shipilev.net/`), watch his videos on YouTube (for example, `https://www.youtube.com/watch?v=4p4vL6EhzOk`), and read some of his papers.

Downloading the source and compiling JHM

Similar to all other OpenJDK tools and projects, there is an option to download the source of the JHM and build it yourself. This might be required if a framework requires customization and an extension fix. Luckily the process is very easy and straightforward.

Getting ready

This recipe requires a machine with an Internet connection that is capable of running Mercurial and Maven. Basically, the requirements are the same as that for compiling and running `jcstress` (see the *Building and running jcstress* recipe).

How to do it...

The following steps will lead you through the process of downloading the source code and building JHM:

1. To start, let's run the following command to download the source files:

   ```
   hg clone http://hg.openjdk.java.net/code-tools/jmh/ jmh
   ```

   This command will download the source files and put them into the jmh folder.

2. The next step is to build the source code. The build requires Maven to be installed on the machine. Change the current folder to jmh and run the following command:

   ```
   mvn clean install -DskipTests
   ```

   This command should generate an output similar to the following:

   ```
   [INFO] ------------------------------------------------------------
   [INFO] BUILD SUCCESS
   [INFO] ------------------------------------------------------------
   [INFO] Total time: 3:14.052s
   [INFO] Finished at: Sat Aug 02 19:43:39 BST 2014
   [INFO] Final Memory: 38M/176M
   [INFO] ------------------------------------------------------------
   ```

   This means that the build was successful.

3. Now, the final step is to change your benchmark project to use the version of JHM that was just built. Assuming the project references of the JHM version are by properties, just change the version of the JHM dependency in your project to 1.0-SNAPHOT:

   ```
   <properties>
       ...
       <jmh.version>0.9.3</jmh.version>
   </properties>
   ```

How it works...

When you run Maven with the install target, it will put the newly built version of the artefact in the local repository. In this case, the version is 1.0-SNAPSHOT. When another project has dependency on that version, Maven will pick the version from the local repository and use it.

10

Contributing to OpenJDK

In this chapter, we will cover the following topics:

- ▶ Becoming a contributor
- ▶ Generating a patch with webrev
- ▶ Backporting OpenJDK v9 patches to OpenJDK v8
- ▶ Understanding OpenJDK groups
- ▶ Understanding OpenJDK projects
- ▶ Suggesting new JSRs
- ▶ Suggesting new JEPs

Introduction

The OpenJDK community consists of lots of people who have different roles and responsibilities in a project. Such a structure evolved as a consequence of the scale of the project and its significance, otherwise it wouldn't be controllable and you wouldn't be able to progress further. The way in which OpenJDK is managed and structured can be described in two hierarchies: one is functional and the other is governance. These two hierarchies intercept, but not much. The only role which is present in both is **JDK Lead**, which is an OpenJDK member appointed by Oracle to manage the Java release project.

Functional hierarchy controls the change and development process. It defines the relationship between all the community members who are involved in proposing and making changes in OpenJDK. On the whole, it can be represented by the structure shown in the following figure:

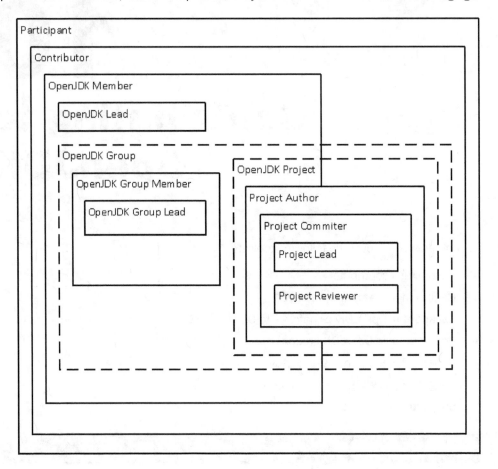

A participant can be anyone who has participated in an OpenJDK project and this can be any type of participation. For example, it can be a discussion on the mailing list or creating a patch to fix a bug. Any participant can sign the **Oracle Contributor Agreement (OCA)** and become a contributor.

A contributor can work on any of the OpenJDK projects and be the **project author** if the project lead approves it. The project author can't push code into the repository and has to ask one of the project committers to do that. After an author gains the trust of the committers, he or she can be elected to become one of them. All code changes have to be approved before they go into the repository. This task is done by the project reviewers who are experienced committers and have a lot of authority. Some projects might not have the project reviewer's role.

Also, a contributor can become an OpenJDK member and participate in the OpenJDK groups. To become an OpenJDK member, the contributor needs to demonstrate a history of significant contribution and should be elected by the votes of the existing OpenJDK members. Being a member allows one to become an OpenJDK group member by joining one or more groups. Group members are nominated by existing group members so, to join a group, a member must have some history of contribution to that group. It is worth adding that the order of membership can be reversed—a contributor can be elected to become a group member and this can then become the route to be an OpenJDK member.

Each OpenJDK group is responsible for the area of JDK. For example, there is a *Swing Group*, *Security Group*, and so on. Each group has a group lead and group members. A group can sponsor projects, for example, as already mentioned, the Swing Group is a sponsor for projects such as *OpenJFX* and *Swing Application Framework*. As we mentioned earlier, any contributor can work on a sponsored project. The contributor is not required to be an Open JDK member or a group member to do this.

The governance structure is represented by the *Governing Board*, which consists of several roles, as follows:

- ▶ **Chair**: This role is appointed by Oracle. This person is the lead of the Governing Board.

- ▶ **Vice Chair**: This role is appointed by IBM

- ▶ **OpenJDK Lead**: This role is appointed by Oracle. This person also leads the Java Release project.

- ▶ **Two At-Large members**: These two members are chosen by a vote of the OpenJDK members.

The governing board's responsibility is to define new processes or refine existing ones, and update and support the Bylaws. The Governing Board is empowered to resolve procedural disputes within community, but it is not an executive body. The latter means that it has no direct authority over the technical or release decisions. Interestingly, the Governing Board and also the OpenJDK group can also sponsor projects.

For those who are interested in the details of the hierarchy of OpenJDK roles, groups, projects, and their relationships, it is worth taking a look at the *bylaws* (`http://openjdk.java.net/bylaws`), which cover all these things in detail.

Becoming a contributor

Becoming a participant is very easy. The only thing that is required is to be interested in OpenJDK and, as a minimum, participate in discussions on mailing lists. Participants can ask OpenJDK members to add code into the code base, but they can't do it themselves. Contributors, however, have a more involved role, These people can submit patches and have more influence on the project.

Getting ready

To get ready to follow this recipe is easy; all that is required is a desire to become a participant. It is important to understand that it is not a quick process and can easily take several weeks or even months. So, be patient and do not give up.

As preparing a patch requires running the Kron shell script, a machine needs to have that shell installed. If a Windows machine is used, then Cygwin is required on the system.

How to do it...

The next steps will describe how to become a participant of OpenJDK. Keep in mind that this is not a deterministic process and, in practice, it might either need a few additional steps or some of the following steps might not be required:

1. The first step is to become visible to other members of the OpenJDK community. This can be achieved by participating in the discussions on mailing lists, and it would be good to suggest a couple of small fixes and ask one of the OpenJDK members or contributors to submit them. This will show that you are interested in OpenJDK and how to contribute to it.

2. Then, create an account in `Java.net` by filling the form at `https://java.net/people/new`. This account is needed for `Java.net`, OpenJDK bug tracking, and the source repository.

3. The next step is to sign the **Oracle Contribution Agreement** (**OCA**). It needs to be downloaded from `http://www.oracle.com/technetwork/oca-405177.pdf`. Read the agreement carefully and understand it, before signing it. Luckily, it is just one page long. Then, sign it and e-mail the scan to `oracle-ca_us@oracle.com`. It might take a couple of weeks to receive a response. So, if the stipulated time has passed and you still haven't heard back, then it is worth sending a reminder.

4. Once you get back the OCA response from Oracle, it's time to find out what your contribution is going to be. Probably, the easiest thing is to find a bug and work on a fix for it. Bugs can be found on the OpenJDK JIRA at `https://bugs.openjdk.java.net/`. Pick something that is not assigned to anyone. Be sure to choose something that will not require interface changes or any significant development.

5. Before doing the actual work, it would be a good idea to discuss the bug and the proposed fix on the mailing list for the appropriate project. It is recommended to use the format, `<bugid>: <bug_description>` as the subject, for example, `JDK-8042253: StressRedefine tests timeout`.

6. Carry out a fix. It is good idea to do the jtreg regression test for any work that was done in the scope of the fix.

7. Generate a patch for review using `webrev`: `[user@localhost hotspot]$ ksh ../make/scripts/webrev.ksh`. Make sure that the generated `webrev.zip` file is available for the relevant community. For example, it can be put on a file hosting with public access. Regular contributors prefer to use `cr.openjdk.java.net` for this purpose. For more details about webrev, see the *Generating a patch with webrev* recipe.

8. To post a patch, use the format `RFR <bugid>: <bug_description>`, as the subject for the mailing list. For example, `RFR JDK-8042253 StressRedefine tests timeout`, where **RFR** refers to **Request for Review**. Give the description of the patch and provide a link to the `webrev` file generated in the previous step.

9. A review always means that there will be some cleanup, code changes, more tests, and so on. Carry out the updates, update `webrev`, and notify other members that changes have been made. Be ready since the process might need several iterations.

10. Once everyone agrees that the fix is of a good quality, the sponsor will push the fix into the repository. At this stage, you might be asked to produce a changeset. Note that this step can take several weeks to execute.

See also

▸ Some additional information on the code review process is available at `http://openjdk.java.net/guide/codeReview.html`. There is also documentation available on the change process as a whole. It is worth having a look at it at `http://openjdk.java.net/guide/changePlanning.html`.

Generating a patch with webrev

Doing any update in a software product normally requires some kind of review process. The code should not be submitted into a repository unless someone else has already looked at it. In OpenJDK, the tool for this purpose is webrev, which allows you to create code reviews that can be shared with other members of the community.

Getting ready

Webrev is a Korn shell script, which means that Korn shell must be installed on the machine before you can use it. On a Linux machine, run `yum install ksh` or an equivalent command. On a Windows machine, ensure that `ksh` in included in the Cygwin installation.

Apart from the environment set up to create the patch review, some changes must be made in the source code as well. As an easy example, we can just modify some comments in a file, as discussed next. Open the file, `hotspot/src/os/linux/vm/jvm_linux.cpp` and update the header or just add a comment.

How to do it...

As webdev is a shell script, start by launching your shell and follow the given steps. It is assumed that the current folder is `jdk` source root and the amended file is `hotspot/src/os/linux/vm/jvm_linux.cpp`:

1. First, change the current folder to `hostpot`; it's not strictly required, but it will make the webrev script do less work:

   ```
   cd ./hostpot
   ```

2. Run the webrev script:

   ```
   [user@localhost hotspot]$ ksh ../make/scripts/webrev.ksh
       SCM detected: mercurial
       No outgoing, perhaps you haven't commited.
           Workspace: /home/user/openjdk/jdk7u/hotspot
       Compare against:
          http://hg.openjdk.java.net/jdk7u/jdk7u/hotspot
            Output to: /home/user/openjdk/jdk7u_clean/hotspot/webrev
       Output Files:
       src/os/linux/vm/jvm_linux.cpp
           patch cdiffs udiffs sdiffs frames old new
          index.html: grep: /home/user/.hgrc:
          No such file or directory
   Done.
   Output to: /home/user/openjdk/jdk7u/hotspot/webrev
   ```

   As can be seen from the output, it detected that `jvm_linux.cpp` was changed and generated review files which were put in the `hotspot/webrev` folder.

3. Now, in the `hotspot` folder, locate the `webrev.zip` file and make it available to anyone who is interested in the changes that you have just made. This file will have the same content as the `webrev` folder.

How it works...

As you have already noticed, webrev is just a shell script and, if you need to see how it works, then it should be relatively easy to do so. All it does is scan your disk for changes and compare them with the parent Mercurial forest. Then, based on the comparison, it generates various reports and a patch file. Finally, all the files are packed into a ZIP file, which is easy to share with other community members or with anyone who just wants to have a look at the change.

There's more...

Webrev has some command options which are displayed if you enter a command, which it doesn't understand. For example, try to run this:

```
[stas@localhost hotspot]$ ksh ../make/scripts/webrev.ksh ?
```

This will print all the available command-line options and environment variables that can affect the execution of the script.

See also

▶ More information and several examples are available on the `openjdk.java.net` website at `http://openjdk.java.net/guide/webrevHelp.html`

▶ The overall OpenJDK code review process is described at `http://openjdk.java.net/guide/codeReview.html`

Backporting OpenJDK v9 patches to OpenJDK v8

In the scope of one of the initiatives for the improvement of the source code structure (`https://bugs.openjdk.java.net/browse/JDK-8051619`) there are some significant changes in the way how the source files are located in OpenJDK v9. It means that if someone is making a patch for OpenJDK v9 and wants these changes to be applied to OpenJDK v8, he/she has to follow a special procedure. That procedure will do the required transformation in the path of changed files.

Getting ready

We need a computer which can run bash shell, that is, a Linux or Windows computer with Cygwin and the source code of OpenJDK v9 and OpenJDK v8.

How to do it...

Following these steps, a developer can learn how to port changes from OpenJDK v9 to OpenJDK v8:

1. There is a special script that was created to help to port patches from OpenJDK v9 to OpenJDK v8. This script is located in `common/bin/unshuffle_patch.sh`. Run this script with the `--help` argument to see its usage:

    ```
    [user@localhost jdk9]$ common/bin/unshuffle_patch.sh --help

    Usage: common/bin/unshuffle_patch.sh [-h|--help] [-v|--verbose]
    <repo> <input_patch> <output_patch>

    where:

    <repo>             is one of: corba, jaxp, jaxws, jdk, langtools,
    nashorn

                       [Note: patches from other repos do not need
    updating]

    <input_patch>      is the input patch file, that needs shuffling/
    unshuffling

    <output_patch>     is the updated patch file
    ```

    If you can see the help output, it means that the script is available and should just work fine.

2. Now. just make the required change in the source tree, commit the code, and generate a patch. For our example, we will edit the `Sockets.java` file. Just add a new line with a few comments in it as shown:

    ```
    [user@localhost jdk9]$ vi ./jdk/src/java.base/share/classes/jdk/
    net/Sockets.java

    now commit the change:

    [user@localhost jdk9]$ cd jdk

    [user@localhost jdk]$ hg commit
    ```

3. Next, get the revision number of the changeset:

    ```
    [user@localhost jdk]$ hg log -l 1

    changeset:    11063:9742f66b011

    tag:          tip

    user:         User <user@user.org>

    date:         Sun Dec 14 21:16:27 2014 +0000

    summary:      test commit
    ```

4. Now, export the changeset that we just created to a patch file in an extended GIT format:

```
[user@localhost jdk]$ hg export -r 11063 --git > 11064.patch
```

5. Then, run the script to make the patch compatible with the OpenJDK 8 source code tree:

```
[user@localhost jdk]$ ../common/bin/unshuffled_patch.sh jdk 11063.
patch 11063_updated.patch
```

6. Finally, change the current folder to the `jdk` directory in the `jdk8u` source root, copy the updated patch to it, and apply it:

```
[user@localhost jdk]$ cp ../../jdk9/jdk9/11063_updated.patch ./
```
```
[user@localhost jdk]$ hg import 11063_updated.patch
```

And that's it. Now all that is required is to commit the changes and then follow the normal process of making the changes in OpenJDK.

See also

> ▶ To get some more information and to be up-to-date with the changes in the utilities, it is recommended that you visit its home page at `http://cr.openjdk.java. net/~chegar/docs/portingScript.html`

Understanding OpenJDK groups

OpenJDK groups look at wide areas of OpenJDK and define what projects are required to support these areas. For example, the Compiler Group's sponsored project Coin added new language features in JDK7, and the HotSpot Group's sponsored project Graal makes VM functionality available via a set of APIs. The groups usually have a much longer life than the projects and do not appear and disappear very often.

Getting ready

All that is required is a computer with access to the Internet, a web browser, and some patience.

How to do it...

The following steps demonstrate documentation and some examples of groups on OpenJDK. They'll also show what groups are, how they are managed, created, and what they do:

1. To become familiar with the definition of groups in OpenJDK, go to `http://openjdk.java.net/groups/`. There is information about various processes and procedures required to support groups and to make them function well. These procedures include the following topics:

   ❑ Proposing a new group.

   ❑ Nominating a contributor to become a group member.

   ❑ Nominating a group member to become an OpenJDK member

   ❑ Nominating a group lead

2. Each group has some web content that is available publically. It can be found on the left-hand side of `http://openjdk.java.net/`, under **Groups**. Usually the content on a group's page has a relatively standard structure and contains information such as the introduction, a list of specifications supported by the group, documentation, some guidelines on how to contribute, where to find the source code, and so on. Also, there are links to the mailing lists, blogs, and contact details. As an example, take a look at the JMX Group webpage at `http://openjdk.java.net/groups/jmx/`.

3. We also recommended that you have a look at the list of projects and see which groups they belong to. This will give some idea about the relationship between groups and projects. The list of projects can be found on the left-hand side of `http://openjdk.java.net/` under **Groups**.

See also

It is worth spending some time exploring `http://openjdk.java.net/` to see what is available and which groups exist. As we have already mentioned, group creation doesn't happen very often and no new groups have been created since 2007. The last one was the Conformance Group, which was proposed in September 2007. You can find the proposal e-mail in the mailing list archive at `http://mail.openjdk.java.net/pipermail/announce/2007-September.txt`. See the last message in that file.

Understanding OpenJDK projects

OpenJDK projects aim to deliver some kind of an artefact, which can be a source code, documentation, or something else. Projects are sponsored by one or more OpenJDK groups. By their nature, projects are much more short-lived than groups and often can cover the implementation of JEPs or JSRs.

How to do it...

This recipe takes you through some sources of information that are available about OpenJDK projects and gives some high-level information about them:

1. Similar to OpenJDK Groups, there is a web page that gives some definitions about the projects and defines how they function. This page is available at `http://openjdk.java.net/projects/`. Among the list of procedures, you will find the following:

   - Becoming an Author
   - Appointing a Contributor to be an Author
   - Nominating a Contributor or Author to be a Committer
   - Nominating a Committer to be a Reviewer
   - Proposing a New Project

2. Very similar to groups, each project also has its own page on `http://openjdk.java.net/`. The list of projects and the links to their pages can be found on the left-hand side of the website under **Projects**. The project page is not very informative, but might have a link to a wiki, which usually contains lots of information.

3. As an example of how projects are created, we can look at the proposal for the project *Sumatra*, which can be found at `http://mail.openjdk.java.net/pipermail/announce/2012-September/000135.html`. This thread also contains the voting results and, therefore, the decision to create that project.

See also

- As usual, it is recommended that you spend some time exploring `http://openjdk.java.net/` to see which projects are available.

Suggesting new JSRs

A **Java Specification Request (JSR)** is the request for a change to the specifications of the Java language, APS, JVM, and so on. Such changes are governed by the **Java Community Process (JCP)**, where every member of the community can register and participate in the review.

This recipe is written as if you were submitting a JSR, but keep in mind that JSRs are not usually submitted by a single individual, but by a group of experts who come out with a proposal. The group has a Spec Lead who submits the JSR. So, this recipe is more about giving you a high-level understanding of the process, helping you to see how JSRs work, and what it is all about. To get some deeper insight, see the resources provided in the *See also* section.

In the following recipe, it can be seen that being a spec lead for JSR is not only a technical position, but it also involves doing lots of work with people and requires one to possess a good amount of soft and leadership skills. The leader has to push the project forward and has to be capable of handling difficult situations. There can be cases when some members of group of experts, for some reason, can't participate any more, or there is clash of personalities. The other possible situation is when the JSR itself faces complicated questions and is challenged by the other community members. Such questions have to be answered clearly and with enough knowledge and passion for people to believe that it's worth going forward and including that JSR into the JDK.

Getting ready

As this is a more procedural recipe, all that is required is a computer with access to the Internet and a web browser.

How to do it...

The following steps, on a high-level, go through the stages of a JSR lifecycle, starting from the idea and finishing with the actual implemented change:

1. As a start, it would be good to create a JCP account. This is required to submit a JSR proposal and to participate in any part of a JCP. The process is very simple. Just go to `https://jcp.org/en/home/index` and follow the steps in the registration link.

2. It is good idea to explore the site and see what's already available there. The list of all JSRs is available at `https://www.jcp.org/en/jsr/all`. Since the whole list can have too much information, there are options to filter JSRs by their stage in the approval process (`https://www.jcp.org/en/jsr/stage`), by technology (`https://www.jcp.org/en/jsr/tech`), by committee (`https://www.jcp.org/en/jsr/ec`), or by the platform (`https://www.jcp.org/en/jsr/platform`). There is also a list of JSRs by the ballot results, where you can find the results of voting for each year at `https://www.jcp.org/en/jsr/vote_summary`.

3. If your proposal is something worth doing, then, similar to all OpenJDK change processes, describe the proposal on the relevant mailing list. This will ensure that the whole thing makes sense and helps to improve the quality of the material. As a spec lead, you need to have followers, that is, a group of experts who will participate in the JCR and push it forward. Such people can be found on mailing lists, relevant forums, or can be anyone who has the right mindset to participate and feels that your idea is worth doing.

4. To make an actual submission, fill the **Java Specification Request Proposal**, which is available at `https://jcp.org/en/jsr/proposal`. After submission, the JSR has to go through the **JSR Approval Ballot**, which will determine whether the initial JSR submission should be approved.

5. In the next stage, the group has to start working as a team, push the proposal forward, discuss it, and answer questions from other members of the community. It would be a good idea to have regular team calls, and regular face-to-face discussions can also be beneficial. This stage is probably the most important one, as it forms the precise shape of the JSR.

6. All discussions have to be publically available and the expert group that has proposed the JSR has to publically answer all the raised questions. This also means that there has to be a publically available archive of all the communication on the matter.

7. When all the responses for all the comments and questions have been received and the JSR is updated accordingly, it is ready for the final submission. The spec lead is responsible for completion and submitting the **Technology Compatibly Kit** (**TCK**) and the **Reference Implementation** (**RI**). If a JSR is targeted to several environments, then it might be required to submit a TCK and RI for each platform. The submission has to follow the process described in the *Final Release* section of the JCP 2 process at `https://jcp.org/en/procedures/jcp2#4`.

8. After the final successful approval ballot, the spec lead will become the maintenance lead and the JSR will move to the maintenance stage. For details, see the *Maintenance* section of JCP 2 process at `https://jcp.org/en/procedures/jcp2#5`.

See also

As the whole process is governed by JCP, it would be a good idea for you to go through the document at `https://jcp.org/en/procedures/jcp2`, which describes the latest version of the process. At the time of writing, the latest version was 2.9.

On the JCP website at `https://jcp.org/en/resources/speclead_life`, there is a good article about being a spec lead that has some good insights and advice. It covers almost all the aspects of the role, starting from the submission of a JSR, and ending with building a team and communicating with people. It is definitely worth reading.

As part of the JSR process, one is required to submit the **Technology Compatibility Kit** (**TCK**). This is the suite of tests that are designed to ensure that a particular implementation is compliant with the JSR. This piece can be considered as one of the most complicated parts of the JSR application. The most common tool to implement the set of tests is JT Harness, but there are also some cases where the TCK might be implemented based on JUnit or TestNG.

The next revision of JCP is going to update some of the current process. This revision is covered by JSR 358. To get more information about it, visit its home page at `https://java.net/projects/jsr358/pages/Home` and the JRS page at `https://jcp.org/en/jsr/detail?id=358`.

Suggesting new JEPs

JEP is the abbreviation for JDK Enhancement Proposal. It means a relatively big change in OpenJDK that requires significant implementation effort, but it doesn't imply changes in the Java specification. The definition of JEP is covered in *JEP 1 JDK Enhancement-Proposal & Roadmap Process* which explains the details of definition of JEP, the process and the required documentation. As defined in JEP 1 (`http://openjdk.java.net/jeps/1`), JEP has to meet at least one of the following criteria:

- ▸ It requires two or more weeks of engineering effort
- ▸ It makes a significant change to the JDK, or to the processes and the infrastructure by which it is developed
- ▸ It is in high demand by the developers or the customers

This recipe will cover the definition of JEPs, their lifecycle, and how to find the latest information about them. It will also go through steps that are required for the creation of a JEP. Such an approach will allow you to get a good understanding of the process and see what JEPs are.

Getting ready

This recipe doesn't require any special tools. All you need is this book and, preferably, a computer with a web browser.

How to do it...

To start with, it is a good idea to have a look at what has already been submitted as JEPs. To get the full list of JEPs, just go to `http://openjdk.java.net/jeps/`. There, you can find the complete list of JEPs with their status, name, and some more information about them. Here is an example of what you can see there:

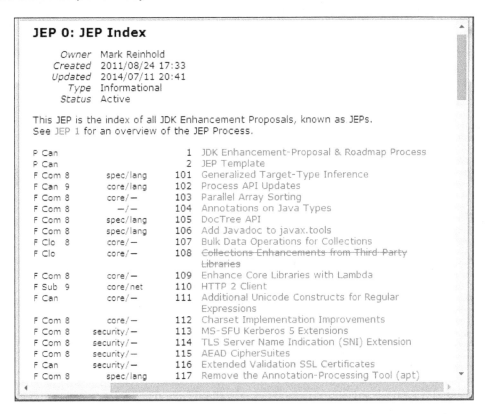

As you can see from the list, the table of JEPs has several columns, which give a brief overview and some additional information. For example, the first column is the type of the JEP, P stands for Process, F for Feature, and so on. It is not that hard to find out the meaning of specific values if you click on **JEP** and have a look at its header:

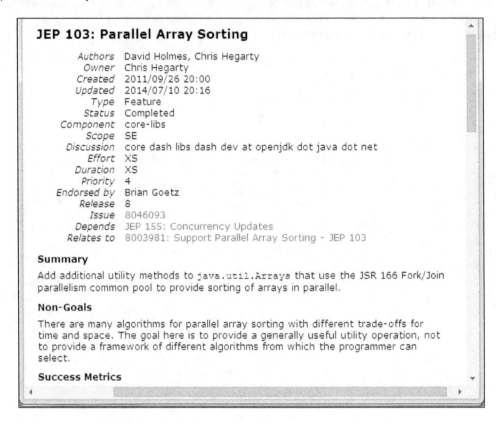

Assuming that we have something completely new that is not in the list, and which definitely has to become a part of OpenJDK:

1. The next step is to read through *JEP 1: JDK Enhancement-Proposal & Roadmap Process*, which is available at http://openjdk.java.net/jeps/1. This covers the process and some mechanics of the process.

2. The next step is to do some more reading. *JEP 2: JEP Template* contains the template of the JEP. This template has to be filled in with the proposal details. The details will cover the overview, testing, dependencies, and so on. It is worthwhile looking at other JEP examples to fill the template. There is also a sample draft, available at http://cr.openjdk.java.net/~mr/jep/draft-mcimadamore-inference-01.md.

3. Before attempting to publish a JEP, it would be a good idea to submit the proposal to the appropriate OpenJDK mailing lists for discussion. This will help you to produce a high quality proposal.

4. When the proposal is ready for submission, send it to `jep-submit@openjdk.java.net`. After this, assuming that the proposal has adequate quality, it will be available in the repository (`http://hg.openjdk.java.net/jep/jeps`) and the webpage which was mentioned in step 1 of this recipe.

5. After this, there will be several rounds of updates and discussions, which might eventually result in the JEP being approved and having its status changed to `Candidate`. This means that it is accepted for inclusion and has a good chance of being funded for one of the next versions. It would be worth mentioning that a JEP can also be rejected, which means that it was decided that it was not worth implementing at all.

6. When a JEP is transferred to the status `Funded`, it means that the group or area lead is happy to fund it. This means that the actual implementation can now be initiated and will be included in one of the future versions.

How it works...

As was already mentioned earlier, the detailed process is described in *JEP 1: JDK Enhancement-Proposal & Roadmap Process*. Similar to all OpenJDK changes, this process requires lots of involvement from the community and OpenJDK members.

See also

- ▶ *JEP 1: JDK Enhancement-Proposal & Roadmap Process* at `http://openjdk.java.net/jeps/1`

- ▶ *JEP 2: JEP Template* at `http://openjdk.java.net/jeps/2`

- ▶ It would be good for you to take a look at some exciting discussions of JEP on mailing lists at `http://mail.openjdk.java.net/pipermail/jdk9-dev/2014-May/000781.html`.

- ▶ There is a JEP at `http://cr.openjdk.java.net/~mr/jep/jep-2.0-02.html` that suggests some changes in the existing process. The current state is *Draft*, but eventually most of the proposals will be applied to the current process.

11
Troubleshooting

In this chapter, we will cover the following topics:

- ▸ Navigating through the process workflow
- ▸ Submitting a defect to the OpenJDK bug systems
- ▸ Creating a patch using NetBeans
- ▸ Creating a code review

Introduction

OpenJDK's openness is its most valuable feature in our fast-paced world. We can be sure that it will never vanish and be forgotten when it is needed. If its support is discontinued, we can support it ourselves. We could fix bugs independently, since the code is open.

However, OpenJDK, as well as the Oracle Java implementation, still contains a lot of issues. Some of them are security issues and should be fixed as soon as possible. Some of the issues may be almost invisible or even valuable only for a virtually nonexistent percent of customers. They might never be fixed in production JDK, but everyone has an opportunity to try to do it for himself/herself.

OpenJDK in the past used a Bugzilla bug tracker to track bugs. Bugzilla is a well-known, but morally outdated project, initially written in 1998 by Terry Weissman. It was open source from the beginning, and it is used even now by thousands of people around the world. It is very simple and easy to use.

However, some time ago, the OpenJDK foundation decided to switch from Bugzilla to JIRA, a proprietary but powerful bug tracking system mostly written in Java. JIRA provides support for different types of workflow, such as Scrum, Kanban, and custom Agile workflows, as well as incorporating all the Bugzilla features.

Sometimes there are opportunities to enlarge the OpenJDK functionality and create a fully-functioning JSR prototype to contribute to OpenJDK development with great benefits to your projects. Sometimes you need to switch to other implementations, such as GNU classpath, or even merge some solutions into your specific version.

In this chapter, we will see how the process workflow is organized, what steps are needed to be followed, and how to cope with the community process. Also, we will see how to submit a bug, and create a patch on it.

Navigating through the process workflow

The knowledge of process workflows, and of how things are done in complex projects like OpenJDK, is critical for a developer. In this recipe, we will explain how things are done while contributing to OpenJDK. We will explain how the work is organized, and how the team co-operates.

Getting ready

We will need an Internet connection and a browser.

How to do it...

We will go through the OpenJDK process workflow and see what to do to contribute to OpenJDK. There are a few initial steps to be followed before you start with the workflow:

1. Firstly, you need to become a contributor. To do so, you need to sign an Oracle Contributor Agreement, and e-mail it to Oracle.

>
> You may find these links useful:
>
> How to become a contributor at `http://openjdk.java.net/contribute/`
>
> Know what is discussed at http://mail.openjdk.java.net/mailman/listinfo

2. Then you need to find something interesting to work with.
3. Now, you are free to discuss and submit patches using the JIRA bug tracking system.

Let's suppose that you've found a bug:

1. When the bug is found, check whether it's already in JIRA.

2. Click on **Issues** and search for issues. You will see the following screen:

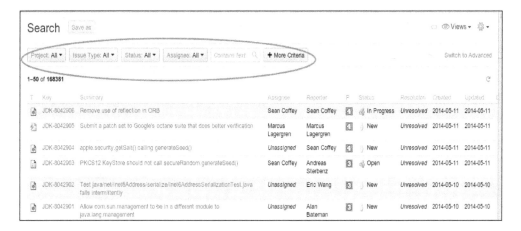

3. In the highlighted section, you can see a filter panel. Use it in combination with the keyword search. Also, notice the **Switch to Advanced** link in the right corner.

4. If the bug is not present already in JIRA, create a JIRA issue.

 JIRA is a commonly used bug tracker tool. You can find how to add issues at `https://confluence.atlassian.com/display/JIRA/`.

5. If you don't know how to resolve the issue, this is the successful ending of your involvement here. The OpenJDK team will be grateful to know all usable information about this problem. If you have anything to add, you are welcome to post information in comments.

6. However, if you feel that you can resolve the issue, comment on it and indicate that you are working on the solution. In some circumstances, you need to wait until the JIRA ticket is assigned to you. Individual workflows use different approaches in this regards.

7. Then, resolve the solution and create the patch.

    The patch creating process is described in the *Creating a patch using NetBeans* recipe in this chapter. you will also find some useful information about building, debugging, and editing OpenJDK code in *Chapter 8, Hacking OpenJDK*.

8. If you are a committer (for example, you have the commit right to the OpenJDK repository), you are free to create a code review using webrev (use information from `https://bitbucket.org/adoptopenjdk/betterrev` to learn how to create a code review). When it is approved, you may commit your changes to the repository and mark your issue as resolved.

9. If you are not a committer, you can also create a webrev review, but the commit process differs slightly. You might push your code changes to the Bitbucket repository along with a `pull` request. It is described in detail in the *Creating a code review* recipe. Read more about the OpenJDK testing process in *Chapter 9, Testing OpenJDK*.

How it works...

OpenJDK has an established workflow, which can differ from one project to another. In all cases, though there are rules of teamwork, one should follow them in order to make the work productive.

Under the hood of this process, there are other team members whose function is to review and test the changes.

Submitting a defect to the OpenJDK bug systems

This recipe will show you how to submit a defect to OpenJDK bug systems. This bug system is used by people who do not have developer access to OpenJDK. For OpenJDK developers, there is JIRA.

How to do it...

We will consider the necessary steps to submit a defect to OpenJDK.

First, we will describe some prerequisites to fill a bug report:

1. First, do a quick search for bugs. It is possible that a similar or even identical bug has already been created. Even if you have something more to say on the subject, please do it in the existing topic without creating a new one.

2. Then, think about the defect's reproducibility. There is a need to describe in detail how to reproduce your defect and cases in which it can and cannot be reproduced.

3. Also, you can make and add logs, traces, and other debug information.

> Please include the fullest possible logs, without cutouts. Even one string in the log may be critical.

4. Also, you may include screenshots along with your logs, especially when you are describing an UI issue.

5. Try to include as much system information as possible. For example, for the *Sumatra* project, even your graphics card driver version may be helpful.

If we need to report an issue without referring to code pieces to describe it generally and not specifically, we can fill the standard bug report as shown here:

1. Fill the fields as shown in the following screenshot:

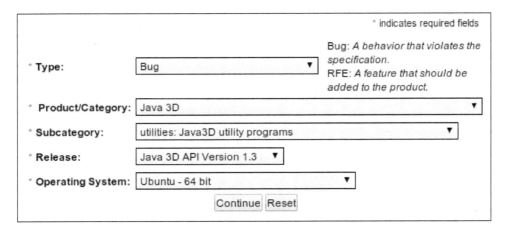

2. Then click on **Continue**.

You will then be required to provide some information to receive the feedback from the team:

User Info

Please give us some information about yourself. Be sure to include a valid email address. You will receive confirmation and subsequent updates regarding your report via email.

* Your Name:
* Company:
* Email:

In addition, Oracle respects your desire for privacy. Personal data collected from this program will not be sold, given or shared with organizations external to Oracle. We will use this data for communications with you to clarify issues regarding the report you submitted and/or status of that report. The issues that you report may be made publicly available, however your personal data will be kept confidential. If you are not comfortable with the above conditions, please do not press the Submit button. If you have any questions, please refer to our Privacy Policy.

How it works...

The OpenJDK project has a bug report system for non-developers to which you can submit your changes where it's convenient. However, it has a JIRA bug tracker, which is used by developers to work in more complex ways with various bugs.

Creating a patch using NetBeans

This section will show you how to create a patch of the OpenJDK project using NetBeans.

Getting ready

You will need a configured development environment. It is preferable that you use NetBeans since NetBeans is a standard tool for developing and debugging OpenJDK.

How to do it...

We will do a simple patch creation with Mercurial and NetBeans by following these steps:

1. Open the OpenJDK project with NetBeans.

2. Make some changes in the project code as shown:

3. Then, follow the chain of context menus, as shown in the preceding screenshot.

4. Click on the **OK** button.

5. Your patch will be saved to the specified directory. Later, you can apply patches using the **Apply Diff Patch** item in the Mercurial context menu.

How it works

NetBeans calls a program that exports a diff (your uncommitted changes versus the head revision in the repository) to a file that can be read and applied when needed.

See also...

Also, diffs between different divisions can also be exported. To do that, simply click on the highlighted item:

Creating a code review

OpenJDK uses webrev as the code review tool. The process of creating a code review and handling lies on the shoulders of the AdoptOpenJDK community, which developed a web tool called **Betterrev**. Review Board along with the Mercurial plugin can be used as well. It automatically generates code reviews, synchronizes with Oracle repository, and performs other useful tasks.

Getting ready

We will need a computer capable of building OpenJDK and which can handle a large amount of code. Also, we will need a development environment installed, as described in *Chapter 8, Hacking OpenJDK*. We will also need Internet access.

How to do it...

We will create a code review using the Betterrev tool, by following the given steps:

1. First, let's clone a repository from Bitbucket.

2. Go to the Betterrev Bitbucket at `https://bitbucket.org/adoptopenjdk/betterrev/src`:

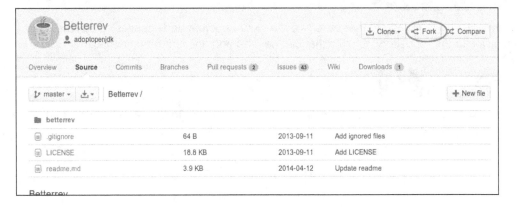

3. Fork it, using the highlighted button:

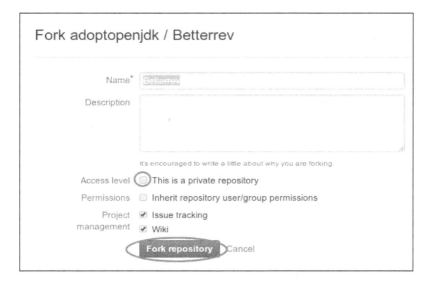

4. Specify the repository name in the **Name** field, and add a description if needed.

5. Check the **This is a private repository** checkbox if you want to make your repository private.

6. Click on the **Fork repository** button.

7. You will see the following screen for a while. It will take some time, but don't worry, all is going well.

8. Make changes that has to be reviewed in the code.

9. Commit them to your local repository.

10. Perform a pull request as shown:

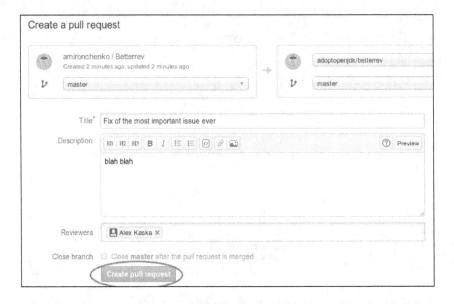

Betterrev will automatically generate a review for your issue.

12
Working with Future Technologies

In this chapter, we will cover the following topics:

- ▶ Building OpenJDK 9 on Mac OS X using Clang
- ▶ Building OpenJDK 9 on Windows using MSYS
- ▶ Running and testing the early access preview of OpenJDK 9
- ▶ Using Jigsaw
- ▶ Building OpenJDK 9 with Graal
- ▶ Building OpenJDK 9 with Sumatra

Introduction

Java is often criticized because of some degree of conservatism, where major language changes are concerned. However, the recent Java 8 release has done a lot to relieve the worry that Java will remain conservative and frozen in time.

However, there are more changes coming. Java 9 is believed to support some long-awaited features that will possibly take it to a completely new market and level of programming.

In the past, annotations support and generics have caused a revolution in Java programming. The way of thinking was changed, and, while nothing completely new was added to the way Java operates in the low-level design, the high-level design and programming techniques were undoubtedly changed. The result was, for example, a rise in annotation-based frameworks and simpler programming as a whole.

Java 8 has been released with lambda expressions support, type annotations, and parameter reflection for public use. But it was possible to use it since late 2012, at least. It was possible to have all this functionality, to write programs with all these features, to have fun with testing new technologies, well before the official release date. Some enterprise developers consider modern Java as unstable and slightly unpredictable even after the release. However, each programmer, who was interested in the new technologies' testing and support and who contributes to it, was able to test and try OpenJDK 8 when it was at development stage.

What is the situation with OpenJDK 9 early access previews were released immediately after the Java 8 release. So we can now try OpenJDK 9. Of course, it is still unstable and doesn't even pass some regression tests, but it is going to change.

What are the main differences between OpenJDK 8 and 9?

There are three main features:

  ▸ The First is the long awaited elimination of type erasure. With new refined generics, it will be possible to determine which type is used in a collection or map, or a tuple—on every generic reference. For all Java programmers this is going to be a major relief.

  ▸ The second feature is intended to bring the Java platform a new ally—the whole might of a GPU will now be in the hands of a programmer, using only standard features without a scrap of native code. It will be explained further in this chapter.

  ▸ And a third one is Graal, the project that exposes Java VM APIs to the end user. It is a great breakthrough since it is possible to change the way Java operates on the fly.

There is more to be done; Java 9 will also contain less GC types without a drop in performance.

> Be aware, underscore (_) will not be a legal identifier name in Java 9, so prepare your code in time. Find more details at `http://openjdk.java.net/jeps/213`.

Also, for those who work with money transactions and financial analytics, there is another Java 9 feature—JSR 354, the Money API. It will implement the ISO-4217 standard currencies along with some additional ones. Currency arithmetics will also be introduced.

> To test the Java Money API, build the source code from `https://github.com/JavaMoney/jsr354-api`. However, this is a Maven project that meets the JSR requirements, and is not a part of the OpenJDK project.

Building OpenJDK 9 on Mac OS X using Clang

At the time of writing, the OpenJDK 9 project was still quite similar to OpenJDK 8. So most of the information about building OpenJDK 9 can be found in *Chapter 4, Building OpenJDK 8.*

One point that differentiates OpenJDK 9 from OpenJDK 8 is the usage of the Clang compiler on Mac OS X. Starting with Xcode Version 5, Clang became the official compiler on Mac OS X instead of GCC. There were plans to use it as an official compiler for OpenJDK 8 on Mac OS X but that switch was postponed to OpenJDK 9.

In this recipe, we will build the current codebase of OpenJDK 9 using Xcode 5 and the Clang compiler.

Getting ready

For this recipe, we will need a clean Mac OS X 10.8 Mountain Lion or 10.9 Mavericks running with Mercurial source control tools installed.

How to do it...

The following procedure will help us to build OpenJDK 9:

1. Download Xcode 5 from `https://developer.apple.com/xcode/` (an Apple developer's account is required, registration is free) and install it.

2. Download the Command Line Tools for the corresponding minor version of Xcode using the same download link mentioned previously, and install it.

3. Run the following command from the terminal to set up the Command Line Tools:

   ```
   sudo xcode-select -switch /Applications/Xcode.app/Contents/
   Developer/
   ```

4. Install JDK 8—Oracle distribution, or prebuilt OpenJDK binaries may be used.

5. Obtain the source code from the Mercurial repository:

   ```
   hg checkout http://hg.openjdk.java.net/jdk9/jdk9/
   bash ./get_source.sh
   ```

6. Run the autotools configuration script:

   ```
   bash ./configure --with-boot-jdk=path/to/jdk8
   ```

7. Start the build:

   ```
   make all 2>&1
   ```

8. The built binaries will be put into the following directory:

```
build/macosx-x86_64-normal-server-release/images/j2sdk-image
```

How it works...

Xcode 5 uses the Clang compiler by default and OpenJDK 9 already has all the adjustments required for switching compiler from GCC to Clang.

There's more...

With the older versions of OpenJDK 9, the installation of the X11 server may be required. The X11 server can be installer from the *XQuartz* project.

See also

▶ Building OpenJDK 8 on Mac OS X recipe from *Chapter 4, Building OpenJDK 8*

Building OpenJDK 9 on Windows using MSYS

The Windows operating system has a long history of different tools providing a Unix-like environment. Tools such as Microsoft POSIX subsystem, Interix, Windows Services for UNIX, MKS Toolkit, Cygwin, MinGW/MSYS, and so on, existed during the various periods of Windows history and provided different levels of Unix compliance.

The three latter tools are most relevant to OpenJDK builds. MKS Toolkit was used for internal builds in Sun Microsystems because it provided better speed than Cygwin. Support for MKS Toolkit was discontinued with OpenJDK 7. Cygwin, that we described in detail in *Chapter 2, Building OpenJDK 6*, was used as the main and only tool to build OpenJDK 7 and 8.

MSYS (short form for minimal system) is a part of the MinGW (Minimalist GNU for Windows) project. The MinGW project was started as a fork of Cygwin with the goal to provide closer integration with Windows API for the cost of lower level Unix support. MinGW-based applications are standalone native Windows applications and do not require the `cygwin.dll` library. Among other things, this can bring better speed for some applications using Windows API through MinGW instead of emulated Unix calls (like fork) through Cygwin. Applications should be changed accordingly, though.

The MSYS project provides a minimalistic shell environment and also provides first-class support for running GNU Autoconf based builds. Actually running Autoconf's configure scripts efficiently was one of the goals of MSYS. In some cases, the configure scripts can be extremely slow in Cygwin because of extensive use of new processes spawning.

Due to better speed in OpenJDK builds, MSYS support was restored in OpenJDK 9 as a second supported environment along with Cygwin.

In this recipe, we will build OpenJDK 9 on Windows 7 using MSYS instead of Cygwin. At the time of writing, OpenJDK 9 was still in development and we have used the latest available source code.

Getting ready

For this recipe, we will need Windows 7 (32- or 64-bit) running.

How to do it...

The following procedure will help us to build OpenJDK 9:

1. Download Microsoft .NET Framework 4 from the Microsoft website and install it.

2. Download Microsoft Windows SDK for Windows 7 (the `GRMSDKX_EN_DVD.iso` file) from the Microsoft website and install it to the default location. The .NET Development and Common Utilities components are not required.

3. Download Visual Studio 2010 Express and install it (C++ variant) to the default location.

4. Download and install Microsoft DirectX 9.0 SDK (Summer 2004) to the default installation path. Note that this distribution is not available on the Microsoft website anymore. It may be downloaded elsewhere online, the file details are as follows:

    `name: dxsdk_sum2004.exe`

    `size: 239008008 bytes`

    `sha1sum: 73d875b97591f48707c38ec0dbc63982ff45c661`

5. Download the prebuilt FreeType libraries from the `openjdk-unofficial-builds` GitHub project (directory `7_64`) and put the binaries into the `c:\freetype\lib` directory and the header files into the `c:\freetype\include` directory.

6. Install the OpenJDK 8 binaries or Oracle Java 8 into `c:\jdk8`.

7. Download and install the Mercurial SCM tool from the `mercurial.selenic.com` website.

8. Clone the current development forest of OpenJDK 9 to the `C:\openjdk` directory:

    `hg clone http://hg.openjdk.java.net/jdk9/jdk9/`

9. Download the `mingw-get` utility (`mingw-get-setup.exe`) from `http://mingw.org/` and install it to the `C:\MinGW` path.

10. Run the `cmd.exe` shell and navigate to the directory.

11. Run the following command to revert the installed version of MSYS from the latest one to 1.0.17:

```
mingw-get install --reinstall --recursive msys-core=1.0.17-1
```

12. Run the following commands to install all required MSYS packages:

```
mingw-get install msys-zip
mingw-get install msys-unzip
mingw-get install msys-diffutils
mingw-get install msys-file
mingw-get install msys-mktemp
mingw-get install msys-tar
mingw-get install msys-xargs
mingw-get install msys-findutils
mingw-get install msys-make
```

13. Run the MSYS shell using the `C:\MinGW\msys\1.0\msys.bat` file.

14. Navigate to the `c/openjdk` directory and download the source code for all OpenJDK subrepositories with the following command:

```
bash ./get_source.sh
```

15. Add a path for the JDK 8 binaries in the `PATH` variable:

```
export PATH=/c/jdk8/bin:$PATH
```

16. Change the filesystem permissions for all source files:

```
chmod -R 777 .
```

17. Run the configure script specifying path to the FreeType binaries:

```
./configure --with-freetype=/c/freetype
```

18. Start the build process writing the output to the screen and logfile simultaneously:

```
make | tee make.log
```

19. Wait for the build to finish.

How it works...

At the time of writing, OpenJDK 9 code uses the same toolchain as OpenJDK 8, so the environment setup is similar.

We use Version 1.0.17 of MSYS because the regression related to multicores support appeared in the 1.0.18 Version. This regression is not fixed at the time of writing but will most likely be fixed in the following versions.

The `mingw-get` utility is a package manager that allows us to install or update the required MSYS packages.

See also

▶ The *Installing Cygwin for Windows builds* recipe from *Chapter 2, Building OpenJDK 6*

▶ The *Building OpenJDK 8 on Windows 7 SP1* recipe from *Chapter 4, Building OpenJDK 8*

▶ The OpenJDK bug related to the restoration of MSYS support in OpenJDK 9 at `https://bugs.openjdk.java.net/browse/JDK-8022177`

▶ The OpenJDK mailing list thread about the regression in MSYS 1.0.18 at `http://mail.openjdk.java.net/pipermail/build-dev/2014-August/012917.html`

▶ The MSYS website at `http://www.mingw.org/wiki/msys`

▶ Information about Windows service for Unix at `http://technet.microsoft.com/en-us/library/bb496506.aspx`

▶ The MKS Toolkit website at `http://mkssoftware.com/`

▶ The Cygwin website at `http://cygwin.com/`

Running and testing the early access preview of OpenJDK 9

We will get the newest OpenJDK code available and will test for feature availability. Don't hesitate to try new features, they may be available in the newer releases. Since the OpenJDK 9 release, it will remain the fastest way to give OpenJDK 9 a test. Hopefully, upon the release, the same thing will work for OpenJDK 10.

Getting ready

You will need an Internet connection. Aside from that, nothing is needed.

How to do it...

We will download, unpack, and run the latest publicly available full OpenJDK build:

1. Open the page `https://jdk9.java.net/`.

2. Download the early access preview, as shown:

Documentation
- JDK Docs (86.75 MB zip | HTML)
- JavaFX Docs (7.55 MB zip | HTML)
- Supported Platforms*

Platforms		JRE	JDK
Windows (WinXP not supported)*	**32-bit**	exe (md5) 61.64 MB	exe (md5) 128.10 MB
	64-bit	exe (md5) 93.54 MB	exe (md5) 132.93 MB
Mac OS X	**64-bit**	dmg(md5) 56.21 MB	dmg (md5) 163.41 MB
Linux	**32-bit**	tar.gz (md5) 61.98 MB	tar.gz (md5) 113.27 MB
	64-bit	tar.gz (md5) 59.63 MB	tar.gz (md5) 110.92 MB
Solaris SPARC	**64-bit**	tar.gz (md5) 61.07 MB	tar.gz (md5) 97.18 MB
Solaris	**64-bit**	tar.gz (md5) 48.08 MB	tar.gz (md5) 94.17 MB

3. Run an installer.

4. You can find out how to install OpenJDK from an archive in *Chapter 1, Getting Started with OpenJDK* of this book.

Test some interesting features that are already included in the early access JDK. Look at the following code:

```
DatagramSocket socket = new DatagramSocket(4445);
System.out.println(socket.supportedOptions());
```

When executed, you may expect it to return the following string, or something similar:

```
[SO_SNDBUF, SO_RCVBUF, SO_REUSEADDR, IP_TOS]
```

Although there are some minor improvements and a lot of bug fixes, there are not yet any major changes in the early access preview.

How it works...

In the source repository on `http://hg.openjdk.java.net/jdk9/jdk9`, there are tags, such as `jdk9-b<build number>`, which are automatically built into the early access releases. Although there are no nightly builds, you can always build them from source, if you have lots of time and a machine that's powerful enough to start with.

Don't forget to update your once installed releases—there will be really major and exciting changes, including those explained next. Sooner or later, developers will come out with Java 9 full, and then there will be time to test it before it becomes production ready.

There's more...

You can also build OpenJDK 9 from source:

1. Clone the source code repository `hg` clone at `http://hg.openjdk.java.net/jdk9/jdk9`

2. Get the source code of the OpenJDK subprojects:

   ```
   chmod 755 ./get_source.sh && ./get_source.sh
   cd jigsaw
   ```

3. Then configure the OpenJDK instance to be built:

   ```
   chmod 755 ./configure.sh && ./configure.sh
   ```

4. And, finally, do the build itself:

   ```
   Make
   ```

5. The final strings of your output will look like this:

   ```
   -------------------------
   Finished building OpenJDK for target 'default'
   ```

Using Jigsaw

Jigsaw is the brand-new modular system for Java. It brings to mind some existing products, such as Maven or Gradle, but its most interesting feature is the possibility of the modularization of the JDK itself. Jigsaw will allow, upon its full completion, to modularize even some features that was thought as unseparable, such as HotSpot binaries.

Jigsaw incorporates proposals about the Java modular system. Modularity means scalability—from small, embedded devices that need only basic functionality and have poor performance, to full-scale data centers with dozens of machines. Some of these goals have already been reached—but Jigsaw presents a universal way to resolve dependencies on all platforms, starting from Java itself.

Several JEPs are part of Jigsaw:

- **JEP 200**: This makes the JDK itself modular
- **JEP 201**: This makes the source code modular
- **JEP 220**: This makes the runtime Java images modular, so they can be loaded in parts

Some information about the progress of the JEPs are found at the following JIRA links:

- `https://bugs.openjdk.java.net/browse/JDK-8051619`
- `https://bugs.openjdk.java.net/browse/JDK-8051618`
- `https://bugs.openjdk.java.net/browse/JDK-8061971`

Also, the core of Jigsaw is JSR 376—the Java platform Module System.

Getting ready

You will need Internet access. Also, some experience with Maven, or similar software is desired. Any knowledge about how the build systems work from the inside will be appreciated.

How to do it...

The following procedure will teach you how to build Jigsaw-enabled Java:

1. First, let's clone a source repo `hg` clone from `http://hg.openjdk.java.net/jigsaw/jigsaw`.

2. Then, let's get the source code of the OpenJDK subprojects:

   ```
   chmod 755 ./get_source.sh && ./get_source.sh
   cd jigsaw
   ```

3. Then configure the OpenJDK instance to be built:

   ```
   chmod 755 ./configure && ./configure
   ```

4. And, finally, do the build itself:

   ```
   make all
   ------------------------
   Finished building OpenJDK for target 'default'
   ```

Congratulations, you've built Jigsaw-enabled Java.

Now, we will do some tests:

1. Let's consider the simple *helloworld1* program:

```
package me.dsmd.jigsawsample
import me.dsmd.helloworldstrings.Strings
public class Main{
  public void main(String [] args){
    System.out.println(Strings.helloworld1());
  }
}
```

2. It has one class, which is imported from a yet nonexistent package.

3. Let's create it.

```
package me.dsmd.helloworldstrings
public class Strings{
  public String helloworld1(){
    return "Hello World";
  }
}
```

Now, we will try to link it using Jigsaw.

Jigsaw stores the module declaration in the file named `module-info.java`.

1. Let's create it for those two packages as follows:

```
module  me.dsmd.jigsawsample @ 1.0{
    requires me.dsmd.helloworldstrings
    class me.dsmd.jigsawsample.Main
}
module  me.dsmd.helloworldstrings @ 0.1 {
    class me.dsmd.helloworldstrings.Strings
}
```

These files are to be placed in the root directory of a package.

2. Let's consider a situation when all those modules are placed in the same directory named `src`:

```
.
├── modules
└── src
     ├── me.dsmd.helloworldstrings
```

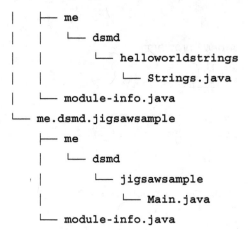

```
|       ├── me
|       |    └── dsmd
|       |          └── helloworldstrings
|       |                 └── Strings.java
|       └── module-info.java
└── me.dsmd.jigsawsample
        ├── me
        |    └── dsmd
        |          └── jigsawsample
        |                 └── Main.java
        └── module-info.java
```

3. Then, let's compile them with `javac` from your jigsaw build:

```
javac -verbose -d modules -modulepath modules -sourcepath \ `find
src -name '*.java'`
```

How it works...

Jigsaw is a modular system that gives Java its very own build system. Similar systems were spawned in the Java world long ago, but they lacked the core support. They were never able to bring the modular support advantages to Java's own features. Of course, there are some downsides as well. The *Write once, run everywhere* slogan is not so applicable as it was before.

We use the newly built OpenJDK commands to create, install, and export modules. Those commands are still under heavy development, but the specification is already written so, hopefully, nothing will significantly change before the production-access release.

There's more...

You also can install a module as a library. To do so, run the following command:

▶ To create a module library:

```
$ jmod -L lib1 create
```

This creates a module library `lib1`.

▶ To install some modules to the library:

```
$ jmod -L lib1 install modules module1 module2
```

This will install your modules under the system parent in the library `lib1`.

Currently, there is no way to remove the module from the library. Maybe, there will not be any in the release either. For now, the simplest way to remove a module from the library is to delete it physically from the repository:

```
rm -rf lib1/module1
```

Also, you can run a module, if it contains a standard entry point:

```
java -L lib1 -m module1
```

 The new -m option is also contained only in the Jigsaw-enabled Java command. As of now (June 2014) it is not contained in any public early access preview.

As a next feature, you can export a module as a file by performing the following command:

```
jpkg -m modules/module1 jmod module1
```

The module1@<module version>.jmod file will be created. It will contain the exported, ready-to-use module.

Building OpenJDK 9 with Graal

As described in the project page, Graal is:

> *A quest for the JVM to leverage its own J.*

Upon completion of this project, JVM functions will be exposed via Java APIs, so the end user will be able to have access to the most low-level manipulation. It will be possible to write a Java compiler in Java, for example. Now, we will try to give it a test.

There is also **Truffle**, a framework that allows you to build your own language using Graal VM. It builds upon a notion of an **abstract syntax tree** (**AST**), and the process, in fact, is really simple. To have a better look, see the following link:

```
https://cesquivias.github.io/blog/2014/10/13/writing-a-language-in-truffle-part-1-a-simple-slow-interpreter/
```

Getting ready

You will need an Internet connection. Also, it's recommended to read the chapters about building OpenJDK.

How to do it...

Have a look at the following procedure to build OpenJDK with Graal:

1. First, clone a source repository:

    ```
    hg clone http://hg.openjdk.java.net/graal/graal
    cd graal
    export EXTRA_JAVA_HOMES=/usr/lib/jvm/java-1.7.0-openjdk
    ./mx.sh build
    ```

2. Enter a selection value, upon which `vm graal` will be built. Unfortunately, it will not be built without modification against the OpenJDK 9-ea preview:

    ```
    ./mx.sh build
    [1]  /usr/lib/jvm/java-1.7.0-openjdk
    [2]  /usr/lib/jvm/java-1.6.0-openjdk-amd64
    [3]  /usr/lib/jvm/java-6-oracle
    [4]  /usr/lib/jvm/jdk1.9.0
    [5]  /usr/lib/jvm/java-7-oracle
    [6]  /usr/lib/jvm/java-8-oracle
    [7]  /usr/lib/jvm/java-6-openjdk-amd64
    [8]  /usr/lib/jvm/java-7-openjdk-amd64
    [9]  /usr/lib/jvm/java-1.7.0-openjdk-amd64
    [10] <other>
    ```

3. Then choose which VM will be executed. There are two types of VM. In a nutshell, `server vm` will use the default hotspot compilation, using Graal itself only for explicit Graal API calls, while `graal VM` will compile everything through Graal. The first option is much more suitable for production VMs, while the second is favorable for testing purposes.

    ```
    Please select the VM to be executed from the following:
    [1] server - Normal compilation is performed with a tiered system (C1
        + C2), Truffle compilation is performed with Graal. Use this for
        optimal Truffle performance.
    [2] graal - Normal compilation is performed with a tiered system (C1 +
        Graal), Truffle compilation is performed with Graal.
    ```

4. Then, make a cup of tea, the process may take several dozen minutes.

5. Then, if you want to initialize your IDE project , run `./mx.sh ideinit`.

6. Then, open your favorite IDE and open a resulting project. It will be shown here with IntelliJ Idea:

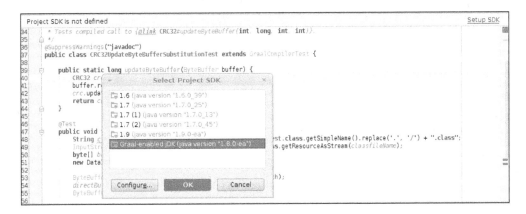

7. Explore various tests.

How it works...

The Graal enabled VM will expose Java APIs to the end user.

There's more...

In *Chapter 8, Hacking OpenJDK*, we added new intrinsics to the HotSpot, using the crc32 calculation as an example. In the Graal project, there is a similar test, which tests the compiled substitution of the `CRC32#updateByteBuffer` method. It is contained in the `com.oracle.graal.hotspot.jdk8.test` package. Run it, and enjoy the performance change.

Building OpenJDK 9 with Sumatra

For a long time, Java was considered as a primarily backend tool, due to its cross-platform vectoring. Only J2ME was capable of achieving long-term superiority in the mobile segment. But now it's going to change. Project Sumatra has the aim of delivering GPU-calculation standards to the Java guys.

Getting ready

You will probably need a GPU that supports CUDA and OpenGL, or a HSAIL simulator running (because on-board GPUs do not support native GPU languages).

How to do it...

Sumatra developers are making wide use of the Graal project, described earlier. The build consists of two stages. Firstly, the Sumatra JDK is built, like a normal OpenJDK build, as shown:

```
make

Building OpenJDK for target 'default' in configuration 'linux-x86_64-
normal-server-release'


## Starting langtools
## Finished langtools (build time 00:00:03)


## Starting hotspot
## Finished hotspot (build time 00:00:01)


## Starting corba
## Finished corba (build time 00:00:00)


## Starting jaxp
## Finished jaxp (build time 00:00:01)


## Starting jaxws
## Finished jaxws (build time 00:00:02)


## Starting jdk
## Finished jdk (build time 00:00:21)


----- Build times -------
Start 2014-07-06 00:17:24
End   2014-07-06 00:17:52
00:00:00 corba
00:00:01 hotspot
```

```
00:00:01 jaxp
00:00:02 jaxws
00:00:21 jdk
00:00:03 langtools
00:00:28 TOTAL

-------------------------

Finished building OpenJDK for target 'default'
```

The second stage consists of building a Graal JDK on top of the Sumatra JDK. It may be tricky, but hopefully it will work:

1. Clone a repository hg clone `http://hg.openjdk.java.net/sumatra/sumatra-dev/`:

   ```
   chmod 755 configure && ./configure
   ```

2. Get the source code:

   ```
   chmod 755 get_source.sh && ./get_source.sh
   ```

3. Then make the source code:

   ```
   make
   ```

4. Export `JAVA_HOME` to the newly built OpenJDK instance:

   ```
   export JAVA_HOME=<path-to-sumatra-dev>/build/linux-<your-arch>-normal-server-release/images/j2sdk-image
   ```

5. Build the HSAIL-enabled grail:

   ```
   /mx.sh --vmbuild product --vm server build
   ```

Congratulations! You have a Sumatra-enabled VM.

Let's do a little test. Consider a code from an official sample:

```
package simple;

import java.util.stream.IntStream;

public class Simple {

    public static void main(String[] args) {
        final int length = 8;
        int[] ina = new int[length];
        int[] inb = new int[length];
```

```
        int[] out = new int[length];

        // Initialize the input arrays - this is offloadable
        IntStream.range(0, length).parallel().forEach(p -> {
            ina[p] = 1;
            inb[p] = 2;
        });

        // Sum each pair of elements into out[] - this is offloadable
        IntStream.range(0, length).parallel().forEach(p -> {
            out[p] = ina[p] + inb[p];
        });

        // Print results - this is not offloadable since it is
        // calling native code etc.
        IntStream.range(0, length).forEach(p -> {
            System.out.println(out[p] + ", " + ina[p] + ", " +
inb[p]);
        });
    }
}
```

It contains two off-loadable lambdas. We will try to make them run in parallel, using the HSA API.

1. First, set JAVA_HOME to the Graal JDK:

   ```
   export JAVA_HOME=/path/to/graal/jdk1.8.0-internal/product/
   ```

2. Then clone the OKRA HSA interface:

   ```
   git clone https://github.com/HSAFoundation/Okra-Interface-to-HSA-
   Device.git
   ```

3. Make it runnable:

   ```
   export PATH=$PATH:/path/to/okra/dist/bin
   ```

   ```
   export LD_LIBRARY_PATH=$LD_LIBRARY_PATH:/path/to/okra/dist/bin
   ```

4. Run the example with and without offloading.

5. You will get the following code in your terminal:

   ```
   $JAVA_HOME/bin/java -server -esa -XX:+TraceGPUInteraction -Dcom.
   amd.sumatra.offload.immediate=true -G:Log=CodeGen  simple.Simple

   ...

   [HSAIL] library is libokra_x86_64.so
   ```

```
[GPU] registered initialization of Okra (total initialized: 2)
[CUDA] Ptx::get_execute_kernel_from_vm_address
[thread:1] scope:
  [thread:1] scope: GraalCompiler
    [thread:1] scope: GraalCompiler.CodeGen
    Nothing to do here
    Nothing to do here
    Nothing to do here
    version 0:95: $full : $large;
// static method HotSpotMethod<Simple.lambda$main$0(int[], int[],
int)>
kernel &run (
    align 8 kernarg_u64 %_arg0,
    align 8 kernarg_u64 %_arg1
    ) {
    ld_kernarg_u64  $d0, [%_arg0];
    ld_kernarg_u64  $d1, [%_arg1];
    workitemabsid_u32 $s0, 0;


@L0:
    cmp_eq_b1_u64 $c0, $d1, 0; // null test
    cbr $c0, @L1;
@L2:
    ld_global_s32 $s1, [$d1 + 12];
    cmp_ge_b1_u32 $c0, $s0, $s1;
    cbr $c0, @L8;
@L3:
    cmp_eq_b1_u64 $c0, $d0, 0; // null test
    cbr $c0, @L4;
@L5:
    ld_global_s32 $s1, [$d0 + 12];
    cmp_ge_b1_u32 $c0, $s0, $s1;
    cbr $c0, @L7;
@L6:
    cvt_s64_s32 $d2, $s0;
    mul_s64 $d2, $d2, 4;
```

```
    add_u64 $d0, $d0, $d2;
    st_global_s32 1, [$d0 + 16];
    cvt_s64_s32 $d0, $s0;
    mul_s64 $d0, $d0, 4;
    add_u64 $d1, $d1, $d0;
    st_global_s32 2, [$d1 + 16];
    ret;
@L1:
    mov_b32 $s0, -6155;
@L9:
    ret;
@L4:
    mov_b32 $s0, -4363;
    brn @L9;
@L8:
    mov_b32 $s0, -6683;
    brn @L9;
@L7:
    mov_b32 $s0, -4891;
    brn @L9;
};
```

```
[HSAIL] heap=0x00007f4c9801de38
[HSAIL] base=0x05a00000, capacity=209190912
External method:simple.Simple.lambda$main$0([I[II)V
installCode0: ExternalCompilationResult
[HSAIL] sig:([I[II)V  args length=2, _parameter_count=3
[HSAIL] static method
[HSAIL] HSAILKernelArguments::do_array, _index=0, 0x82b20888, is a
[I
[HSAIL] HSAILKernelArguments::do_array, _index=1, 0x82b208b8, is a
[I
[HSAIL] HSAILKernelArguments::not pushing trailing int
   [thread:1] scope: GraalCompiler
     [thread:1] scope: GraalCompiler.CodeGen
     Nothing to do here
```

```
    Nothing to do here
    Nothing to do here
    version 0:95: $full : $large;
// static method HotSpotMethod<Simple.lambda$main$1(int[], int[],
int[], int)>
kernel &run (
    align 8 kernarg_u64 %_arg0,
    align 8 kernarg_u64 %_arg1,
    align 8 kernarg_u64 %_arg2
    ) {
    ld_kernarg_u64  $d0, [%_arg0];
    ld_kernarg_u64  $d1, [%_arg1];
    ld_kernarg_u64  $d2, [%_arg2];
    workitemabsid_u32 $s0, 0;


@L0:
    cmp_eq_b1_u64 $c0, $d0, 0; // null test
    cbr $c0, @L1;
@L2:
    ld_global_s32 $s1, [$d0 + 12];
    cmp_ge_b1_u32 $c0, $s0, $s1;
    cbr $c0, @L12;
@L3:
    cmp_eq_b1_u64 $c0, $d2, 0; // null test
    cbr $c0, @L4;
@L5:
    ld_global_s32 $s1, [$d2 + 12];
    cmp_ge_b1_u32 $c0, $s0, $s1;
    cbr $c0, @L11;
@L6:
    cmp_eq_b1_u64 $c0, $d1, 0; // null test
    cbr $c0, @L7;
@L8:
    ld_global_s32 $s1, [$d1 + 12];
    cmp_ge_b1_u32 $c0, $s0, $s1;
    cbr $c0, @L10;
```

```
    @L9:
        cvt_s64_s32 $d3, $s0;
        mul_s64 $d3, $d3, 4;
        add_u64 $d1, $d1, $d3;
        ld_global_s32 $s1, [$d1 + 16];
        cvt_s64_s32 $d1, $s0;
        mul_s64 $d1, $d1, 4;
        add_u64 $d2, $d2, $d1;
        ld_global_s32 $s2, [$d2 + 16];
        add_s32 $s2, $s2, $s1;
        cvt_s64_s32 $d1, $s0;
        mul_s64 $d1, $d1, 4;
        add_u64 $d0, $d0, $d1;
        st_global_s32 $s2, [$d0 + 16];
        ret;
    @L1:
        mov_b32 $s0, -7691;
    @L13:
        ret;
    @L4:
        mov_b32 $s0, -6411;
        brn @L13;
    @L10:
        mov_b32 $s0, -5403;
        brn @L13;
    @L7:
        mov_b32 $s0, -4875;
        brn @L13;
    @L12:
        mov_b32 $s0, -8219;
        brn @L13;
    @L11:
        mov_b32 $s0, -6939;
        brn @L13;
    };
```

```
[HSAIL]  heap=0x00007f4c9801de38
[HSAIL]  base=0x05a00000, capacity=209190912
External method:simple.Simple.lambda$main$1(([I[I[II)V
installCode0: ExternalCompilationResult
[HSAIL]  sig:([I[I[II)V  args length=3, _parameter_count=4
[HSAIL]  static method
[HSAIL]  HSAILKernelArguments::do_array, _index=0, 0x82b208f8, is a
[I
[HSAIL]  HSAILKernelArguments::do_array, _index=1, 0x82b20888, is a
[I
[HSAIL]  HSAILKernelArguments::do_array, _index=2, 0x82b208b8, is a
[I
[HSAIL]  HSAILKernelArguments::not pushing trailing int
3, 1, 2
3, 1, 2
3, 1, 2
3, 1, 2
3, 1, 2
3, 1, 2
3, 1, 2
3, 1, 2
```

How it works...

Sumatra runs on top of the Graal project. Since all operations with GPU are implemented on the VM level, Sumatra uses Graal to gain access to them. Sumatra features are at the heavy development stage, and they are subject to various unpredictable changes.

But the end user can use some of them, even now, to gain a new level of Java productivity at the expense of some compatibility and standardization.

There's more...

In the Graal suite, there is a possibility to test the Sumatra HSAIL feature.

To do so, run the following code:

```
./mx.sh --vm server unittest -XX:+TraceGPUInteraction -XX:+GPUOffload
-G:Log=CodeGen hsail.test.IntAddTest
```

The output should look like the following (for Linux Mint 15, or for other distributions\OS, results may slightly differ):

```
[HSAIL] library is libokra_x86_64.so
[HSAIL] using _OKRA_SIM_LIB_PATH_=/tmp/okraresource.
dir_2488167353114811077/libokra_x86_64.so
[GPU] registered initialization of Okra (total initialized: 2)
[CUDA] Ptx::get_execute_kernel_from_vm_address
JUnit version 4.8
.[thread:1] scope:
  [thread:1] scope: GraalCompiler
    [thread:1] scope: GraalCompiler.CodeGen
    Nothing to do here
    Nothing to do here
    Nothing to do here
    version 0:95: $full : $large;
// static method HotSpotMethod<IntAddTest.run(int[], int[], int[], int)>
kernel &run (
    align 8 kernarg_u64 %_arg0,
    align 8 kernarg_u64 %_arg1,
    align 8 kernarg_u64 %_arg2
    ) {
    ld_kernarg_u64  $d0, [%_arg0];
    ld_kernarg_u64  $d1, [%_arg1];
    ld_kernarg_u64  $d2, [%_arg2];
    workitemabsid_u32 $s0, 0;
@L0:
    cmp_eq_b1_u64 $c0, $d0, 0; // null test
    cbr $c0, @L1;
@L2:
    ld_global_s32 $s1, [$d0 + 12];
    cmp_ge_b1_u32 $c0, $s0, $s1;
    cbr $c0, @L12;
@L3:
    cmp_eq_b1_u64 $c0, $d2, 0; // null test
    cbr $c0, @L4;
@L5:
```

```
    ld_global_s32 $s1, [$d2 + 12];
    cmp_ge_b1_u32 $c0, $s0, $s1;
    cbr $c0, @L11;
@L6:
    cmp_eq_b1_u64 $c0, $d1, 0; // null test
    cbr $c0, @L7;
@L8:
    ld_global_s32 $s1, [$d1 + 12];
    cmp_ge_b1_u32 $c0, $s0, $s1;
    cbr $c0, @L10;
@L9:
    cvt_s64_s32 $d3, $s0;
    mul_s64 $d3, $d3, 4;
    add_u64 $d1, $d1, $d3;
    ld_global_s32 $s1, [$d1 + 16];
    cvt_s64_s32 $d1, $s0;
    mul_s64 $d1, $d1, 4;
    add_u64 $d2, $d2, $d1;
    ld_global_s32 $s2, [$d2 + 16];
    add_s32 $s2, $s2, $s1;
    cvt_s64_s32 $d1, $s0;
    mul_s64 $d1, $d1, 4;
    add_u64 $d0, $d0, $d1;
    st_global_s32 $s2, [$d0 + 16];
    ret;
@L1:
    mov_b32 $s0, -7691;
@L13:
    ret;
@L4:
    mov_b32 $s0, -6411;
    brn @L13;
@L10:
    mov_b32 $s0, -5403;
    brn @L13;
@L7:
```

```
     mov_b32 $s0, -4875;
     brn @L13;
@L12:
     mov_b32 $s0, -8219;
     brn @L13;
@L11:
     mov_b32 $s0, -6939;
     brn @L13;
};
```

[HSAIL] heap=0x00007f95b8019cc0

[HSAIL] base=0x05a00000, capacity=210763776

External method:com.oracle.graal.compiler.hsail.test.IntAddTest.
run([I[I[II)V

installCode0: ExternalCompilationResult

[HSAIL] sig:([I[I[II)V args length=3, _parameter_count=4

[HSAIL] static method

[HSAIL] HSAILKernelArguments::do_array, _index=0, 0x82b21970, is a [I

[HSAIL] HSAILKernelArguments::do_array, _index=1, 0x82b477f0, is a [I

[HSAIL] HSAILKernelArguments::do_array, _index=2, 0x82b479e0, is a [I

[HSAIL] HSAILKernelArguments::not pushing trailing int

Time: 0.153

OK (1 test)

The completion of this test will mean that the HSAIL functions are working OK, so the cutting-edge Java already benefits from your GPU.

13
Build Automation

In this chapter, we will cover:

- ▶ Installing VirtualBox
- ▶ Preparing SSH keys
- ▶ Preparing VirtualBox machines with Linux
- ▶ Preparing VirtualBox machines with Mac OS X
- ▶ Preparing VirtualBox machines with Windows
- ▶ Automating builds
- ▶ Building cross-platform installers

Introduction

Automated builds are widely used in cross-platform software development. *Build farm* with build machines for each supported operating systems is required to build projects remotely and run tests on all platforms. With the rising popularity of software virtualization tools, it became possible to deploy a *virtual build farm* using a single physical machine.

Besides the build environment in each OS, the essential part of an automated build is the communication between the *master* machine and the *build* machines. The following communication jobs might be required:

- ▶ The master should prepare and start the build machine
- ▶ The master should send the source code directly to the build machine or fire sources fetching process from the build machine itself
- ▶ The master should start the build process
- ▶ The build machine should send build logs to the master during the build

  ▸ The build machine should send result binaries to the master

  ▸ The master should shut down the build machine

In this chapter, we will prepare the OpenJDK build environment for Windows, Linux, and Mac OS X. This task can be done using a high-level build automation (or Continuous Integration) tool. However, such tools can be limited in functionality and inflexible for our task. While all such tools should do similar jobs (as listed previously), different tools can have different configurations and peculiarities, and the knowledge of one tool can be less useful for another. Also, such tools bring in an additional level of complexity with possible tool-specific problems.

You will learn how to perform build automation using the most basic tools for a better understanding of the process. The bash shell is already used for OpenJDK builds on all platforms (natively on Linux/Mac and through Cygwin on Windows), so we will use bash scripts for setting up and starting to build virtual machines. For communication (sending commands and data), we will use the SSH protocol; implementation for this is usually preinstalled on Unix-like operating systems and can also be installed on Windows. For virtualization, we will use the popular VirtualBox tool from Oracle.

Installing VirtualBox

VirtualBox is a popular virtualization toolbox from Oracle Corporation that allows us to run *virtual* instances of other operating systems on top of the *host* operating system. In this recipe, we will install VirtualBox and configure host network interfaces. Such a configuration will allow us to connect from host to guest and back during the automated builds.

Getting ready

For this recipe, we will require the Ubuntu 12.04 amd64 operating system running.

How to do it...

The following procedure will help you to install VirtualBox:

  1. Download the installation package from the VirtualBox website (`https://www.virtualbox.org/`) and install it.

  2. Install the virtual network interface package:

     ```
     sudo apt-get install uml-utilities
     ```

  3. Create a virtual interface `tap0` that will be used for connections to and from the guest machine:

     ```
     sudo tunctl -t tap0 -u your_username
     ```

4. Configure the interface `tap0`:

   ```
   sudo ifconfig tap0 192.168.42.2 up dstaddr 192.168.42.1 netmask
   255.255.255.0
   ```

5. Create an arbitrary VirtualBox machine using GUI forms.

6. Navigate to **Settings | Network form** and check whether the **tap0** network interface is available in the interfaces drop-down list when the **Bridged Adapter** mode is used.

How it works...

VirtualBox supports different networking options for guest machines. One of them—Bridged Adapter—allows us to connect from host to guest and back using static IP addresses. To set up this mode on the host side, we need an additional virtual network interface with a separate address. The `tunctl` utility that comes as part of the `uml-utilities` package allows us to create a virtual interface such as `tap0`.

There's more...

Multiple virtual interfaces can be created with different addresses to run multiple virtual machines simultaneously. Mac OS X can be used as a host machine, the `tuntaposx` kernel extensions are required to use the `tunctl` utility.

See also

▶ The Oracle VirtualBox user manual at `https://www.virtualbox.org/manual/UserManual.html`

Preparing SSH keys

In this chapter, we will use virtual machines to build OpenJDK. During the build source code, control commands, logs, and result binaries should be sent between host and virtual machines. We will use the ubiquitous **Secure Shell** (**SSH**) protocol and its most popular implementation **OpenSSH** for these tasks.

SSH allows us to send data between the machines and run the commands remotely. When the client performs an SSH connection, it should be authenticated against the server. Besides the user/password authentication, OpenSSH also supports authentication using asymmetric cryptography (RSA or similar) keys. With SSH keys configured, a client can connect to server without manual intervention. This eases the scripting for copying multiple files or running remote tasks.

In this recipe, we will prepare a set of public and private keys and use these on all virtual machines and on the host machine during the build.

Getting ready

For this recipe, we will need a Unix-like operating system running with an OpenSSH server and client installed. For example, the Ubuntu 12.04 operating system can be used.

How to do it...

The following procedure will help us to install VirtualBox:

1. Generate client RSA keys pairs for the host and guest machines:

    ```
    ssh-keygen -q -P "" -t rsa -f vmhost__id_rsa
    ssh-keygen -q -P "" -t rsa -f vmguest__id_rsa
    ```

2. Generate server RSA key pairs for the host and guest machines:

    ```
    ssh-keygen -q -P "" -t rsa -f vmhost__ssh_host_rsa_key
    ssh-keygen -q -P "" -t rsa -f vmguest__ssh_host_rsa_key
    ```

3. Create a new user on the host machine that will be used to manage builds, and login under this user:

    ```
    sudo adduser packt
    ```

4. Run VirtualBox and configure networking as described in the previous recipe, *Installing VirtualBox*, with the `192.168.42.2` host IP address and the `192.168.42.1` guest IP address.

5. Create a user with the same name on the guest machine and login under this user:

    ```
    sudo adduser packt
    ```

6. Check whether the `ping` command works successfully from host to guest and back from guest to host:

    ```
    ping 192.168.42.1
        PING 192.168.42.2 (192.168.42.2) 56(84) bytes of data.
        64 bytes from 192.168.42.2: icmp_req=1 ttl=64 time=0.181 ms
        ...
    ```

7. On the host machine, set up the client keys:

    ```
    cp vmhost__id_rsa.pub ~/.ssh/id_rsa.pub
    cp vmhost__id_rsa ~/.ssh/id_rsa
    chmod 600 ~/.ssh/id_rsa
    ```

8. On the guest machine, set up server keys:

   ```
   sudo rm -rf /etc/ssh/ssh_host_*
   sudo cp vmguest__ssh_host_rsa_key.pub /etc/ssh/ssh_host_rsa_key.
   pub
   sudo cp vmguest__ssh_host_rsa_key /etc/ssh/ssh_host_rsa_key
   sudo chmod 600 /etc/ssh/ssh_host_rsa_key
   ```

9. On the guest machine, set up the host client public key:

   ```
   cp vmhost__id_rsa.pub ~/.ssh/authorized_keys2
   ```

10. On the host machine, try to connect to the guest and confirm the new guest server key:

    ```
    ssh packt@192.168.42.1
    ```

11. On the host machine, save the obtained fingerprint of the guest server key:

    ```
    cp ~/.ssh/known_hosts vmhost__known_hosts
    ```

12. On the host machine, check whether we can now connect from host to guest without any passwords or additional confirmations:

    ```
    ssh packt@192.168.42.1
    ```

13. Repeat steps 7 to 11, swapping host and guest sides to set up connections from guest to host.

14. Save the following keys for use later during the builds:

    ❑ vmhost__id_rsa: This is the host client private key

    ❑ vmhost__id_rsa.pub: This is the host client public key

    ❑ vmhost__ssh_host_rsa_key: This is the host server private key

    ❑ vmhost__ssh_host_rsa_key.pub: This is the host server public key

    ❑ vmhost__known_hosts: This is the guest server key fingerprint to be used on the host

    ❑ vmguest__id_rsa: This is the guest client private key

    ❑ vmguest__id_rsa.pub: This is the guest client private key

    ❑ vmguest__ssh_host_rsa_key: This is the guest server private key

    ❑ vmguest__ssh_host_rsa_key.pub: This is the guest server public key

    ❑ vmguest__known_hosts: This is the host server key fingerprint to be used on guest

How it works...

The `ssh-keygen` command generates a pair of asymmetric cryptography (in our example, RSA) keys.

SSH supports passwordless authentication based on keys. We prepared the set of keys that can be loaded to host and guest side (for all guest machines) to allow seamless connections from host to guest and back. So, now we can a call script on the host machine that will connect (or send files) to the guest and will be able to connect back to the host from the same guest session.

All keys are deliberately generated with an empty passphrase to allow connections without manual passphrase input.

There's more...

Connections over SSH are secure and this can be useful if you want to perform builds using remote machines instead of local virtual ones. If security is not required, then other protocols can be used. They do not require authentication or a keys setup, for example, some custom protocol over HTTP with support for commands and sending files.

The DSA or ECDSA keys can be used instead of the RSA keys.

A shell automation tool like `expect` can be used to set up automated connections with passwords instead of client keys.

See also

- ▸ The *Installing VirtualBox* recipe
- ▸ The OpenSSH manual on key generation that is available at `https://www.virtualbox.org/manual/UserManual.html`

Preparing VirtualBox machines with Linux

Many Linux-based operating systems have decent support for virtualization using VirtualBox. They also usually have an OpenSSH client and server preinstalled or available in the main packages repository.

In this recipe, we will set up an Ubuntu Linux virtual machine that can be used for automated OpenJDK builds.

Getting ready

For this recipe, we will require the Ubuntu 12.04 amd64 operating system with VirtualBox installed and a virtual network interface configured.

How to do it...

The following procedure will help us to prepare the Linux virtual machine:

1. Prepare the SSH keys as described in the recipe *Preparing SSH keys*.

2. Download the Ubuntu 12.04 server amd64 image from the Ubuntu website (http://www.ubuntu.com/).

3. In VirtualBox, create a virtual machine instance using the IDE storage controller and default values for other settings.

4. Install Ubuntu on to the virtual machine, set up networking as described in the recipe, *Installing VirtualBox*, and boot the virtual machine.

5. Create a user with the same name on the host machine, and login under this user:

   ```
   sudo adduser packt
   ```

6. Set up the client keys:

   ```
   cp vmguest__id_rsa.pub ~/.ssh/id_rsa.pub
   cp vmguest__id_rsa ~/.ssh/id_rsa
   chmod 600 ~/.ssh/id_rsa
   ```

7. Set up the server keys:

   ```
   sudo rm -rf /etc/ssh/ssh_host_*
   sudo cp vmguest__ssh_host_rsa_key.pub /etc/ssh/ssh_host_rsa_key.pub
   sudo cp vmguest__ssh_host_rsa_key /etc/ssh/ssh_host_rsa_key
   sudo chmod 600 /etc/ssh/ssh_host_rsa_key
   ```

8. Set up the host client public key:

   ```
   cp vmhost__id_rsa.pub ~/.ssh/authorized_keys2
   ```

9. Set up the host key fingerprint:

   ```
   cp vmguest__known_hosts ~/.ssh/known_hosts
   ```

10. Check whether the connection from host to guest and back works seamlessly:

    ```
    ssh packt@192.168.42.1
    ```

11. Complete the manual build of OpenJDK using the recipe, *Building OpenJDK 8 Ubuntu Linux 12.04 LTS*, from *Chapter 4, Building OpenJDK 8*.

How it works...

In this recipe, we created a virtual machine instance with Ubuntu Linux and configured SSH keys to enable seamless automated connections to it.

The manual build was done on this VM to be ensure all environment the is correct.

There's more...

Other Linux-based OSs can be used instead of Ubuntu 12.04. Other protocols/tools can be used for interaction between the host and guest machine instead of OpenSSH.

See also

▸ The *Building OpenJDK 8 Ubuntu Linux 12.04 LTS* recipe from *Chapter 4, Building OpenJDK 8*

▸ The *Installing VirtualBox* recipe

▸ The *Preparing SSH keys* recipe

▸ The Oracle VirtualBox user manual at `https://www.virtualbox.org/manual/UserManual.html`

Preparing VirtualBox machines with Mac OS X

Modern versions of the Mac OS X operating system support run in a virtualized environment using VirtualBox. Instructions to prepare the Mac OS X image for virtualization might differ vastly depending on the Mac OS X version and the host operating system. Exact instructions lie outside the scope of this book and can be found on the Internet.

Please note that running a guest Mac OS X on a non-Mac host operating system can violate your end user license agreement with Apple Inc., it's better to consult your lawyer about this.

Mac OS X has an OpenSSH client and server preinstalled.

Getting ready

For this recipe, we will require a ready-to-use Mac OS X image (for VirtualBox-VDI) Version 10.7 or later.

How to do it...

The following procedure will help us to prepare the Mac OS X virtual machine:

1. Prepare SSH keys as described in the *Preparing SSH keys* recipe in this chapter.
2. In VirtualBox, create a virtual machine instance using at least 2048 RAM, PIIX3 Chipset, disabled UEFI, single CPU, and IDE storage controller.
3. Set up networking as described in the *Installing VirtualBox* recipe in this chapter and boot the virtual machine.
4. Create a user with the same name on the host machine and login under this user.
5. Set up the client keys:

   ```
   cp vmguest__id_rsa.pub ~/.ssh/id_rsa.pub
   cp vmguest__id_rsa ~/.ssh/id_rsa
   chmod 600 ~/.ssh/id_rsa
   ```

6. Set up the server keys:

   ```
   sudo rm -rf /etc/ssh_host_*
   sudo cp vmguest__ssh_host_rsa_key.pub /etc/ssh_host_rsa_key.pub
   sudo cp vmguest__ssh_host_rsa_key /etc/ssh_host_rsa_key
   sudo chmod 600 /etc/ssh_host_rsa_key
   ```

7. Set up the host client public key:

   ```
   cp vmhost__id_rsa.pub ~/.ssh/authorized_keys2
   ```

8. Set up the host key fingerprint:

   ```
   cp vmguest__known_hosts ~/.ssh/known_hosts
   ```

9. Check whether the connection from host to guest and back works seamlessly:

   ```
   ssh packt@192.168.42.1
   ```

10. Complete the manual build of OpenJDK using the *Building OpenJDK 8 on Mac OS X* recipe from *Chapter 4, Building OpenJDK 8*.

How it works...

In this recipe, we created a virtual machine instance with Mac OS X and configured SSH keys to enable seamless automated connections to it.

The manual build was done on this VM to ensure that the environment setup was correct.

There's more...

In some Mac OS X versions, the preinstalled OpenSSH might not support the ECDSA SSH keys. This won't prevent us from finishing this recipe as we have used the RSA SSH keys. However, if you want to use ECDSA keys you can update the OpenSSH installation relatively easily using the Homebrew packaging system and its system duplicates repository, `homebrew/dupes`.

Other protocols/tools can be used for interaction between the host and the guest machine instead of OpenSSH.

See also

- ▶ The *Building OpenJDK 8 on Mac OS X* recipe from *Chapter 4, Building OpenJDK 8*
- ▶ The *Installing VirtualBox* recipe
- ▶ The *Preparing SSH keys* recipe
- ▶ The Oracle VirtualBox user manual at `https://www.virtualbox.org/manual/UserManual.html`

Preparing VirtualBox machines with Windows

Popular virtualization tools have very good support for virtualizing Windows. The VirtualBox setup for Windows can be easier than with Mac OS X. However, the SSH protocol is less popular on Windows than on Unix-like operating systems, and the SSH server's setup on Windows might be complex.

In this recipe, you will learn how to set up a Windows virtual machine for automated builds. A set of in-depth instructions about configuration of free SSH servers on Windows will constitute a significant part of the recipe.

Getting ready

For this recipe, we will require a Windows 7 virtual machine VirtualBox image.

How to do it...

The following procedure will help us to prepare the Windows virtual machine:

1. Prepare the SSH keys as described in the *Preparing SSH keys* recipe in this chapter.

2. Download the Copssh SSH server implementation Version 3.1.4. Unfortunately, it was removed from public downloads by the authors, but still can be found on the Internet with these file details:

   ```
   Copssh_3.1.4_Installer.exe
   size: 5885261 bytes
   sha1: faedb8ebf88285d7fe3e141bf5253cfa70f94819
   ```

3. Install Copssh into any Windows instance using the default installation parameters and copy the installed files somewhere for later usage.

4. In VirtualBox, create a virtual machine instance using the IDE storage controller and the default values for other settings.

5. Set up networking as described in the *Installing VirtualBox* recipe in this chapter and boot the virtual machine.

6. Create a user with the same name on the host machine and login under this user (we will use the name `packt`).

7. Download Windows Server 2003 Resource Kit Tools from the Microsoft website and extract `ntrights`, `instsrv`, and `srvany` utilities from it.

8. Copy the extracted Copssh files into the `c:\ssh` directory.

9. Set up users and rights for the SSH service using the following script:

   ```
   net user sshd sshd /ADD
   net user SvcCOPSSH SvcCOPSSH /ADD
   net localgroup Administrators SvcCOPSSH /add
   ntrights +r SeTcbPrivilege -u SvcCOPSSH
   ntrights +r SeIncreaseQuotaPrivilege -u SvcCOPSSH
   ntrights +r SeCreateTokenPrivilege -u SvcCOPSSH
   ntrights +r SeServiceLogonRight -u SvcCOPSSH
   ntrights +r SeAssignPrimaryTokenPrivilege -u SvcCOPSSH
   ntrights +r SeDenyInteractiveLogonRight -u SvcCOPSSH
   ntrights +r SeDenyNetworkLogonRight -u SvcCOPSSH
   ```

10. Generate internal Copssh login and password information, and register Copssh as a Windows service:

    ```
    c:\copssh\bin\mkpasswd -l > c:\obf\copssh\etc\passwd
    c:\copssh\bin\cygrunsrv.exe --install OpenSSHServer --args "-D"
    --path /bin/sshd --env "CYGWIN=binmode ntsec tty" -u SvcCOPSSH -w
    SvcCOPSSH
    ```

11. Install the Cygwin tools and run the bash shell.

12. Set up the client keys:

```
cp vmguest__id_rsa.pub /cygdrive/c/ssh/home/packt/.ssh/id_rsa.pub
cp vmguest__id_rsa /cygdrive/c/ssh/home/packt/.ssh/id_rsa
chmod 600 /cygdrive/c/ssh/home/packt/.ssh/id_rsa
```

13. Set up the server keys:

```
rm -rf /cygdrive/c/ssh/etc/ssh_host_*
cp vmguest__ssh_host_rsa_key.pub /cygdrive/c/ssh/etc/ssh_host_rsa_key.pub
cp vmguest__ssh_host_rsa_key /cygdrive/c/ssh/etc/ssh_host_rsa_key
chmod 600 /cygdrive/c/ssh/etc/ssh_host_rsa_key
```

14. Set up the host client public key:

```
cp vmhost__id_rsa.pub /cygdrive/c/ssh/home/packt/.ssh/authorized_keys2
```

15. Set up the host key fingerprint:

```
cp vmguest__known_hosts /cygdrive/c/ssh/home/packt/.ssh/known_hosts
```

16. Check whether the connection from host to guest and back works seamlessly:

```
ssh packt@192.168.42.1
```

17. Register the Windows service that will be used to start the build process using the `instsrv` and `srvany` utilities:

```
instsrv.exe packt_build c:\path\to\srvany.exe
reg add "HKEY_LOCAL_MACHINE\SYSTEM\CurrentControlSet\Services\packt_build\Parameters" /v Application /t reg_sz /d "C:\packt\build.bat"
```

18. Configure the service to avoid starting automatically on OS boot:

```
sc config obf_build start= demand
```

19. Complete the manual build of OpenJDK using the *Building OpenJDK 8 on Windows 7 SP1* recipe from *Chapter 4, Building OpenJDK 8*.

How it works...

In this recipe, we created a virtual machine instance with Windows and configured the SSH server to enable seamless automated connections to it.

Binaries of Copssh SSH server Version 3.1.4 were released by the authors as free software under the terms of GNU General Public License Version 3. This means that we can publish or use unchanged binaries for any purposes without additional licensing limitations.

Copssh uses the Cygwin environment and the OpenSSH server under the hood. It also provides integration with the Windows user rights system.

Authorization roles given to the SvcCOPSSH user are required to support the SSH key authentication.

We used Cygwin to set up key files to support the proper setting of Cygwin file rights.

Copssh uses parts of the old version of the Cygwin environment and we need the additional full Cygwin installation for the OpenJDK build process. Different Cygwin versions running on the same machine might interfere with each other causing errors. Although during heavy use of such a setup, I never observed any problems, it is better to keep this point in mind for instances of cryptic Cygwin/Copssh errors/crashes.

Two additional Windows users for the SSH server (sshd and SvcCOPSSH) are used internally by Copssh.

The `ntrighs` utility was used to assign additional roles to the SvcCOPSSH user. This utility is not officially supported in the newer versions of Windows but should work fine anyway.

Windows service registration will be required for automated builds to start the actual build process over an SSH connection. For a proper environment setup, the build process on Windows should be started from the `cmd.exe` shell (usually running a batch file). It cannot be started directly from the SSH session that works in the guest Windows machine inside the Cygwin environment. The `instsrv` and `ntrighs` utilities allowed us to create a Windows service that will run the batch file (that in turn will start the actual build process) on a path preconfigured in the registry. This `packt_build` service can be started from the SSH session using the `net start` command, effectively starting the build process.

The Manual build was done on this VM to ensure that the environment setup was correct.

There's more...

Other SSH servers can be used in theory, although I am not aware of other free (as in "free speech") SSH server implementations for Windows, which support key authentication.

Other protocols/tools can be used for interaction between the host and guest machine instead of OpenSSH.

See also

- ▸ The *Building OpenJDK 8 on Windows 7 SP1* recipe from *Chapter 4, Building OpenJDK 8*
- ▸ The *Installing Cygwin for Windows builds* recipe from *Chapter 2, Building OpenJDK 6*
- ▸ The *Installing VirtualBox* recipe
- ▸ The *Preparing SSH keys* recipe

> ▸ The Oracle VirtualBox user manual at `https://www.virtualbox.org/manual/UserManual.html`
>
> ▸ The Copssh website at `https://www.itefix.net/copssh`

Automating builds

This recipe joins together all the previous recipes in this chapter. Prepared virtual machine images and SSH with key authentication will allow us to build OpenJDK in fully automated mode using simple bash scripts without additional tools.

Getting ready

For this recipe, we will require a Linux or Mac OS host machine running.

How to do it...

The following procedure will help us to prepare the Windows virtual machine:

1. Prepare SSH keys as described in the *Preparing SSH keys* recipe in this chapter.

2. Set up the VirtualBox installation and its network settings as described in the *Installing VirtualBox* recipe in this chapter.

3. Prepare the virtual machine images as described in the previous recipes in this chapter.

4. For each VM image, prepare a list of environment variables, which will be used by the build script (for example, Windows):

   ```
   export VM_ADDRESS=192.168.42.1
   export VM_NAME=jdk7-windows-amd64
   export VM_OSTYPE=Windows7_64
   export VM_MEMORY=1780
   export VM_IOAPIC=on
   export VM_NICTYPE=82545EM
   export VM_MACADDR=auto
   export VM_OBF_DIR=/cygdrive/c/packt
   export VM_START_BUILD="net start obf_build >> build.log 2>&1"
   export VM_SHUTDOWN="shutdown /L /T:00 /C /Y"
   export VM_IDE_CONTROLLER=PIIX4
   ```

5. Add the snippets from the following steps (steps 6 to 12) to the main build script.

6. Create a virtual machine instance using the `VBoxManage` utility:

```
SCRIPT_DIR="$( cd "$( dirname "${BASH_SOURCE[0]}" )" && pwd )"

VBoxManage createvm --name "$VM_NAME" --register --basefolder
"$SCRIPT_DIR"/target >> "$SCRIPT_DIR"/build.log 2>&1

VBoxManage modifyvm "$VM_NAME" --ostype "$VM_OSTYPE" >> "$SCRIPT_
DIR"/build.log 2>&1

VBoxManage modifyvm "$VM_NAME" --memory "$VM_MEMORY" >> "$SCRIPT_
DIR"/build.log 2>&1

VBoxManage modifyvm "$VM_NAME" --nic1 bridged --bridgeadapter1
tap0 >> "$SCRIPT_DIR"/build.log 2>&1

VBoxManage modifyvm "$VM_NAME" --nictype1 "$VM_NICTYPE" >>
"$SCRIPT_DIR"/build.log 2>&1

VBoxManage modifyvm "$VM_NAME" --macaddress1 "$VM_MACADDR" >>
"$SCRIPT_DIR"/build.log 2>&1

VBoxManage modifyvm "$VM_NAME" --cpus 1 >> "$SCRIPT_DIR"/build.log
2>&1

VBoxManage modifyvm "$VM_NAME" --audio none >> "$SCRIPT_DIR"/
build.log 2>&1

VBoxManage modifyvm "$VM_NAME" --usb off >> "$SCRIPT_DIR"/build.
log 2>&1

VBoxManage modifyvm "$VM_NAME" --vrde on

VBoxManage modifyvm "$VM_NAME" --ioapic "$VM_IOAPIC" >> "$SCRIPT_
DIR"/build.log 2>&1

VBoxManage modifyvm "$VM_NAME" --mouse usbtablet >> "$SCRIPT_DIR"/
build.log 2>&1

VBoxManage modifyvm "$VM_NAME" --keyboard usb >> "$SCRIPT_DIR"/
build.log 2>&1

VBoxManage setextradata global GUI/SuppressMessages
remindAboutAutoCapture,remindAboutMouseIntegrationOn,
showRuntimeError.warning.HostAudioNotResponding,
remindAboutGoingSeamless,remindAboutInputCapture,
remindAboutGoingFullscreen,
remindAboutMouseIntegrationOff,confirmGoingSeamless,
confirmInputCapture,remindAboutPausedVMInput,
confirmVMReset,confirmGoingFullscreen,
remindAboutWrongColorDepth >> "$SCRIPT_DIR"/build.log 2>&1

VBoxManage storagectl "$VM_NAME" --name "IDE" --add ide >>
"$SCRIPT_DIR"/build.log 2>&1

VBoxManage internalcommands sethduuid "$SCRIPT_DIR"/target/$VM_
NAME.vdi >> "$SCRIPT_DIR"/build.log 2>&1
```

```
VBoxManage storageattach "$VM_NAME" --storagectl "IDE" --port 0
--device 0 --type hdd --medium "$SCRIPT_DIR"/target/"$VM_NAME".vdi
>> "$SCRIPT_DIR"/build.log 2>&1
```

```
VBoxManage storagectl "$VM_NAME" --name "IDE" --controller "$VM_
IDE_CONTROLLER"
```

7. Start up the virtual machine instance:

```
VBoxManage startvm "$VM_NAME" --type headless >> "$SCRIPT_DIR"/
build.log 2>&1
```

```
ssh "$VM_ADDRESS" "ls" > /dev/null 2>&1
```

```
while [ $? -ne 0 ]; do
```

```
echo "Waiting for VM ..."
```

```
    sleep 10
```

```
    ssh "$VM_ADDRESS" "ls" > /dev/null 2>&1
```

```
done
```

```
echo "VM started"
```

8. Enable remote logging back to the host machine over SSH:

```
ssh "$VM_ADDRESS" "cd "$VM_OBF_DIR" && echo 'Starting build' >
build.log"
```

```
nohup ssh "$VM_ADDRESS" "tail -f "$VM_OBF_DIR"/build.log | ssh
192.168.42.2 'cat >> "$SCRIPT_DIR"/build.log'" >> "$SCRIPT_DIR"/
build.log 2>&1 &
```

```
LOGGER_PID="$!"
```

9. Copy the OpenJDK sources into the build VM and start the build:

```
scp "$SCRIPT_DIR"/openjdk.zip "$VM_ADDRESS":"$VM_OBF_DIR"
```

```
ssh "$VM_ADDRESS" "cd "$VM_OBF_DIR" && unzip -q openjdk.zip >>
build.log 2>&1"
```

```
ssh "$VM_ADDRESS" "cd "$VM_OBF_DIR" && "$VM_START_BUILD""
```

10. Poll the build machine periodically looking for the build_finished.flag file that should be created after the build is finished:

```
ssh "$VM_ADDRESS" "if [ ! -f "$VM_OBF_DIR"/build_finished.flag ];
then exit 1; else exit 0; fi" > /dev/null 2>&1
```

```
while [ $? -ne 0 ]; do
```

```
    echo "Waiting for build ..."
```

```
    sleep 300
```

```
ssh "$VM_ADDRESS" "if [ ! -f "$VM_OBF_DIR"/build_finished.flag ];
then exit 1; else exit 0; fi" > /dev/null 2>&1
```

```
done
```

11. Copy the build results, stop the logger, shut down the virtual machine instance, and unregister it from VirtualBox:

```
scp -r "$VM_ADDRESS":"$VM_OBF_DIR"/dist/* "$SCRIPT_DIR"/dist

kill -9 $LOGGER_PID >> "$SCRIPT_DIR"/build.log 2>&1

ssh "$VM_ADDRESS" "$VM_SHUTDOWN" >> "$SCRIPT_DIR"/build.log 2>&1
|| true

sleep 15

VBoxManage controlvm "$VM_NAME" poweroff > /dev/null 2>&1 || true

VBoxManage unregistervm "$VM_NAME" >> "$SCRIPT_DIR"/build.log
```

12. To start the build with the chosen virtual machine image, use the following commands:

```
. windows_amd64.env # please not the dot before the command

nohup build.sh >> build.log 2>&1 &

echo "$!" > .pid

tail -F "$SCRIPT_DIR"/build.log
```

13. After the build is finished, the OpenJDK binaries will be copied back to the host machine.

How it works...

We use the low-level VBoxManage tool to manipulate virtual machine instances for better control over this process.

To ensure that the virtual machine instance actually starts, we poll it periodically over SSH and stop polling after the first successful connection.

For remote logging, we run the `tail -f` process on the build machine that sends its output back to the host machine immediately over SSH. We start this process with a connection from the host machine in the background using the `nohup` utility and write the host process `pid` to the `.pid` file to kill the process after the build.

We use `scp` to copy sources to a build machine and commands over SSH to decompress the sources and start the build.

After the build is started, we poll the build machine periodically over SSH to look for the `build_finished.flag` file that should be created by the build script on the build machine.

After the build is finished, we copy OpenJDK binaries back to the host machine and shut down the virtual machine instance gracefully before unregistering it.

Different virtual machine configuration and environment options are listed in the `.env` file for each virtual machine image. We use the "dot first" syntax to import variables from the `env` file to the current shell. This allows us to use a generic build script for all virtual machine images.

There's more...

This recipe can be seen as a basic example of build automation. Different commands, tools, and protocols can be used to achieve the same goal.

The `build_finished.flag` file (with custom content) can also be used to end the build prematurely after the error.

See also

- The *Installing VirtualBox* recipe
- The *Preparing SSH keys* recipe
- The *Preparing VirtualBox machines with Linux* recipe
- The *Preparing VirtualBox machines with Mac OS X* recipe
- The *Preparing VirtualBox machines with Windows* recipe
- *Chapter 4, Building OpenJDK 8*
- The Oracle VirtualBox user manual at `https://www.virtualbox.org/manual/UserManual.html`

Building cross-platform installers

When cloud services became the ubiquitous way to install desktop software, classic GUI installers became almost obsolete. Cloud package repositories or stores can be much more convenient to install and, in the first place, update the desktop application.

At the same time, GUI installers are still widely used for various free and commercial applications. Especially for cross-platform applications, GUI installers should show the same behavior on all supported platforms despite not being fully native on those platforms. Some applications require complex environment changes at the time of installation, for example, registering themselves as Windows services or setting environment variables.

In this recipe, we will prepare a cross-platform installer for OpenJDK that will work on all supported platforms (Windows, Linux, and Mac OS X). We will use a popular open-source installation tool, `IzPack`, written in Java.

Getting ready

For this recipe we will require the OpenJDK binaries (to wrap into the installer).

How to do it...

The following procedure will help us in preparing the installer:

1. Download IzPack compiler Version 4.3.5 from the IzPack website (`http://izpack.org/`) and install it.

2. Download the sample installation config file from the documentation section of the Izpack website.

3. Move the `jre` directory from the OpenJDK image one level up, next to the `openjdk` directory.

4. Add the `jre` directory to the installer configuration as a "loose" pack using the following configuration snippet:

   ```
   <pack name="OpenJDK RE" required="yes" loose="true">
       <description>OpenJDK Runtime Environment</description>
       <file src="jre" targetdir="$INSTALL_PATH"/>
   </pack>
   ```

5. Add the `openjdk` directory (that now does not contain JRE) as a normal pack:

   ```
   <pack name="OpenJDK DK" required="no">
       <description>OpenJDK Development Kit</description>
       <fileset dir="openjdk" targetdir="$INSTALL_PATH"/>
       <file src="uninstall" targetdir="$INSTALL_PATH"/>
   </pack>
   ```

6. Adjust labels, GUI forms, locale, and icons as you like.

7. Run the IzPack compiler:

   ```
   ./izcomp/bin/compile ./config.xml -h ./izcomp -o installer.jar
   ```

8. Put the generated `install.jar` and `jre` directory in the `openjdk-installer` directory.

9. Add the bash/batch script to the `openjdk-installer` directory which will allow us to run the installer using the relative path to the `jre` directory:

   ```
   ./jre/bin/java -jar install.jar
   ```

10. Compress the `openjdk-installer` directory—it now contains the OpenJDK installer.

How it works...

The main feature of our installer is that the installer itself runs on the same version of Java that it will install. The `loose="true"` configuration in the JRE pack instructs the installer to find this pack on a relative path outside of the main installation `.jar` file, without duplicating the contents of the `jre` directory.

There's more...

The IzPack installer supports a lot of configuration options, we highlighted only the basic one in this recipe. Besides the GUI and installation forms customizations, the one feature that can be useful, especially for OpenJDK, is running scripts at installation time. We can prepare scripts to adjust the environment and add them to the corresponding packs using the executable configuration element. On simple Unix-like operating systems, such scripts can simply append the PATH variable changes to ~/.bashrc or ~/.bash_profile files. On Windows, utilities such as `pathman`, `setx`, and `reg` can be used to adjust the environment variables or the Windows Registry.

Instead of running scripts at the time of installation, you can extend the IzPack itself (adding new forms, and so on) and perform environment registration directly from Java code.

See also

 ▸ *Chapter 2, Building OpenJDK 6*

 ▸ *Chapter 3, Building OpenJDK 7*

 ▸ *Chapter 4, Building OpenJDK 8*

 ▸ The IzPack installer website at `http://izpack.org/`

Index

Symbols

Thank you for buying
OpenJDK Cookbook

About Packt Publishing

Packt, pronounced 'packed', published its first book, *Mastering phpMyAdmin for Effective MySQL Management*, in April 2004, and subsequently continued to specialize in publishing highly focused books on specific technologies and solutions.

Our books and publications share the experiences of your fellow IT professionals in adapting and customizing today's systems, applications, and frameworks. Our solution-based books give you the knowledge and power to customize the software and technologies you're using to get the job done. Packt books are more specific and less general than the IT books you have seen in the past. Our unique business model allows us to bring you more focused information, giving you more of what you need to know, and less of what you don't.

Packt is a modern yet unique publishing company that focuses on producing quality, cutting-edge books for communities of developers, administrators, and newbies alike. For more information, please visit our website at www.packtpub.com.

Writing for Packt

We welcome all inquiries from people who are interested in authoring. Book proposals should be sent to author@packtpub.com. If your book idea is still at an early stage and you would like to discuss it first before writing a formal book proposal, then please contact us; one of our commissioning editors will get in touch with you.

We're not just looking for published authors; if you have strong technical skills but no writing experience, our experienced editors can help you develop a writing career, or simply get some additional reward for your expertise.

Instant Web Scraping with Java

ISBN: 978-1-84969-688-3   Paperback: 72 pages

Build simple scrapers or vast armies of Java-based bots to untangle and capture the Web

1. Learn something new in an Instant! A short, fast, focused guide delivering immediate results.

2. Get your Java environment up and running.

3. Gather clean, formatted web data into your own database.

4. Learn how to work around crawler-resistant websites and legally subvert security measures.

Java EE 7 Developer Handbook

ISBN: 978-1-84968-794-2   Paperback: 634 pages

Develop professional applications in Java EE 7 with this essential reference guide

1. Learn about local and remote service endpoints, containers, architecture, synchronous and asynchronous invocations, and remote communications in a concise reference.

2. Understand the architecture of the Java EE platform and then apply the new Java EE 7 enhancements to benefit your own business-critical applications.

3. Learn about integration test development on Java EE with the Arquillian framework and the Gradle build system.

Java EE 7 with GlassFish 4 Application Server

ISBN: 978-1-78217-688-6   Paperback: 348 pages

A practical guide to install and configure the GlassFish 4 application server and develop Java EE 7 applications to be deployed to this server

1. Install and configure GlassFish 4.

2. Covers all major Java EE 7 APIs and includes new additions such as JSON Processing.

3. Packed with clear, step-by-step instructions, practical examples, and straightforward explanations.

Learning JavaScriptMVC

ISBN: 978-1-78216-020-5   Paperback: 124 pages

Learn to build well-structured JavaScript web applications using JavaScriptMVC

1. Install JavaScriptMVC in three different ways, including installation using Vagrant and Chef.

2. Document your JavaScript codebase and generate searchable API documentation.

3. Test your codebase and application as well as learn how to integrate tests with the continuous integration tool—Jenkins.

Please check **www.PacktPub.com** for information on our titles